Discourse Analysis

Discourse Analysis

An Introduction

Alexandra Georgakopoulou
and
Dionysis Goutsos

EDINBURGH UNIVERSITY PRESS

© Alexandra Georgakopoulou and Dionysis Goutsos, 1997

Edinburgh University Press
22 George Square, Edinburgh EH8 9LF

Typeset in 10/12.5pt Palatino by
Koinonia, Manchester
and printed and bound in Great Britain by
Hartnolls Ltd, Bodmin, Cornwall

A CIP record for this book is available from the British Library

ISBN 0 7486 0834 6

Contents

Transcription Symbols

The transcription symbols used for the oral, conversational texts in this book are as follows (adapted from Button and Lee 1987: 9–17):

//	overlapping utterances ([ ] is another common symbol , but not used here)
=	continuous utterances
:	extension or prolongation of a sound
::	longer extension
?	rising intonation
!	animated tone
><	delivery at a quicker pace than the surrounding talk
(( ))	editorial comments, transcriptionist's description
hh hh, heh, he, huh	laughter
,	continuing intonation
.	stopping fall in intonation

Numbers in parentheses mark the seconds and tenths of seconds of timed intervals within an utterance or between utterances

(.)	a micro-pause that is less than 0.1 seconds
..	a pause of less than 0.1–0.5 seconds
...	a pause greater than 0.5 seconds
–	an abrupt cut-off or self-interruption of the sound in progress

An arrow is placed in front of the speaker designation to draw the reader's attention to an utterance. <u>Underlining</u> serves the same purpose.

The above symbols are only a modest sample of the sum of symbols that figure in conversation analytic transcripts in the literature.

Preface

Discourse analysis, the study of the use of language for communication in context, is a rapidly-expanding field which is characterised by proliferating analytical methods and continuously renewed tools. Its scope embraces a broad range of disciplines from sociology to anthropology, and from education to psychology, among others. At the same time, discourse analysis has built a significant foundation for itself in linguistics – theoretical, descriptive and applied. This is a fairly recent development. Despite the centuries-old tradition of the mother discipline of rhetoric, three decades ago there were only two isolated attempts to study language beyond the sentence with specifically linguistic methods, namely Harris (1952) and Mitchell (1957) (see Coulthard 1985: 3). The first edition of Coulthard (1983), the earliest fully-fledged textbook of discourse analysis, dates back to just 1977. Its appearance coincided with the full bloom of structuralism, which established the key concepts of analysis and set its distinctive mark on the development of language sciences. The explosion of discourse studies that followed was accompanied by the appearance of general descriptions of the field, of which the most prominent date back to the early 1980s (de Beaugrande and Dressler 1981; Brown and Yule 1983).

At the end of the founding decades and before the beginning of a new era, now is the time to take stock of the contribution of discourse analysis to language sciences and theories of communication. Rapid developments within linguistics call for an immediate review of the major findings in the field. In addition, the proliferation of diverse approaches necessitates a careful reflection on the state of the art and an equally careful planning ahead. It is not a coincidence that, whereas the first endeavours in discourse analysis appeared at the same time as the peak of linguistic approaches which disregarded the study of language-in-use, the former's reaching of maturity has run parallel with the latter's widely-felt decline. One of the major consequences of this development has been the reassessment of the central concerns of discourse studies since the beginning of the 1980s. For instance, the prominence of approaches based on speech act theory has given way to a broader conception of the interaction between functions and patterns. The area has now been cleared for a discourse analysis which would be ready to critically absorb the full impact of insights from neighbouring disciplines and to provide integrated theories of discourse, based on a constructive dialogue between different approaches.

Nevertheless, it is our belief that the opening of discourse analysis to the surrounding fields of discourse studies should not be taken as an excuse to throw the baby out with the bathwater, that is, to overthrow the positive contributions of structuralism and, especially, its main thrust, which J. Sinclair (1992) aptly summarised as the injunction to 'trust the text'. This belief in the text has helped formulate the distinctive mark and identity of discourse analysis as an area of linguistics. It also constitutes the driving force behind this book and the principle underlying our view of discourse. Texts are meant to be the protagonists of the discipline (and our book). Texts, however, can only be understood in their immediate and wider contexts of occurrence. Texts are communicative units embedded in social and cultural practices, shaping and being shaped by them. In our view, texts can also be understood as instances of one of the two fundamental modes of discourse, the narrative and the non-narrative mode. We intend to use this central distinction to provide an accessible introduction to discourse analysis which will familiarise the reader with the linguistic construction of different text-types and the ways in which they can be analysed from a variety of perspectives. Our book has thus a twofold aim: to provide a state-of-the-art reference textbook and to offer an exemplar of practical text analysis in a coherent way by integrating foundational research with more recent approaches.

The organisation of the book follows upon our view of the area. We first discuss the notions of discourse and text and provide an overview of key concepts in the analysis of discourse, whose systematic study is a concern which different approaches to discourse share (Chapter 1). Then we introduce and discuss the fundamental distinction between narrative and non-narrative discourse (Chapter 2). Thereafter, we deal with the *how*, the *what* and the *why* of narrative and non-narrative discourse. Chapter 3 develops the question of *how* units are related in discourse, while Chapter 4 is concerned with *what* the basic elements of discourse organisation are and Chapter 5 with *why*, or the purposes and functions for which specific units and devices are used in discourse. Finally, we bring the two modes of discourse together and closely describe their interaction, in terms of their text constitution, contexts and methods of analysis (Chapter 6).

Although we have assumed a familiarity with basic notions from other areas of linguistics (e.g. syntax, semantics, etc.), the design of our presentation takes into consideration the newcomer to the field. Our description is illustrated throughout with the analysis of authentic data comprising a wide range of narrative and non-narrative texts, both spoken and written. It is also combined with activities addressed to the reader (preceded or followed by clues for their appropriate responses). Reader activities are intended as a

means of checking the basic concepts of analysis and further expanding on
the notions presented. They can well be used both for self-study and as
material for workshops in the classroom. Readers are invited to work on
them as they read through or after they have completed the study of the relevant section. For a more thorough study, some readers might wish to work
on them in relation to the sources, to which they should refer for further
guidance and assistance. Similarly, the section on further reading at the end
of each chapter involves both elementary research for the aid of the student
and more advanced research (more appropriate for the teacher). Both reader
activities and further reading sections are designed to encourage further
discussion and research and to provide students and teachers alike with
ideas for assignments of various kinds.

A book on discourse analysis demands the use of data from various
languages and cultures and should not by any means rely exclusively on
English. Thus, our discussion will at various points bring in texts which
originate in non-English-speaking environments; in addition, it will
constantly emphasise the context-sensitivity of discourse as well as the problems of applicability and universality of discourse concepts and tools. We
would also like to invite readers to test models and descriptions in their own
native linguistic varieties (e.g. language/dialect, idiolect). Extended cross-
linguistic and cross-cultural research are necessary in order to emphasise the
fact that discourse analysis should not just mean English discourse analysis.

Many people have contributed directly and indirectly to this book. From
the academic environments which shaped our ideas (i.e. the Universities of
Athens, Strathclyde, Birmingham and Edinburgh), special thanks go to
Elizabeth Black, Susan Hunston, Carol Marley and Hugh Trappes-Lomax
for their seminars on stylistics and discourse studies, to which our discussion
owes a lot. We would also like to credit the Greek discourse analysis groups
of students at King's College London for showing us what does and what
doesn't work in the classroom when they were exposed to various activities
and preliminary chapters of the book. Useful suggestions as to how the book
might be made more user-friendly to linguists and non-linguists were kindly
made by Philip Carabott, Malcolm Coulthard, Philip King, David Ricks and
Michael Toolan, who read parts of drafts. We are particularly grateful to
Malcolm Coulthard for his encouragement and watchful eye on the book.
We would also like to thank Jonathan Price for his enthusiasm for the project
in its initial stages and our current editor Jackie Jones, of Edinburgh University
Press, for her constant support and encouragement throughout its completion. Our respective families have been a big part of this book by providing
distraction and motivation at the same time. Alex Nunes, in particular, with
his probing questions and appetite for after-hours academic discussion, has
been a source of inspiration. This book is a dream come true for us, since it
was initially conceived in our undergraduate years as a vague idea for the
remote future. We apologise to the people whom we will disappoint by
dedicating it to the abstract notions of youthful dreams and friendship.

London, 1996

The Study of Discourse

1.1 DISCOURSE: THE TEXT-LINGUISTIC PERSPECTIVE

How do people communicate with each other? Language is obviously the most elaborate semiotic system among those that human beings have developed for their social need of communication. If we observe language in use, we will find that linguistic communication is not achieved by individual units of language such as sounds, words or sentences. People, primarily and essentially, communicate through combinations of these language units, which themselves constitute distinct units of expression. We call these combinations of language units texts; we can, therefore, say that people, when using language, communicate through texts.

A first objection could be raised here. If texts are the units of linguistic communication, how do the following instances of language manage to communicate?

    (1) Help!
    (2) Work in Progress.
    (3) Kilroy was here.

These are, certainly, examples of an isolated word, a phrase and a sentence that can be (and have been) used in communication through language. However, there is more to them than we can see at first glance. First of all, if examples (1) to (3) are real instances of language in use (and not, for example, abstract illustrations of notions discussed by linguists), they appear in a specific material form that may vary: (1) they may be a desperate cry of agony or a mild request; (2) they may be printed in thick letters on a sign or appear in the agenda of a meeting; (3) they may be scribbled on a wall or typed in neat letters in a novel. We thus have to clarify which particular instantiation we have in mind when we talk of linguistic communication through these pieces of language. Furthermore, these instances could be produced by a different speaker or writer: a skier in free fall or a pop singer, the Department of Transport or a business secretary, a school student or a middle-aged novelist. Similarly, they could be received by different audiences: a fellow skier or a concert-hall crowd, a driver or a business person, a passer-by or a class of students. The activity in which the participants are involved as well as the setting of communication would then also vary accordingly. As a consequence, in each case we would have to do not with abstract linguistic units but with wholes of language, intentions and situations. These wholes that combine speech, writing, gesture, posture and so on and integrate linguistic organisation and action can be defined as texts. Provided that these conditions are fulfilled for (1), (2) and (3), these examples are texts.

A further objection needs to be dealt with, as well: is every combination of language units in use a text? The answer to that must be that only meaningful combinations of units constitute texts. However, what does 'meaningful' mean? Meaning derives first from the rules of a specific language which suggest that only some combinations of sound (phonemes) and form (morphemes) are possible, namely the syntax and semantics of a language. Notice however the following combination of well-formed sentences:

(4) Excuse me, could you tell me where Frith Street is?
(5) Thank you so much.

'Thank you so much' is not by any means the answer you would expect from a stranger in the street when asking her for directions. In such a context, the combination of the sentences in this sequence would not be meaningful because it would fail to perform the act of giving directions. This leads us to a fundamental tenet of our linguistic communication, which is that not only say things with language; we also do things, we perform actions. The identification of the *speech acts* which we perform is a prerequisite for establishing meaning in communication. The philosopher Austin (1962), who systematically looked at what speakers do with language, started off from clear examples of speech acts:

(6) I name this ship Aurora.
(7) I pronounce you husband and wife.
(8) I find the accused guilty as charged.

Such examples occur in ritual and ceremonial settings and, when uttered by authorised individuals, they are capable of bringing about a new state of affairs, of saying and doing at the same time. Their *illocutionary force* (the act performed in saying them) is thus easily identifiable. In less conventionalised settings, though, the illocutionary force of speech acts is not always easily defined. It is not always easy to discern the speaker's true intention, in particular because what is said can differ dramatically from what is meant. Furthermore, what is meant can be said in many words and in many different ways with various degrees of indirectness (see Grice 1975). Notice some of the forms which a request can take. A request belongs to the class of speech acts called directives:

    (9) Close the window.
   (10) Can/could you close the window?
   (11) Would you mind closing the window?
   (12) It's cold in here. (very indirect request in the form of a hint)

Similarly, a phrase like 'I think I deserve a drink too' could be factually stating the speaker's wish to buy herself a drink; or it could be expressing a complaint to the person who has not bought the speaker a drink; or it could be indirectly soliciting the hearer's offer: 'Why don't you join us in the pub?'

The above may suggest that there is no hope for successful communication in our everyday life, since we can utter so many speech acts in so many different ways. However, in actual fact, we manage to interpret speech acts with surprising accuracy. We do that because we establish the link between linguistic forms and functions not in a vacuum but in the specific environments in which they occur. There, our sentences are utterances: not just grammatically complete units in isolation, but communicative units used in context to perform functions. For instance, if we go back to our example (3), 'Kilroy was here', this is meaningful as a text only to the extent that some speakers of English (text-receivers) recognise the intentions of the text-producer and the conventions of using the specific message for communication. Similarly, 'I deserve a drink too' can be assigned the appropriate illocutionary force if looked at in a specific context: where and when it was uttered, why, by whom, to whom etc.

The term 'context' is commonly used to encompass all those choices that suggest different conditions for texts, along with the interaction of these conditions with exclusively linguistic choices. (Context will be discussed in detail in section 1.5 below). Looking at speech acts in whole stretches of text in context is something which both Austin and Searle (1969), who further developed the theory of speech acts, failed to do. They instead tried to formalise the speakers' intentions, which is a very complicated task. Intentions are unobservable psychological states which are hard to define and assign. Currently though, speech acts are increasingly focused upon as part of texts in contexts, in particular in discourse analysis.

Going back to the notion of a text, in the area of discourse analysis this involves the material aspect of language communication referred to above, the semiotic aspect of communication (the combination of sounds with meanings), the specific linguistic choices and their organisation into meaningful combinations. When we refer to the ongoing use of texts in their communicative environments, that is, in their contexts, we talk of discourse. 'Discourse' and 'text' have been used in a variety of ways in the literature. In some cases the two terms have been treated as synonyms, while in others the distinction between discourse and text has been taken to apply to units of spoken versus written communication. Consequently, discourse analysis is, in some accounts, regarded as concerned with spoken texts (primarily conversation). Text-linguistics, as a different discipline, has mainly been associated with written texts. In our view, the terms do not refer to different domains (speech and writing) but reflect a difference in focus. Discourse is the umbrella term for either spoken or written communication beyond the sentence. Text is the basic means of this communication, be it spoken or written, a monologue or an interaction. Discourse is thus a more embracing term that calls attention to the situated uses of text: it comprises both text and context. However, text is not just the product of discourse, as customarily assumed (cf. Brown and Yule 1983), that is, the actual (written or spoken) language unit produced on the page. Text is the means of discourse, without which discourse would not be a linguistic activity.

In our everyday life, we engage in discourse in a multiplicity of roles. When we write a letter to a friend or an essay for a course, pick up the telephone, visit our local shop or the doctor, look up a word in a dictionary, tell a joke, watch TV or listen to the radio, we actively engage in discourse as speakers and hearers, or writers and readers. In these activities, we continuously produce and interpret discourse. Every human act that involves language necessarily makes use of texts in context. Using language is thus synonymous with engaging in discourse.

READER ACTIVITY

Make a rough list of the things you did today. Which of them involved language? Which ones involved texts? What was your role?

The ubiquity of discourse in language and human life accounts for the central role of the notion in many disciplines. At the same time, the development of a specialised branch of linguistics to study discourse is a rather recent phenomenon. At the beginning of the 1980s, van Dijk and Petöfi (1981) remarked that 'both the humanities and the social sciences are progressively discovering the discourse dimension of language, language use and communication'. Since then, discourse has become a central object of study in a variety of disciplines, including anthropology, history, sociology, information science, psychology and psychotherapy, education, neurolinguistics, semiotics, philosophy. The scope of 'discourse' has thus been widened, as can be evidenced, among other things, by the broad use of the basic term associated with it, namely text. As Geertz notes, text has been extended to cover things as distinct as 'Apache jokes, English meals, African cult sermons, American high schools, Indian caste or Balinese widow burning' (1983: 32).

A different use of discourse appears in social sciences. Here the notion has been mainly employed by studies of ideology to signify 'all the non-verbal as well as the verbal construction of meanings occurring in the wider sphere of "ideological" practices' (Macdonnel 1986: 4). More a theoretical given than an analytical concept, discourse has been viewed here from a wide range of perspectives. Some theoretical views focus on discourse as the sum of the socially-instituted modes of speech and writing and the related forms of power (Foucault's sociological tradition). Other approaches employ the term as a synonym for the social space for rational debate that is as free of domination as possible (Habermas' view).

This social sciences' conception of discourse, if not in disagreement, takes an explicitly different standpoint from the way the notion is used in discourse analysis, the discipline concerned with the systematic study of discourse. As a sub-discipline of linguistics, discourse analysis primarily regards discourse as consisting of language complexes that are to be studied in their own terms. Thus, it is more concerned with the ways in which socio-cultural and ideological practices take effect in language. At the same time, discourse analysis is a cross-discipline ('Textwissenschaft', in van Dijk and Petöfi's terms, 1981) and, as such, finds itself in interaction with approaches from a wide range of other disciplines. Discourse analysis is thus an inter-disciplinary study of discourse within linguistics.

In order to clarify this alliance of affiliations in discourse analysis, we need to turn our attention to precisely the distinctive approach to discourse within linguistics, that is, discourse analysis as a sub-discipline of linguistics. What differentiates the analysis of discourse within linguistics from the same practice in other social and human sciences is, essentially, the access to discourse through texts rather than through other semiotic systems like arte-facts, systems of beliefs, or even a social and cultural organisation as a whole. Although the study of texts may be a central concern of other disci-plines, it does not constitute the axis of their founding assumptions, as is the case with discourse analysis. These assumptions, which specify what we can call the text-linguistic perspective to discourse, include the following:

1. The basic unit of analysis is text.
2. The focus of examination is the language of the text.
3. Text is structured.
4. Texts are meaningful language units, which primarily derive their meaning from their situated use.
5. There are no privileged texts, but only authentic, attested texts can be the basis of analysis.

We have hinted at this set of assumptions in our discussion above; this chap-ter is devoted to their detailed explanation. The sum of these assumptions constitutes the distinctive feature of the text-linguistic approach to discourse, as opposed to other approaches within other disciplines in the humanities and social sciences. The vast amount of research presented in this book is characterised by these underlying assumptions. This is the reason why the book is called a text-linguistic introduction to discourse rather than a sociological or an anthropological introduction.

1.2 TEXT AS A UNIT

By taking text as the basic unit of analysis, we assume that it can be considered as an autonomous unit, an entity that has some unity or self-sufficiency, 'a single unified construction' (Fowler 1981: 14). This assumption partly stems from the notion of text as a concrete, material record of the process of communication, which has been mentioned above. As a record, every text has discrete limits (beginning and end) and constitutes a self-contained whole.

From a diachronic point of view, technological advancements of media such as the system of writing and the introduction of the book have played a prominent role in this conception of the text. Ong (1982) has lucidly explained the effects of writing and typography by talking about the sense of 'closure' created by the physical properties of written text. The title on the page, the various headings, the justification of lines, all convey the impression that the text is complete and somehow self-contained. This view is not restricted to the product of written communication. The development of technology for recording and storing sound in a tape or disc has conferred the same sense of closure to the spoken text, which can now be defined, segmented and analysed bit by bit. In the same way that the invention of the phonetic alphabet by the Greeks moulded the assumption of the autonomous word as a linguistic unit, the advent of typography influenced the assumption of the autonomous text. By the same token, the introduction of new electronic media has already challenged this view of the text. A text stored in the form of bytes has a less permanent dimension and is always subject to change and always identified in relation to other texts.

The sense of text unity is not simply an effect of recording. Discourse behaviour is, in general, characterised by a similar sense of closure. As Pike observes, 'certain chunks of human behaviour can be taken as culturally given, that is recognizable to those who participate in them and often a bystander who understands the cultural systems involved as having a definite beginning and end' (cited in Grimes 1975: 21). This is true of many social artefacts. A symphony or a dance sequence, for instance, exhibits certain characteristics that allow us to identify a specific beginning and end, as well as some internal unity. Pike has developed the notion of behavioreme to characterise these cultural chunks of behaviour and has claimed that discourse is a verbal behavioreme with a beginning, an end and an internal structure. As a consequence, the products of this behaviour (i.e. texts) also have definite limits and constitute individual units.

The assumption of text as a unit can be justified in many ways, and so can the delimitation of text units. What is particularly significant is that this conception constitutes the founding assumption of discourse studies. Text is a *primum datum*, a primary notion, for discourse analysis, in the same way that phoneme is for phonology, or morpheme for morphology. It is the smallest definable entity. Its existence allows us to study discourse on its own and not from a phonological, syntactic, lexical or other point of view –

READER ACTIVITY

Study the following extract from a conversation.

Text 1.1
((Doctor leads patient into the consultation room, talking as he does so))
D: that's only the clutter in the (.) background (.)
P: yeah
D: no problem (.)
   so (.) take your coat off
P: sure
   (4.0) ((Doctor helps patient to remove his coat))
   thanks
D: don't think Philip's got any clothes pegs in here so uh (1.5)
   ((Doctor hangs up coat))
   I don't usually use thi– sit down
P: fine
D: I don't usually use this room it's erm (.)
   Philip's (1.0)
P: yes of course
D: anyway (.) going through the whole thing (2.0)
   you've changed your job (.) in effect (.)
P: well (.) an additional responsibility
                          Source: Montgomery 1986: 154–5)

Can you find evidence to suggest that there are definable units in the participants' behaviour? Is there an all-encompassing unit and by what could this be defined?

---

although, of course, discourse can also be studied from all these perspectives. Taking text as the unit of study also distinguishes the text-linguistic perspective from other discourse studies in ethnography, anthropology, sociology etc. Finally, the employment of text is what distinguishes discourse analysis from the field of pragmatics, the study of 'the general conditions of the communicative use of language' (Leech 1983: 10). Although both disciplines are concerned with linguistic communication, pragmatics does not study texts as a whole. Even if, in theory, pragmatics is concerned with language in context, in practice most approaches in pragmatics analyse isolated, invented or idealised sentences.

For the text-linguistic perspective, text is both the upper and the lower limit of analysis. This means that discourse analysis is not interested in the internal construction of sentences, or the combination of morphemes in discourse, but subsumes the analysis of such 'lower' units within the study of texts. Of course, as we will see in Chapter 3, texts are composed of sub-units, some of which may coincide with sentences or clauses. These latter, however, are treated from an exclusively discourse point of view and with regard to their functions in the overall text. In consequence, whereas text may be conceived as a suprasentential unit, it is unequivocally not dependent on sentence for its definition. This text-linguistic perspective presupposes a paradigm shift: more than the ways in which sentences combine with each other, we are interested in the meaningful wholes that they form. As a result, grammar, like lexis, can be seen as a useful access road to text rather than the reverse. This concurs with recent views of grammar as a dynamic entity which is not reducible to a set of fixed and predetermined rules: it is instead an entity emerging from discourse and constituting a set of strategies for building discourses (see Hopper's 'emergent grammar', 1988).

It should be emphasised that this view of text is a matter of theoretical standpoint, accepted for methodological reasons rather than dictated by the nature of text itself. It is clearly impossible to study text without reference to both the surrounding context and the building blocks of grammar and lexis. There is a close interaction between discourse, grammar and the lexicon as well as between discourse and phonology or morphology. The study of discourse, however, can and must be independent from the study of other aspects of language. This may seem obvious nowadays, but it is a truth that has only lately been made welcome in linguistics.

1.3 CONTENT, FORM AND STRUCTURE

The second assumption of the text-linguistic perspective is that the language of the text is the focus of study. This assumption, first of all, excludes all non-linguistic or prelinguistic material. Thus the focus of discourse analysis is not on the ideas, thoughts, plans, goals etc. which exist independently of language. It is, instead, both on what is said or done in the text, a text's subject matter, and on how something is said, that is, the total of the language mechanisms and strategies that operate in discourse.

The distinction between prelinguistic substance, subject matter and form of discourse is one of the fundamental issues of concern in discourse analysis. We can exemplify it by looking more closely at the primary material to which language is called to give form and expression.

READER ACTIVITY

In groups of two or more, write a short description of a photograph or describe orally what the picture shows (one person taking notes.). Compare the texts produced. How is the same information related by the different groups?

Evidently there are many different ways to describe the same event or talk about the same information. In a famous research project, linguists compared the written and oral texts produced by speakers of different languages and cultures when relating a simple story that had been shown to them in a silent film (Chafe 1980). In one of his lectures, Becker (1988) also had a group of linguists describe a simple action which he performed in front of the audience. The texts produced in both cases were intriguingly variable: people differed in the amount and type of information that they included in their description, the complexity of syntactic and other organisation, the perspective adopted and so on.

Why should texts on the same extralinguistic entity vary to such an extent, if all text producers start from the same basic bare facts, such as the same dots on the picture? First, it must be noted that a photograph is itself a selection from the multiplicity of entities available in the world out there. Not everything is represented in the picture, and what is selected is always presented in a specific way, for example, the camera is focused on certain people or objects, leaving others outside the frame. Second, the information given by the picture follows certain conventions dictated by the medium of photography itself: there is a certain amount and direction of light, objects are two-dimensional, there are certain shades of colour etc. All these clearly influence our linguistic ways of describing the picture.

Third, and most important, what is mentioned in a text does not automatically follow from its substance, that is the domain of knowledge described in the text, or the 'knowledge base' that contains the information provided by the text. There can be different selections from the same knowledge base. What is mentionable or tellable does not depend on substance, since 'there is no inherent irrelevance in any information contained in a knowledge base' (Hughes and McCoy 1993). Finally, different selections from the same information base may be organised in differing ways. The same information base can give rise to different forms of expression. Texts, correspondingly, may have different structures. Emphasis on different aspects, different selections from the material available and different organising principles allow for an extremely large variety of text structures.

One of the best ways to formalise our discussion so far would be to adopt Hjelmslev's (1954) distinction of four planes in semiotic systems. His stratification model of language suggests that we can distinguish between form and substance, on the one hand, and between content and expression, on the other. Thus we have two pairs of terms corresponding to four different planes of discourse: the form of content and the substance of content, on the one hand, and the form of expression and the substance of expression, on the other. Table 1.1 presents these four planes and what they consist of in the case of discourse.

Table 1.1 is useful in suggesting that both substance and form in language are articulated. Substance is not an undifferentiated, unstructured whole. Its content includes all the elements on the agenda of discourse, all information

	content	expression
substance	information base	subject matter
form	entities, events, relations	structures

Table 1.1: Discourse planes

available, as well as the 'ongoing docket of actions, needs, motives and goals', in de Beaugrande's words (1992: 246). In the case of the photograph, this would include information about shapes and figures, foreground and background, etc. This content takes a specific expression and constitutes the subject matter of any discourse regarding the object under description. The expression of substance would include, for example, the representation of people and objects, their relative position etc. When substance takes a specific form through a text, we can again distinguish between content and expression planes in the discourse produced: on the one hand, we have entities such as characters and settings, their actions and their relations (e.g. a woman crosses the street, a car stops in front of a hospital), and, on the other hand, we have the specific structures created in our texts (e.g. we start the description from the woman, then go on to the car etc.).

Different approaches to discourse analysis study discourse from a different point of departure in the pattern of discourse planes. Some analysts are concerned with the articulation of linguistic substance. Applications of discourse analysis to language teaching fall into this category. Johns (1994), for instance, distinguishes between several types of expression that subject matter takes in postgraduate reading texts (e.g. tree-diagram, matrix or flow-chart) (cf. Ball 1992). Pedagogical applications of discourse analysis are also interested in the kinds of subjects raised and the legitimacy of topics in such reading material.

One of the most influential traditions of research, the 'critical paradigm' as van Dijk (1990) has named it, also focuses on the articulation of substance and its socio-political and ideological constraints. Critical discourse analysis has focused on the social and political issues related to texts and text production. It has also systematically studied the subject matter of discourse and the social relations, assumptions and ideological complexes informing it. In interaction with the sociological concept of discourse explained above, this research has affirmed that language substance always comes 'pre-packaged', that is, it depends on the prevailing ideologies and the socio-political context. There are specific cultural and political constraints on what can be talked about and how this is thought of, before it is even expressed. At the same time, critical discourse analysis has emphasised that it would be simplistic to consider substance the base on which a superstructure of text is raised. Language form does not simply reflect our external reality, its entities and its relations. It is, in fact, constitutive of that reality and our knowledge about it. The process of linguistic articulation shapes our perception of things. The understanding of how language works and the awareness of the repertoires available to people for constructing texts are thus crucial for examining how knowledge is constructed.

In this book, we are concerned with describing the planes of discourse and the relations of mapping between them. We are interested in the ways in which substance and form interact with each other in narrative and non-narrative discourse. Our primary focus is on the linguistic form of texts and their linguistically describable structure. However, as implied by the articulation of planes shown in Table 1.1, we cannot have a full picture of the discourse under analysis without referring to the planes of linguistic substance in the text.

1.4 STRUCTURE AND COHESION

We have so far touched upon only one aspect of unity in text, namely the definable limits of beginning and end. We have also mentioned that the other aspect of unity, namely structure, is not synonymous with form but may refer to the organisation or articulation of both form and content. We can understand the concept of structure by drawing a parallel from the grammatical unit of sentence. In a sentence like *The Brangwens had lived for generations on the Marsh Farm*, all the constituents (the parts of a sentence) have a number of specific relations with the whole and with each other. First of all, there are only some possible combinations of the parts; so we can have *On the Marsh Farm the Brangwens had lived for generations, For generations the Brangwens had lived on the Marsh Farm*, but not **Had lived the Brangwens for generations on the Marsh Farm*. The same holds for the order of elements within constituents; we cannot, for instance, have **Brangwens the*. This happens because English allows only for some possible combinations of syntactic roles (e.g. subject before predicate) or word classes (e.g. article before noun) in specified sentence types. We can say that structure here applies to the part–whole relations as they appear in the sentence, and the limited number of possible configurations. Structure thus refers to the forces that keep the sentence together in a certain configuration.

It would be interesting to see whether something similar applies to texts. We can check this by rearranging the normal order of sentences in a text.

READER ACTIVITY

A. Try to find the original order of the sentences that has been changed in the extract below. What is the linguistic evidence that helps you decide?

B. Can you make any necessary changes in the wording of the extract below so as to have a 'normal' text? What are these changes?

Text 1.2

1 These two roles can be traced back to two important influences of his childhood. 2 Ruskin's choice of phrase reflects the second influence in his life: his daily Bible-readings under the direction of his mother. 3 His father, a wealthy wine merchant, was fond of travels, and on tours of the Continent he introduced his son to the landscape, architecture, and art. 4 John Ruskin was both the leading Victorian critic of art and an important critic of society. 5 In his autobiography he describes his first view of the Swiss Alps at sunset: 'the seen walls of lost Eden could not have been more beautiful'. 6 From this exposure John Ruskin acquired a zest for beauty that animates even the most theoretical of his discussion of aesthetics.

(*Source: The Norton Anthology of English Literature*, 4th edn, vol. 2 (New York: Norton, 1979), p. 1,317)

We can see that the analogy of texts with sentences holds in some ways but falls in others. Whereas some reordering seems more probable than others, we cannot say that there is an impossible combination. At the same time, in order to find the order with which most people agree, we rely on linguistic elements such as the relation between *two roles* and *both*, which suggests that sentence 1 above follows 4, or between *his father* and *Ruskin*, which implies that 3 also follows 4. These semantic relations between sentences, achieved through links between grammatical and lexical items, are the forces of unity in text. They are also the relations which we rely on when changing the wording of the text so as to 'glue' one sentence to another in the order that they appear above.

These semantic relations have been called cohesive ties by Halliday and Hasan (1976) in their classic study of *Cohesion in English*. Cohesive ties are the forces that keep the text together in the original order and what we manipulate when we try to regain a text's meaning after a reordering of its sentences. Halliday and Hasan have distinguished the following types of the general phenomenon of cohesion in English:

- Reference: the use of pronouns (*John Ruskin – his father* in text 1.2), demonstratives, comparatives and the definite article to indicate the semantic identity of an item with another: <u>Pencey Prep</u> *is this school that's in Agerstown, Pennsylvania. You probably heard of <u>it</u>.*
- Substitution: when an item like *one, same, do, so, not* is used for another, in the case of a different referent: *I've heard some strange <u>stories</u> in my time. But <u>this one</u> was perhaps the strangest of all.*
- Ellipsis: when a zero element appears to link to a previous part of the text: *John brought some carnations. Catherine Ø some sweet peas* (ellipsis of *brought*).

- Conjunction: the use of connective forms such as *and, because, or, though* to indicate semantic relations: *I was not informed. <u>Otherwise</u> I would have taken some action.*
- Collocation: the presence of lexical ties such as repetition (*influences – influence* in text 1.2), synonymy, antonymy and metonymy (the name of a referent is replaced by the name of an attribute as in the example below) to establish a link: *Can you tell me where to stay in <u>Geneva</u>? I've never been to <u>the place</u>.*

As can be seen from text 1.2, cohesive ties may operate within the boundaries of the sentence. Cohesive ties also may be anaphoric or cataphoric, that is, an item may relate to something that has gone before or point forwards to something that follows. For instance, *these two roles* points back to *critic of art* and *critic of society* in the original order of text 1.2 (anaphoric link). If we changed the respective sentence into something like *John Ruskin had <u>two roles</u> that can be traced back …*, we could establish a cataphoric link to the phrases *critic of art* and *critic of society*. There is a rich literature distinguishing other types of cohesive ties (e.g. endophoric and exophoric) and making fine classifications according to individual cases. We should particularly notice that, in Halliday and Hasan's view, cohesion in text is largely responsible for giving a text its 'texture', that is, its property of being a text.

READER ACTIVITY

Find the cohesive ties in the following text. Are there any ambiguous cases? Are there any ties that continue for more than one sentence?

Text 1.3
I said we had the same name. She said she had had another name, before. I asked her to say it. She wouldn't say it. She said, 'Now just Indun Fanny'. She said this place was called Klatsland. There was a village here, on the creek above the beach. Another up near the spring on Kelly's place on Breton Head. Two down past Wreck Point, and one at Altar Rock. All her people. 'All my people,' she said. They died of smallpox and consumption and the venereal disease. They all died in the villages. All her children died of smallpox. She said there were five women left from the villages. The other four became whores so as to live, but she was too old. The other four died. 'I don't get no sickness'. Her eyes are like turtle's eyes. I bought a little basket from her for two bits. It's a pretty little thing. Her children were all born before the whites settled here and all died in a year. All of them died.

(*Source*: Ursula Le Guin, *Searoads*,
(New York: HarperPerennial, 1992), p. 125)

It is easy to observe that many cohesive ties do not just bind two sentences together but run through the whole of the text, forming some sort of backbone for the text. In Chapter 4, we will examine the effects of this linking for text as a whole. Here, it suffices to note that cohesion is only one aspect of a texts organisation. Cohesive ties point out certain relations that bind parts of the text (mainly sentences) to each other. In the following chapters, we examine the more general issue of relations between parts and between parts and whole of a text. The sum of these relations constitutes the hierarchy of part–whole relations in a text, which is what is commonly referred to as a text's structure (Becker 1988).

1.5 TEXT, MEANING AND CONTEXT

What happens when we establish a cohesive tie? Finding a link between two sentences is not a mechanical function that arises automatically from the presence of linguistic forms. Instead, it is we, as readers or hearers, who make an active interpretation which allows us to find a connection between two parts of a text. For instance, in text 1.3 above, we have to make an interpretation of what *All her people* refers to, in order to identify the cohesive ties of this sentence to the rest of the text. This does not only happen in ambiguous cases like this one. It is rather the norm in the establishment of cohesion in a text. Thus *she* in the second sentence of text 1.3 becomes understood as a subordinate of *we* in the first sentence. This is a result of an act of interpretation, that is, a mental representation of the entities described in the text.

More generally, as we noted in our mention of speech acts, finding the structure of a text cannot be dissociated from the identification and understanding of its functions. This constant engagement with meaning relies on the assumption that people do not produce texts at random and without any purpose but have specific intentions to communicate and certain goals to achieve. Language is capable of realising numerous functions. Jakobson's (1960) influential scheme of language functions included, among others, the *referential function* (conveying information), the *emotive function* (expressing inner states), the *phatic function* (establishing or maintaining a channel of communication: e.g. the British favourite of 'talking about the weather'), the *poetic function* (when the choice of the form is the essence of our message), the *metalinguistic function* (when the language talks about itself: e.g. 'The word "computer" means ...'), the *directive function* (seeking to affect the behaviour of the addressee: e.g. 'Come back') and the *contextual function* (framing communication as a particular kind: 'Let's start our discussion by ...'). In addition to these functions, there are numerous others such as requesting, offering, apologising, pleading, complimenting, advising, warning etc.

There is no end to the number of such functions, and it is difficult to classify them into a small number of well-defined, neat categories. Searle's attempt (1976) to regroup Austin's hundreds of speech acts into a small number was not free from problems. Where one speech act ended and another began was not clear. It was equally unclear how different sub-categories of speech acts related to each other and to the overarching category of speech act. However difficult to define rigorously and compute, language functions are an integral part of our search for meaning both in the production and in the reception of discourse.

A major assumption in this pursuit of meaning is that all the parts of a text contribute to it, no part being random or purposeless. This is the assumption of a text's coherence, which is one of the major forces in interpretation. Its function can be seen in cases of 'disturbed' texts.

READER ACTIVITY

Produce a short text by picking out some extracts from other texts, each one from a different source (a sentence from a novel, a newspaper title, a snippet of telephone conversation etc.). Can you make any sense out of it? What would help for the text to be fully understood?

It seems that it is almost impossible to produce a totally meaningless text. In our interpretation, we strive to find as much coherence as we can, based on the fact that as rational beings we engage in meaningful activities. As Halliday and Hasan have observed, 'we insist on interpreting any passage as text if there is the remotest possibility of doing so' (1976: 23). The assumption of text as a unit plays a fundamental role in the search for coherence, since we assume that all individual chunks of language, by belonging to the same text, refer to the same central entity or topic. We also assume that a text is a product of one speaker, or at least, that a single intention underlies a text. Finally, we presuppose that there can only be one interpretation at a time, that meaning is attributable by a single intention of the interpreter. As Reddick argues, 'intentionally or unintentionally, our claims about meaningful features of discourse are simultaneously claims about language users' (1986: 41).

Discourse analysis is fundamentally concerned with the 'general principles of interpretation by which people normally make sense of what they hear and read' (Brown and Yule 1983). However, interpretation is not simply a matter of individual, mental activity. In trying to derive a text's meaning, language users actually relate the text to the situation, environment or context in which it is found. For instance, in order to justify our interpretation of a problematic text, we try to invent possible circumstances or contexts in which this would be accepted without any difficulty. At the same time, we can never fully interpret a text without taking its context into consideration, even if we consider its coherence to be a function of the intentions of text-producer and text-receiver. Take for instance text 1.4:

Text 1.4
The iron that will spoil the sword;
The sword that will cut the iron;
The tree in the farm that can swim like a canoe;
Cast for Oshe
When he was going to ask for all destinies from Olodumare.

(*Source*: Du Bois 1993: 55)

Although we can identify the cohesive ties in this text and can produce a partial interpretation on the basis of the assumption of coherence, what really happens here eludes us and thus we cannot achieve a full interpretation. What we need to know is who the text-producer is, what the intended audience is, what the time and place of text-production and reception are. Furthermore, any understanding of the text would be deficient if we did not know the purpose or the function of the text in the speech community in which it has been created. For text 1.4 we need to know, for instance, that it is a Yoruba divinatory spell. Once this information is available, a lot of things fall into place. The people and things mentioned assume a specific role, the underlying purposes of the text-producer begin to emerge, even the syntactic relations between noun and verb phrases become disambiguated. This reviewed understanding of the text occurs because we know what 'language game' is played. To complete our interpretation, we further need to know how this text relates to other, prior or contemporaneous texts and text constraints (patterns, rules etc.) that account for its production. In other words, the full meaning of a text is a set of relations (of speaker and writer, audience, purpose, previous history etc.) whose sum constitutes the context for a text.

READER ACTIVITY

Describe the context in which the following texts have taken place. What is the most crucial element of the situation we need to know in order to interpret the texts in each case?

Text 1.5
Shut Down Windows

Are you sure you want to:
- Shut down the computer?
- Restart the computer?
- Restart the computer in MS-Dos mode?

Yes   No   Help

Text 1.6
Kathy: Let's say I was really bad to you.
Heather: Mother I'm sorry about that!
           I'm very angry!
           Bye!
           And I closed the door,
           and you start to cry,
           and I make you some wedding cake,
           Mommy I did something once for you.
           I made you a wedding ring cake that you can eat for your
           own self.
           ((She offers empty angel food cake pan to Kathy))
           You can eat it with the spoon if you want.
           I made something cute for you.
Andy: ((into toy phone)) So she can bring all of her toys.
Kathy: No, I'm not crying yet.
Heather: I made something cute for you.
           Here's one piece of candy.
           She's my mother.
           I do nice stuff for her.
Andy: Heather, I called her gramma.
           And she's gonna keep …
           she gonna keep care of her.
Heather: Gramma's gonna keep care of you.
Andy: And she can bring all her toys.
Heather: Yay!

(*Source*: Sawyer 1993)

Although context is relatively easy to conceive and describe, it is quite hard to delimit and define in a precise, formal way. The origins of the notion of context are interdisciplinary. Its use in linguistics dates from the mid-1960s, when by the influence of work in sociology and anthropology it was realised that language cannot be analysed as a formal system which can be abstracted from society and culture. The notion has already been used in varying ways by many different traditions and schools of linguistics. This certainly is the strength of the notion and a proof of its relevance for analysis; however, the broad range of views may confuse the notion. A rather general definition considers context 'a world filled with people producing utterances: people who have social, cultural, and personal identities, knowledge, beliefs, goals and wants, and who interact with one another in various socially and culturally defined situations' (Schiffrin 1994a: 364). We can perceive this world as a frame that surrounds the text under analysis and provides resources for its appropriate interpretation (cf. Duranti and

Goodwin 1992).

The dimensions, scope and coverage of context have also been viewed in varying ways. Two unifying components among the different definitions can be identified: situation and knowledge. Situation includes the immediate setting and behaviour (as in the notion of 'context of situation', originating in Malinowski's work) or the broader, surrounding culture, including the norms of discourse choices and socio-cultural processes invoked by the text. Knowledge refers to the general background information of text-recipients. In addition to this abstract, cognitive knowledge of context, there is the specific knowledge of the actual social circumstances in which the text is produced. Our general expectations about situations and activities are adapted to the specific circumstances, the 'here and now' of a text.

A widespread view of context also includes text among the components of context. If we accept that situations provide a context for a text's interpretation, the previous text can also provide a context of interpretation for what follows. Brown and Yule (1983) refer to this type of contextual environment as 'co-text'. The 'text as context' view draws attention to the fact that our meanings and understandings of a text are dynamic and sequentially emergent, which means that they are constantly readjusted in the progression of communication. Gumperz (1982) has provided a different perspective of co-text by the notion of contextualisation cues. This notion refers to the sum of signals that allow participants to evoke the cultural background and the social expectations that are necessary to interpret text. Contextualisation cues cover all verbal and non-verbal indicators that help speakers or writers and their addressees to invoke such inferences. This view of co-text as composed of linguistic signals is discussed in detail in the following chapters of the book. Table 1.2 presents the main conceptions of context discussed above. It must be stressed that these dimensions of context are not fixed and immutable; instead they are dynamically and socially constituted by the discourse activities themselves. Communication is constrained by context, but it also reveals, sustains and provides context.

There have been many descriptions of contextual parameters in the literature. Possibly the best codification of context elements is Hymes' (1964, 1974) classification of components of speech events, based on Jakobson's

Context of situation:
who is speaking to whom, when, where and for what purpose; the physical setting, the social scene in which the discourse occurs; the roles and status of the participants involved.
Context of culture:
the speech community; what is possible for, or normally done by, members of the community; the speech events participated in, the speech acts performed, the topics talked about.
Context as co-text:
the prior and upcoming text; what has just been said, what was earlier said, what comes next.
Cognitive context:
knowledge as a set of recognisable conventions, rules, norms and shared assumptions; the process of inferencing tied to current activity and general expectations.

Table 1.2: Types of context

classification of language functions. In Hymes' description, speech events are the largest units of language activity (cf. Pike's behavioreme), which occur in a non-verbal context, the speech situation. The important components of every speech event are setting, participants, purpose, key, channel, topic and message form. Hymes uses a mnemonic device for these factors, the SPEAKING grid, in which each letter is an abbreviation for a different component:

S for setting or scene (time and place)
P for participants and their roles
E for their ends or purposes
A for the act sequence including the message form, medium and content
K for key, i.e. the manner or mood of communication (formal, informal, casual, relaxed etc.)
I for instrumentalities, i.e. the (verbal or non-verbal) channel
N for the norms of interaction
G for genre (see Chapter 2).

In order fully to understand text 1.6 above, for example, we would have to describe the time and place of the event, the participants (three children from 3½ to 5 years of age), the purpose (language play), the key or 'tone, manner or spirit' of the conversation (informal, pretend play), the channel or medium (spoken), the topic or what is discussed and the form or the grammatical and lexical composition of utterances (i.e. the pet names characteris-

---

READER ACTIVITY

Complete the following table by filling in the details about the components of speech events.

	a sermon	a BR announcement	Queen's message	a passport	balcony scene
setting	church				
participant	priest, congregation				
purpose	spiritual, uplifting				
key	formal, exhortative				
channel	written to be spoken				
content	obituary etc.				
form	'God saves you!' 'Let us pray.'				

Table 1.3: Components of some speech events

tic of child language etc.).

In Hymes' view, the specific components of various communicative situations form part of our social and cultural knowledge, or 'communicative competence', in his term. In various approaches, context components like the ones found in Hymes' grid are treated as discrete, codable and detachable factors that can serve text comparison. Such approaches aim at isolating and counting, to the extent that something like this is possible, the effect of a specific contextual factor (e.g. addresser and addressee roles, relations, formal or informal style etc.) on textual choices.

Different descriptions of context include the notion of register in Functional Grammar. Register refers to 'a configuration of meanings that are typically associated with a particular situational configuration of field, mode and tenor' (Halliday and Hasan 1985: 38; see also Chapter 2 below). Field refers to the role or purpose of discourse (e.g. technical discourse etc.). The mode or medium of communication coincides with Hymes' channel (i.e. spoken vs written, spontaneous or not, written to be spoken, written to be read etc.: Gregory and Carroll 1978). Tenor or tone parallels Hymes' key and refers to the social relationships of participants in their roles as addresser and addressee (i.e. formality vs informality etc.).

Discourse analysis is interested in the analysis of contexts mainly because text and context provide evidence for each other. Halliday and Hasan (1985: 36) observe that 'in the normal course of life, all day and every day, when we are interacting with others through language, we are making ... inferences from the situation to the text, and from the text to the situation'.

READER ACTIVITY

Can you reconstruct a context for the following extracts from texts? Who is speaking? Can there be more than one context for each extract?

Once upon a time, there was a fairy prince ...
This is to certify that ...
Four hearts.
On your marks ...
Just a trim, is it?
Rail strike threat averted.
Sea slight on a low swell.

(*Source*: Halliday and Hasan 1985: 37)

In the same way that only some kind of language is allowed in certain contexts, the language used provides indications for the kinds of contexts for which it is fit. In text 1.6, for instance, *let's say* provides from the very beginning a means of understanding the context of the conversation. More generally, our social and cultural knowledge allows us to discover what is going on in the text. However, not only does text invoke social organisation but also social organisation is itself interactively sustained and constructed. Every new utterance indicates an ever-expanding context, which is necessary for the performance and understanding of the discourse. A text does not statically mirror or reflect its context. It also provides for this context by invoking larger social and cultural processes and by organising a framework for them. Individual linguistic participants produce and reproduce their social knowledge through their actions. Context, therefore, is always part of the analysis, because it is an indispensable part of the text (cf. Schiffrin 1988). As a consequence, rather than talking about contexts that determine the use of linguistic elements or the opposite, it is more helpful to consider text and context as ongoing dialogical processes which mutually feed into one another in a dynamic and complex relationship.

Discourse forms and patterns have thus very broad meanings for both participants and interpreters. The use of specific vocabulary and patterns of storytelling in text 1.6 indexes (points to, shapes) an imaginary world (pretend playworld) created by the interaction of the three participants. Recourse to this world is necessary in order to understand the text produced. In Gee's formulation, 'certain forms of language ... are intimately connected to forms of life' (1990: 120ff.). The same is true of less 'fictional' discourse such as text 1.5 above, which is a perfect example of how texts are designed to fit their situated use, on which they also depend for their interpretation. The specific conventions of linguistic form indicate a separate 'form of life' for this discourse.

Discourse analysis is committed to an investigation of what language is used for, and it cannot be restricted to the description of linguistic forms 'independently of the purposes or functions that those forms are designed to serve in human affairs' (Brown and Yule 1983: 1). The study of discourse is not an investigation of signs in abstraction but an investigation of them in the common world in which we all live and act (cf. Geertz 1983).

1.6 THE DATA OF DISCOURSE ANALYSIS

Discourse analysis endorses its own distinctive view of data. In the same way that, for example, experimental phonology has to work with isolated words or sentences in an artificial environment, the study of discourse calls for the analysis of real texts in actual environments and the spurning of fabricated examples. Actual (as opposed to invented) texts are critically important because they constitute the appropriate evidence for studying the function of linguistic devices. As stressed above, the study of discourse is a study of contexts and situated use. Only actual data can be relied upon in studying important aspects of the context such as the stance of discourse participants towards the texts which they create. The main interest in discourse studies is not to make a point of theory; texts, instead, are both the starting and end point of analysis. In consequence, discourse analysis subscribes to the principle of the empiricist tradition that 'language should be studied in actual, attested, authentic instances of use, not as intuitive, invented, isolated sentences' (Stubbs 1993).

From this point of view, it is important to point out that the most spontaneous type of data is oral material, normally recorded or (less frequently) videotaped in natural contexts, mainly in conversational settings. These data should be distinguished from material elicited in sociolinguistic interviews. Interviews are a distinct speech event following its own rules and conventions that are very different from everyday contexts of communication, as can be seen in the range of their variations (television chat shows, radio phone-ins, live interviews etc.). This should not mean that they cannot be employed as a source of data but only that the researcher should be fully aware of the limitations following from their context. Their idiosyncrasies should be taken into account when setting specific research questions and objectives.

In addition and in contrast to other disciplines in the humanities, discourse analysis does not privilege a certain type of text. Contrary to literary studies, it does not work with the concept of a canon, a body of works that share an assumed aesthetic or cultural value. In contrast to stylistics, it is not constrained in the study of literary texts. Finally, it does not privilege – at least, in theory – oral or written texts. Discourse analysis in its everyday practice deals with texts as heterogeneous as advertisements (Cook 1992), biomedical research articles (Dubois 1987), police interviews (Coulthard 1992b), psychotic narratives (Chaika and Alexander 1986), CB talk (Montgomery 1986), newspaper editorials (Bolivar 1994), Beowulfian speech (Shippey 1993) and life stories (Linde 1993).

Furthermore, size is not a principle in excluding texts from analysis. As we saw in the first section of this chapter, texts may be of varying length, even that of a single word. Of course, there are theoretical and practical considerations related to size. First of all, there is the issue of the limits of text as a unit: is a section, a chapter, a whole book, an encyclopaedia a whole and autonomous text or a collection of texts? What is the cut-off point? These questions cannot be answered in an *a priori*, abstract fashion but have always to be addressed in the frame of the current research questions. Let us also note that, although discourse analysis is based on analysing a text as an entity, a unit from beginning to end, the advent of new paradigms such as corpus studies is expected to challenge this perspective and allow for complementary approaches that study a large amount of material for its textual properties. As we have already noted, the increasing spread of new electronic media is also bound to influence our conception of text and redefine its limits in a radical way.

From a practical point of view, there are difficulties in the analysis and presentation of results related to very large texts. As a result, most applications have been limited to rather small texts – although there is a whole range of very small texts that have not been systematically studied: answering-machine talk, e-mail messages, headlines and captions, small ads etc. In this book we are necessarily constrained in the analysis of very large texts for reasons of space, but, as a compensation, we mostly work with complete texts from beginning to end.

1.7 THE SCOPE OF THE BOOK

It must be clear by now that people do not communicate with words. Similarly, they do not (or not exclusively) communicate with sounds, morphemes or sentences, nor with notions, concepts or propositions. They, instead, communicate with meaningful combinations of these entities, namely texts, that integrate meaning and structure and combine language in the form of speech or writing and paralanguage. Furthermore, language units are not produced in a vacuum, and neither are their meaningful combinations. Texts are produced and received in distinct socio-cultural environments imbued with personal and interpersonal goals. The ongoing use of texts in these communicative environments constitutes discourse.

The text-linguistic perspective to discourse analysis consists in the view that discourse is to be studied by taking text as the basic unit of analysis and the language of the text as the main focus of examination. This view allows for identifying the articulation of both linguistic substance and form, as well as for acknowledging the relations between them as legitimate objects of analysis. Text is assumed to be structured or organised in a multiplicity of ways, which our book will aim at helping to reveal. This assumption is based on the presupposition that texts have a coherent, interpretable meaning, derived from their textual and contextual relations. As we will argue in Chapter 2, the most fundamental organising principle of a text's textual and contextual parameters is its construction according to the narrative or the non-narrative mode. Finally, only authentic, attested texts can form the basis of our analysis. No texts are privileged on the basis of some (aesthetic or other) value. As a result, our presentation will rely on all kinds of discourse with emphasis on the most typical and fundamental types of text that speakers and writers produce and consume in their everyday interaction.

Tannen has talked of the basic concern of discourse analysis as the explanation of 'that mysterious moving force that creeps in between the words and between the lines, sparking ideas, images and emotions that are not contained in any of the words one at a time – the force that makes words into discourse' (1988: xi). Our book aims at exploring this force by mapping the area of narrative and non-narrative discourse. In addition, we intend to provide an exemplar of text analysis in practice and to indicate a coherent framework for integrating traditional and foundational research with more recent approaches. It falls outside the book's scope to deal in detail with production and composition aspects of texts (for an overview, see de Beaugrande and Dressler 1981 and Nystrand et al. 1993, respectively), principles of reading (see de Beaugrande 1981) or discourse pragmatics (see

Leech 1983; Blakemore 1988), although the relevance of all these will be made clear at many points. Although not claiming to be exhaustive, our presentation intends to give the reader a sense of the state of the art at the end of the twentieth century.

FURTHER READING

Some of the most fundamental references for the use of discourse outside discourse analysis are: in anthropology, Geertz (1983) and Clifford (1988); in history, White (1981) and Schöttler (1989); in sociology, Drew and Heritage (1992); in information science, Brady and Berwick (1983) and Rambow (1993); in psychology and psychotherapy, van Dijk and Kintsch (1983) and Labov and Fanshel (1977); in education, Cazden (1988); in neurolinguistics, Bloom et al. (1994).

Classic textbooks on discourse analysis within linguistics are: de Beaugrande and Dressler (1981), Brown and Yule (1983), Stubbs (1983) and the less sophisticated, more basic Cook (1989). Particularly strong on conversation analysis are Coulthard (1985) and Schiffrin (1994a). Hatch (1992) and McCarthy (1992) provide a discussion of different methods and models of discourse analysis in terms of their usefulness to (foreign) language teachers and students. The best collection of papers on individual issues of discourse analysis are the three volumes of van Dijk (1985). Finally, the analysis of narrative discourse is equipped with a useful dictionary, Prince (1987), which explains terms from a wide perspective of approaches, and one of the best introductory textbooks, Toolan (1988).

For the use of the term 'discourse' and 'text', see, among others, Coulthard (1985) and Lavandera (1988).

Williams (1977) is a basic, if somewhat peripheral, reference on the issues of substance, expression and the effect of media on the conception of text. Specifically, for the effect of the alphabet and typography, see Ong (1982) and the further references given there. For the effect of the book on the concept of text, see Illich (1993).

For a detailed discussion of the theory of speech acts and its implications on approaches to discourse, see Schiffrin (1994a: ch. 3). There is also a vast literature, mainly of a sociolinguistic nature, on the cross-cultural differences and realisations of speech acts (e.g. Blum-Kulka, House and Kasper 1989; Wolfson 1981).

Basic references in the school of critical discourse analysis include Fowler (1981), Hodge and Kress (1988), Fairclough (1989), Kress and Hodge (1990). Two unrelated approaches that also emphasise the importance of the substance plane are Davies and Greene (1984) and Connor and McCagg (1987).

A parallel description of cohesion to that of Halliday and Hasan (1976) is Gutwinski (1976). A more detailed picture of cohesive relations in English can be found in Martin (1992). Further references are given in the more advanced discussion of cohesion in Chapter 4.

The best introduction to context, although mainly within a Functional Grammar perspective, is Halliday and Hasan (1985). The most detailed, Halliday (1978), is also illuminating for many aspects of context. Hymes' articles (1964, 1972, 1974) are always worth studying closely, and so is Malinowski's early study (1946). Schiffrin (1994a) provides a thorough but too advanced discussion on the different views of context within models of discourse analysis. Duranti and Goodwin (1992) include a useful state-of-the-art section on context in its many facets. The whole volume is also commendable for bringing together research on context from different analytic traditions. Particularly for the notion of register, see Gregory and Carroll (1978). For the role of the audience in shaping discourse, see papers in Duranti and Brenneis (1986). Finally, for the parallel notion of context in pragmatics, see Levinson (1983: 47ff.) and Horn (1988).

Finally, for a guide to collecting and analysing data, see Silverman (1993). The state-of-the-art paper on recording natural data is Goodwin (1993). For the central issue of elicited data in interviews, see Churchill (1978), Wolfson (1982) and Linde (1993).

The Modes of Discourse

2.1 SPEECH EVENTS AND SCHEMATA

In Chapter 1, we defined discourse as texts (meaningful combinations of language units) which serve various communicative purposes and perform various acts in situational, social and cultural contexts. These texts make up the discourse system of our communication. However, in real life, we do not produce or construct and participate in the same kinds of discourse all the time. Our communication takes various forms, to which we orient ourselves in different ways. We talk to our friends in face-to-face interactions, on the phone or on the computer, we tell jokes or relate events which happened to us or others, we write essays for our courses, we give or attend lectures and pre-sentations, we write notes, we participate in meetings, we read or less com-monly write articles in academic journals or newspapers, novels, poems etc.

All these different discourse activities form sub-groupings within the overall system of our linguistic communication. In numerous cases, they are predictably associated with certain situations and speech events, that is, discourse structures which exhibit conventional speech acts, settings, topics, participants, purposes and other context features. All of us are familiar with such conventional associations. We know for instance that a sexual joke is normally told in a company of intimates in a relaxed and informal setting. We know that the format of an invited lecture in university consists of a monologic lecture followed by open discussion. We know about participant roles too. They can also vary predictably in different discourse activities. We are more aware of a power differential when we are in a meeting with the president of the company in which we work than when we have a chat with friends. Comparably, different speech events are associated with different topics, more or less conventionalised. In a business meeting, there is normally limited flexibility and freedom in the topics to be discussed. Similarly, the communication between a salesperson and a customer in a shop is expected mainly to revolve around a sales request and the response to it. In such speech events, even the internal structure of our communication is conventionalised: it has clear beginnings, carefully-organised closings and a recognisable overall organisation in between. Knowing this internal structure is essential for our successful communication.

READER ACTIVITY

What are your expectations about the internal structure of a telephone call and a message in an answering machine? Try to invent some examples. How do they relate to the following instances of discourse?

Text 2.1
```
 0  ring
 1  Hello::,
 2  H'llo, Arthur?
 3  Yes.
 4  Hi. It's Alex.
 5  Oh hi.
 6  How's life?
 7  Fine.
 8  And the school?
 9  It's alright. It's half-term next week.
10  Right. And you're doing your music course?
11  Yeah, I am.
12  Right. Is Aubrey around?
```
(*Source*: Authors' data)

Text 2.2
```
 1  hi
 2  only me
 3  I hope you're enjoying yourselves
 4  and having a good evening out.
 5  Give me a ring sometime tomorrow
 6  one of you or other
 7  if you've got time.
 8  I'll probably be in evening
 9  sort of ...
10  well, I'll be in most of the time.
11  But I'm off to Paris with Pam
12  from Tuesday morning early
13  till Friday .. Friday midday
14  just to sort of have a flip.
15  Wonderful cheap
16  el cheapo journey on the Eurostar
17  sixty-eight pounds return.
18  Lots and lots of love.
19  Bye.
```
(*Source*: Authors' data)

We form our expectations about speech acts, events and the situations in which they are embedded on the basis of our participation in them in our speech community. The more conventionalised a speech act or event is, the more expectations we seem to have about its setting, participant roles and internal structure. If two people belong to different social and cultural groups, their expectations are likely to differ. Even the most convention-alised speech events have been found to vary socio-culturally in certain respects. Within a given culture too, discourse structure varies in different social, professional, age, gender groups etc. Telephone conversations, in particular their openings and closings, provide a classic instance of docu-mented variation. American telephone conversations show a preference for the caller to be identified by recognition from the answerer (see 2 in text 2.1 above) rather than by explicit self-identification (Schegloff 1986). This pref-erence has been found in other societies too (e.g. in Greece: Sifianou 1989). Swedish and Dutch data, on the other hand, suggest a preference for self-identification rather than other-recognition (Lindstrom 1994: 248). Similarly, the rest of the opening sections, namely the answer to a telephone summons (see 1 in text 2.1), the greeting sequence (4–5) and the 'how are you?' sequences (6–9) are socio-culturally variable.

The situational, social and cultural variability of speech acts and events has been mainly documented by sociolinguistic research on the expression of politeness. Speech acts such as apologies, compliments, offers and requests have been looked into systematically in different situations and socio-cultural groups (e.g. see Blum-Kulka, House and Kasper 1989; Brown and Levinson 1987). The well-known speech act of thanking, for instance, has been found to vary according to the situation, setting, relationship of the participants and culture involved. In Italian, the expression of thanks often seems to call for an acknowledging response in closing, whereas comparable forms (e.g. *don't mention it* etc.) are rare in British English (Aston 1995: 60). The predictability of the speech act is also variable in different discourse settings. In Nepali, service encounters may end directly on provision of the service, whereas in the USA they require a thanking sequence.

In general, the results of studies on speech acts and events suggest that the same speech act or event may be used and interpreted differently in different contexts. Even the same utterance of a speech act may perform a range of functions and convey a range of meanings. These may range from the encoding of solidarity and intimacy with the addressee to the expression of an asymmetrical power relation between the interactants. All these gain their force from the context in which they are employed. The domain of gender differences in linguistic usage has provided us with ample examples of this variability. For instance, despite our intuitive association between insults and rude behaviour, it has been found that insults may be used by men as a device for expressing closeness and solidarity with their interlocu-tors. Women tend to prefer compliments for that function (for a lucid discus-sion, see Holmes 1995: 115–153).

READER ACTIVITY

The following texts are examples of apologies. Based on the internal structure of each apology, what do you understand about the relationship of the people involved in each case? (The effect of the presence vs absence of the addressee on the expression of the apology needs to be taken into account.) To what extent do the examples confirm your expectations about as well as your own preferences for apologies?

Text 2.3: Note
I'm really sorry I haven't been in. I've been trying to get in touch with you for the past week or so, and it's either busy or not in. I've been really sick and now I've got all this work to catch up with at UCL. So, it has been really hectic and because it's been reading week I'm trying to catch up with my work. I will definitely come in on Wednesday because I'll have got most of my work done by then. Once again I'm really sorry.

(*Source*: Authors' data)

Text 2.4: From a letter
I'm sorry I haven't got around to responding until now, but I've been quite busy (same old excuse). Christine's old tenants have moved out, so it's been a mad rush at the weekends to get the house in good shape again for the new tenants, which move in on the 15 Dec. With that out of the way, I thought it would be great to get together some time over Christmas …

(*Source*: Authors' data)

Text 2.5: E-mail message
Congratulations on your marriage. Sorry for not having come but I couldn't understand the directions. Simon.

Text 2.6: Reply to 2.5
Well I don't believe a clever chap like you couldn't follow the directions but I'll let that wash over … (just kidding)

(*Source*: Authors' data)

Text 2.7: Avril is a guest at Jenny's place
Avril: I'm terribly sorry I've done a terrible thing. I've broken that little knob on the dryer. It's fallen inside the filter and I can't get it out.
Jenny: Oh that's easily fixed. And it'll run OK without the filter.

(*Source*: Holmes 1995: 176)

Text 2.8: In a college refectory
Student: I'm sorry but I don't have anything smaller.
Salesperson: That's okay love.

(*Source*: Authors' data)

As with other speech events, the strategies and norms for appropriate use of apologies are contextually variable. As a general rule of thumb, we can expect the degree of explicit expression of an apology to reflect the level of formality of the situation and the participants' relationship. The better we know people and the more friendly we are with them, the less explicit we need to be when apologising. It has been found that male friends tend to apologise less to each other than female friends and to regard explicit apologies as less important in maintaining relationships (see Holmes 1995: 159). The humorous and teasing (almost insulting) tone of our example of the e-mail messages (texts 2.5 and 2.6 above, exchanged between two male friends) seems to confirm this.

So far, it must have become apparent that a lot of our everyday discourse communication exhibits certain conventionalised components which are associated with certain contextual configurations. As communicative speakers of a language and members of a society, we have knowledge of and expectations about such components. There have been a lot of attempts to characterise and formally represent this knowledge. One general unifying principle in these attempts is the assumption that the mind analyses and interprets experience with the help of highly abstract mental patterns that are available for recall, revision and reinterpretation in new situations. These mental patterns are stored in long-term memory as data structures that represent sets of associations and (general and specific) knowledge about commonplace and stereotypical situations: for example, going to a restaurant, having a birthday party, going to the dentist etc. (see Mandler 1978; Minsky 1985; Schank 1982; Schank and Abelson 1977).

Such mental patterns have been labelled as scripts, frames or schemata. While not immediately interchangeable, these terms stand for notions which reveal a substantial convergence of different scholars on the components for representing knowledge. The term 'frame' originates in Minsky's (1985) influential framework of knowledge representation and has been used mainly by scholars in artificial intelligence. Minsky saw a frame as a remembered framework of knowledge, a network of nodes and relations, which is adapted to fit reality by changing details as necessary. The top levels of this network are fixed and represent things that are always true about various situations. The lower levels have many terminals or slots which are filled by specific instances of data. Some of them are default but attached loosely to their terminals, so that they can be easily displaced by new items that fit the current situation better.

The term 'schema' has a long history in psychology, starting from Bartlett's work on memory (1932) which put forward a reconstructive approach to information retrieval and recall. According to this theory, recall is not a passive reproduction of information but an inferential reconstruction of it, in the light of a person's active schemata. Like frames, schemata have constant relationships within them and variables that may become associated with, or bound by, different aspects of our environment. On different occasions, these variables take on different values.

The notion of a script is used by various scholars as hyponymous in rela-tion to schemata. It is reserved for a number of stereotypic situations in which human behaviour is highly predictable and narrowly defined. Schank and Abelson's (1977) scripts refer to a class of rigid schemata, which are subtly distinguished from other forms of knowledge structure, namely the plans, the goals and the themes. Scripts are spatially- and temporally-organ-ised representations specialised to deal with event sequences. A detailed account of the differences between frames, schemata and scripts is beyond the scope of this discussion. For our purposes, it is useful to think of them as data structures which represent generalised concepts stored in our memory: concepts which underlie objects, situations, events, actions and sequences of events or actions. In the view of numerous scholars, they are expressions of so-called episodic or situation models (e.g. Johnson-Laird 1983; van Dijk 1987a). A model is a mental representation of a situation or an episode, that is, an event or action taking place in a specific social situation. It embodies personal, general (i.e. scriptal, schematic) knowledge and information derived from textual representation. Speakers and hearers in the course of production and comprehension of discourse make strategic uses of their models. They retrieve, activate and update them on-line (e.g. Johnson-Laird 1983; van Dijk 1987a). In interpreting discourse, participants also draw upon their knowledge of context models (i.e. social and cultural properties, shared assumptions, addresser–addressee roles and relations etc.).

READER ACTIVITY

It is very easy to find evidence for the schematic knowledge which we employ in our discourse production and reception. Look at the three extracts of texts below and provide a possible continuation for each of them. Then, look at the three continuations given by the authors and correspond each of them to each of the three texts.

Text 2.9
Australia from 798 for 14 nights
Cairns is the gateway to the tropical north of Queensland, an area endowed with two of nature's greatest treasures – the world's largest and most famous coral reef and some of the oldest and finest rain-forests. Cairns is a compact and friendly city of gardens, set between the sea and the mountains.
                    (*Source*: *The Guide*, 16–23 March 1996, p. 10)

Text 2.10
Donation and membership form
If you want to help ...

Your donation towards asthma research will help us to find new ways of treating this devastating disease. We rely almost entirely on voluntary contributions.

(*Source*: National Asthma Campaign leaflet)

Text 2.11

NEWS FLASH: <u>YOU</u> MUST DECIDE

HAS PERFECT PIZZA FINALLY GONE CHEESY MAD?

OR

ARE WE SIMPLY GIVING YOU AN OBSCENE NUMBER OF GREAT OFFERS?

(*Source*: Perfect Pizza advertisement)

Text 2.12

The accommodation is in beach front apartments (all with sea views) with a large pool on site.

Prices (all dates subject to availability):

4 sharing (2 bedrooms, bathrooms) £798 per person;

3 sharing (2 bedrooms, bathrooms) £848 per person;

2 sharing £898 per person.

The prices include: • return scheduled flights • return transfers • 14 nights' accommodation.

Text 2.13

Dear Customer,

Order today and you can get:

FREE EVENING STANDARD NEWSPAPER to all our customers

FREE 2 OFF VOUCHER for a great home movie

GREAT REGULAR MEAL DEAL for £7.99   SAVE £2.21

THE BIG MEAL DEAL for £9.95   SAVE £3.75

Full details of these great offers are in the enclosed menu. ...

Text 2.14

Last year we spent nearly £2,000,000 on vital research.

I would like to make a donation of:
•£50 •£25 •£12 •£5 •Other

Method of payment:
•I enclose a cheque payable to ...

2.2 GENRES OR DISCOURSE TYPES: SPOKEN AND WRITTEN

It must be evident by now that there are certain systematic co-patternings between the form, content, function and context of our discourse activities. A standard term that captures such co-patternings is 'genre', which is also well known outside linguistics. The genre is essentially a classificatory

---

READER ACTIVITY

Try to form a list of specific names for genres that are part of our everyday vocabulary. Can you think of terms which denote relatively recent genres?

---

concept, referring to a class of communicative events, the participants in which share a certain set of conventions defined in terms of formal, functional and contextual properties. Both linguistic and non-linguistic criteria enter its definition. The boundaries of a genre are not only determined by reference to form (e.g. lexical and grammatical patterns etc.) and content. They are also determined by reference to social and cognitive criteria, such as norms, conventions, rules of use, schemata and, on the whole, our perceptions of and expectations about textual boundaries (Paltridge 1995: 288–99).

Each society has its own particular configuration of genres, which are in particular relationships to each other. This system is not static but open to change. Certain genres gradually become less popular in certain communities (e.g. folktales in western communities), while others gain in popularity following upon social, technological and other changes (e.g. telephone conversations, computer-mediated communication). In addition, each society also has its own particular nomenclature for genres, for example distinguishing between novels and short stories, or assigning even more specialised descriptions such as science-fiction novels, scientific textbooks or repair manuals.

Systematic co-patternings between elements of form, content, functions and context have been given various names in the literature. Style (the language habits shared by a group of people at one time, according to Crystal and Davy 1969: 10) and register (see 1.5) are as a rule overarched by the term 'genre'. A genre tends to be identified with a specific style and register. A much broader term that is chosen over 'genre' by numerous discourse analysts is 'discourse type' (see Cook 1989; Fairclough 1989) or 'text type' (mainly in the continental tradition: see de Beaugrande and Dressler 1981).

One of the main advantages of using terms like 'genre' and 'discourse type' in discourse analysis is that 'they enable us to pick out major differences of type between the elements of orders of discourse which we might otherwise lose sight of. In so doing the conventional associations between discourse form and content become much clearer' (Fairclough 1989: 124). As a result, we can formalise the ways in which our communication practices are constrained by conventions. In general, genres are helpful as means of constructing, organising and interpreting meaning, as well as of controlling its function in audiences and discourse communities. However, the main disadvantage of working with classificatory terms such as 'genre' is the absence of broadly-accepted, clear-cut criteria and definitions. As a result, groupings of discourse activities by genre tend to multiply into minutely detailed and fragmented categories. To take the logic of this tendency to extremes, each new different text should be classified as a separate genre. Alternatively, it could be treated as a new sub-genre of a genre. Where you draw the line between different genres and sub-genres of a genre is another problematic enterprise. It has thus become increasingly apparent that genres are not fixed or static categories which fall into rigid dichotomies. Instead, they should be viewed as dynamic compilations of textual and contextual dimensions that form a continuum. These dimensions serve as the basis for operationalising the notion of a genre and exploring relationships of similarity and difference between genres as points on a continuum.

One of the dimensions that has commonly been employed for these purposes is medium or modality, that is, the spoken–written dimension. The spoken and the written media each seem at first glance to be neatly associated with a set of contextual features of their own. In speech, interlocutors normally share the same spatio-temporal context. Communication thus exhibits an 'on-line' monitoring which benefits from the addressees' immediate feedback and the abundance of contextual clues (e.g. visual clues such as body language and gestures, auditory clues such as variations in stress and tone of voice, hesitations, pauses etc.). By contrast, written language is decontextualised or 'autonomous' since it cannot depend on the addressees' contributions or on other contextual clues.

At the same time, the speed and manner of production afford speech with less forethought, planning and prior organisation than written discourse (see Ochs 1979 for the differences between planned and unplanned discourse). Writing is inevitably a slower activity; thus, writers have time to mould their ideas into a more complex, coherent and integrated whole, making use of complicated lexical and syntactic devices. Instances of writing are also characterised by (at least, relative) permanence, and they allow for future survey and consultation. Written texts are the product of extensive checking and editing. From the moment they reach their addressees, they can be examined and re-examined and be portable to new contexts. By contrast, spoken discourse is transient and does not outlive its moment of production (unless recorded). Thus, it can afford imperfections and on-line editings and negotiations.

READER ACTIVITY

The following is a transcript of a spoken text. How does it confirm the features of spoken discourse discussed above?

Text 2.15
A: Apparently, there's some scandal now, that there's mm there was er a dirty war, conducted by the Gonzalez // government

B: yeah

A: and and, there's now a scandal, when we were there

C: oh .. it was a huge affair // when we were there //

A: that Gonzalez seemed to be // aware of this //

B: well, they were tapping the phone of the king

A: no no, // they actually //

B: that's pretty serious (laughing)

A: they actually // had //

B: (laughs)

A: no no .. listen, they had – they had their own death squad, as a government

B: possibly

D: who's to cook this meat now, // is this

B: I'm gonna cook the meat, I didn't – I didn't know when I

C: so how many days are you going to spend in France?

B: well ... that's not clear. // What I initially wanted us to do //

D: well, well the plan is, our, er, we're going on a Sunday, and then, and we're coming back two weeks on, and then

B: and two more days

D: and then two more days

C: so you're going for seventeen days

D: so we're going for a bit more than // a fortnight //

C: and so you are

D: we're planning to er shoot down to Brittany // and //

B: we think sort of between one and five days in Brittany

D: so what what, well we want to shoot down from from from // Brittany to

B: I mean the, er, we maybe, we are not committed ...

(*Source*: Authors' data)

Transcripts of natural conversational data, even when they lack details about paralinguistic features as above, show a picture of messiness, with their amount of interruptions, overlaps, repetitions, hesitations, false starts, after-thoughts and back-channelling, to mention only some of the typical features of face-to-face interactions.

On the basis of the above features, the initial hypothesis in discourse analysis was that spoken discourse types were bound to be less complex and more implicit than written discourse types. They were expected to present very little abstraction and density of ideas, more repetitious use of language and avoidance of syntactically complex categories such as participial and passive constructions. In addition, they were assumed to draw more on expressive, interpersonal and, on the whole, subjective features of communication to suit their participatory framework (for a more detailed discussion, see Chapter 5).

These hypotheses encouraged an oversimplified view of the relationship between spoken and written genres. This was congruent with the creation of dissociated mentalities regarding the voice (speaking) vs print (writing) divide which prevailed in numerous disciplines at one time in their history. Numerous empirical studies not only in linguistics but also in anthropology, psychology and other areas gradually cast doubt on various long-standing assertions in relation to speech and writing. First of all, the allegedly general differences between oral or non-literate societies (i.e. with no writing or schooling) and literate societies turned out on examination to be difficult to prove. Along with their hypothesised formulaic, additive (strung together by simple relations like those with *and*) and redundant thought and expression, oral cultures were also found to have linguistic formality, explicitness and complexity associated with writing. The claim that literacy leads to higher cognitive skills and analytical thought was also hard to bear out. Scribner and Cole's (1981) groundbreaking work on the Vai in Liberia demonstrated that literacy in and of itself does not lead to any grandiose cognitive abilities. It is literacy associated with formal schooling (i.e. school-based or essayist literacy) that leads to quite specific abilities (e.g. abstract reasoning, talking about tasks in contrived situations). Writing may help the capacity for analytical and critical expression, but it does not promote its automatic development.

In the light of numerous studies in various contexts, currently the standard view is that there are no absolute differences between spoken and written discourse. Spoken and written genres form a continuum and not the opposites of a rigid dichotomy. The prototypical communicative contexts of spoken and written discourse only offer the potential for certain features: immediacy, formulaicity and rhythmicity, participatory engagement and implicitness in spoken discourse; explicitness, integrated expression and abstraction in written discourse. Nonetheless, all these features can in fact cut across the distinction between spoken and written. Thus, particular types of speech and writing may be more or less similar with respect to several dimensions of variation. As a result, spoken and written genres should be seen as ways of using the language which cannot form unitary and independent links with speaking and writing respectively. Different social and cultural practices in certain contexts call for certain uses of language. These are diversely patterned and trade on features like implicitness–explicitness, simplicity–complexity and immediacy–decontextualisation in varying degrees.

READER ACTIVITY

In what ways do texts 2.1 and 2.2 not fit the prototypical communicative context of spoken discourse?

Numerous genres that lie neither on the spoken nor on the written end of the genre continuum appear prominently in cases of technologically-mediated communication: for example, fax, answering-machine talk, e(lectronic)-mail, e-chat, e-conferencing etc. For instance, answering-machine talk, an instance of spoken discourse with, however, no addressee feedback or interaction, has been found to draw on a mixed repertoire of prototypically spoken and written language (Gold 1991) and at times to behave more like letters than telephone calls, that is, to be closer to the written end of the speaking–writing continuum (Liddicoat 1994).

The various forms of electronic discourse clearly throw the book at some of our well-established conceptions about spoken and written genres. The new electronic medium allows for texts that do not fall neatly into any particular category. Thus, despite the fact that they are written, interactive forms like e-mail and e-chat are highly dialogic and relatively unplanned, with a potential for broad, rapid dissemination and quick feedback (see Foertsch 1995).

READER ACTIVITY

Study the following e-mail messages. Would you agree with the following view: 'Electronic discourse is neither here nor there, neither pure writing nor pure speech but somewhere in between. ... Studying it as one and not the other will force us to exclude certain factors that influence its construction' (Foertch 1995: 304)?

Text 2.16
> It seems the problem with my car is nothing a new engine won't
> sort out. I'm not kidding, apparently gas is seeping around the side
> of the pistons building up pressure in the cam head. The cure is
> usually an engine re-bore and new pistons (or a new engine).

It's times like these when I'm glad I don't have a car!
A new engine, wow! Wasn't it a new car?

BTW, what are you doing on the weekend?

Text 2.17 (reply to text 2.3)
This weekend is the Logica 25th anniversary in London. All employees + guests are invited which means attendance may be around 4000 people! To accommodate this many people the whole of Spitalfields market has been hired out.

Some bright spark came up with the idea that the theme for the party should be the wild west so Yvette and I are getting fitted out with cowgirl/boy outfits on Saturday. It seems to be the ideal opportunity for a corporate piss-take so keep an eye on Computing's 'Back Bytes' for any pics.

I hope you're over your colds. Now I've got the bug!

(*Source*: Authors' data)

E-mail messages are only one example of the combination of diverse elements in discourse activities. There is an indeterminate list of genres in every community and at times it is infinitely difficult to decide whether something is or is not a separate instance of a genre. There are numerous forms of discourse based on further combinations, recombinations and blendings of various kinds of resources that are already conventionally attached to a genre. Genre approaches to discourse fail to account for those cases. They also fail to consider 'the differentially weighted potential which the meanings of the resources themselves have in being open to possible modification or transformation by an individual at any particular moment of use' (Kelly 1994: 221).

To cope with the continuous proliferation of distinct discourse activities we would need to set up never-ending lists of genres. But that is where we started from and that clearly does not work. However, neither does the opposite strategy of trying, instead, to group distinct speech events as conventional forms of discourse (discourse types) in well-motivated ways, accepting that each category would cover a diverse and heterogeneous domain. Working with the spoken–written distinction represents such an attempt. As we saw, however, it too can create a too-rigid framework if applied too narrowly and can lead one to lose sight of the complexities of discourse. In addition, the distinction between spoken and written or orality and literacy is ultimately based on a difference in technology and has been challenged for various societies. As already suggested, various oral societies have been found to be literate in terms of the complexity of their cognitive systems and of the form and content of their discourse. Comparably, various literate types of discourse exhibit an impressive affinity with our prototypical features of an oral discourse. Any differences that speaking and writing are usually alleged to involve arise from various communicative context features and cut across the medium difference (see Tannen 1982, 1984, 1985). In consequence, although genre and discourse type are in principle useful means of categorisation, they can be overridden by a much more powerful basis for a typology of texts, that of (rhetorical) mode.

2.3 DISCOURSE MODES

As a way of categorising the seamless web of linguistic communication, the taxonomic principle of rhetorical mode (or stance) is as old as any metalanguage on discourse, traceable to Aristotle's *Poetics*. From Aristotle to modern-day rhetorical theory, texts (and genres) have been classified by reference to general modes of organisation basically including (cf. de Beaugrande and Dressler 1981: 184):

> narration: the telling/writing of a story, consisting of a unique sequence of events that took place at a specific point in time;
> description: presentations of how something looks (smells, tastes etc.);
> argumentation: the process of supporting or weakening arguments, views, theories etc.

Many models (e.g. Kinneavy 1971; Werlich 1976) add a fourth category, namely exposition, including texts like essays, summaries etc. However, this lacks a clearly-defined status. Other models include distinct persuasive, poetic and scientific (rhetorical) modes (e.g. Moffett 1968; Britton et al. 1975).

Mainly developed for pedagogical purposes, models that classify texts according to mode have mostly relied on intuition and, in general, have shunned the formulation of precise criteria. A more systematic taxonomy of genres is provided by Longacre (1976). His criteria combine features of 'surface' and 'deep' levels. Surface-level criteria refer to the appearance or not of a chronological linkage in the text and the presence of prescription (instructions or injunctions for something to be done). The corresponding deep-level criteria deal with the succession of elements and the presence of time as projected (e.g. in future plans and wishes) or not projected (e.g. occurring in the past). These criteria reflect on specific linguistic choices such as the use of pronouns (e.g. notice the generic 'you' in procedural texts), modality, tenses and cohesion. The sum of these features can be employed to distinguish four major categories of discourse genres as shown in Table 2.1.

Longacre's classification is clearly a neat and economical way of distinguishing between discourse genres. However, as Reddick (1992) has noticed, many definitions of categories are negative rather than positive:

DEEP		– projected	+ projected
	SURFACE	– prescription	+ prescription
+ succession	+ chronological framework	NARRATIVE	PROCEDURE
– succession	– chronological framework	EXPOSITORY	HORTATORY

Table 2.1: Longacre's taxonomy of 'discourse genres'

thus expository genres are those which are *not* chronological, *not* prescriptive, *not* based on succession etc.

Another, more important, drawback in Longacre's taxonomy is that it fails to recognise an even more fundamental division of modes, transcending individual genres and texts. This is the distinction between narrative and non-narrative discourse. This distinction is overrriding and cuts across other major divisions such as the spoken–written, which, as we have shown in section 2.2, has been seriously challenged on more than one ground. Traditional rhetorical models implicitly recognise the fundamental division of discourse (compare the fictive vs non-fictive 'kinds' in Moffett 1968, the expressive vs informative functions in Brittion et al. 1975 etc.). More recent studies, based on a statistical analysis of sets of variable features, also point to a major division between fictional and informative types (see Grabe 1987). The use of the terms 'fiction' and 'non-fiction' in the world of book publishing is a further recognition of a basic dichotomy.

Bruner's influential studies acknowledge the centrality of narrative as a mode of organising not just discourse but also human knowledge and interaction. As Bruner has asserted, 'we organise our experience and our memory of human happenings mainly in the form of narrative – stories, excuses, myths, reasons for doing and not doing and so on' (1991: 4). Narrative is so powerful as to encapsulate an individual's sense of the world (i.e. our subjective reality). As such, it is a form not only of representing but also of constituting reality (cf. ibid.: 5). Bruner identifies (1986, 1990) two major ways of knowing: the 'narrative mode' is a way of knowing human reality, experiences, beliefs, doubts and emotions; the 'paradigmatic mode' deals with natural (physical) reality, truth, observation, analysis, proof and rationality. The latter is normally described in terms of science and, according to Bruner and other scholars, has been mistakenly favoured over the narrative mode by the models of rationality that have characterised western thought from Descartes to the present.

Lately though, this non-narrative bias has given way to the recognition of narrative as an alternative, equally important, mode of making claims about knowledge, presenting viewpoints and constructing and challenging theories about ourselves and others. In addition to all its other functions, narrative is thus projected as a major vehicle for the cultivation of critical skills and for socialisation into the rudiments of scholarly discourse (e.g. Ochs et al. 1992: 37–72). Furthermore, both traditional and modern societies rely upon the narrative mode for children's socialisation into a specific cultural reality.

The results of various experiments strengthen the validity of these views. The truth established in a story appears to have a stronger cognitive effect on people than the truth established through rationality and informative texts. People also remember things better when they are presented to them in a narrative mode (Bruner 1986). Infact, numerous (basically, non-western) societies encode their claims about knowledge and their views about the world almost exclusively in narrative mode.

An interesting case in point is Maranhão's research which suggested that, in the community of Icarai (north-east Brazil), the stories with which the fishermen answered the researcher's questions were in fact substitutes for the expected short speech acts (turns in conversation, reactions, corrections etc.). In other words, the stories were devices for encoding knowledge in the place of explanations and other non-narrative types of discourse. As Maranhão describes: 'the fishermen who told me long fishing stories were demonstrating their knowledge to an ethnographer whose "scientific" curiosity was interpreted as scepticism' (1993: 265). He adds: 'at times they made poignant efforts to persuade me that they knew what they were talking about by building narratives which were truly gems, illustrating all aspects of their nautical and ichthyological knowledge, as well as the forms of social etiquette which were important within their social milieu' (ibid.: 266). At the end, the ethnographer realised that for him knowledge was defined in terms of explanatory eloquence, while for various communities knowledge partakes in different, narrative spheres of discourse.

In addition to its status as a device for sharing knowledge and theorising, narrative discourse exhibits an unquestionable primacy in our everyday social lives. Narratives do not only permeate our lives in their different shapes but also form a constitutive element of them, a fundamental principle of organising and making sense of our experience. In the last two decades, the recognition of their importance as a key element in every person's identity has given rise to new approaches in personality studies and psychoanalysis. Therapeutic sessions capitalise on the fact that we exist through our stories. The only way to discover and be ourselves is by recollecting and possessing the narrative of ourselves (see Johnstone 1990: 110–11). Narrative discourse even plays a critical role in spheres of public life, which are the stronghold of non-narrative. The domain of law is such an example: for instance, social psychologists have found that jurors use narrative structures of expectation in arriving at their verdicts (Pennington and Hastie 1993).

READER ACTIVITY

The narrative mode of discourse can be found to operate in, among others, the following texts: everyday stories about various events, retellings of plots of movies and TV series, comic strips, autobiography, personal letters, gossip, news reports, legal testimonies, history books, fairytales etc. Which of these do you usually produce or receive in a day? Which other texts would you add to the above list?

Narrative analysis is one of the best and most extensively researched areas of the multi-disciplinary study of discourse (van Dijk 1993). The term 'narrative' is itself one of the most standardised and widely-accepted terms.

How will we label collectively what is juxtaposed to narrative? Expository discourse? Argumentative discourse? Analytical? Elaboration or presentation (as suggested by various scholars)? Such terms are either felt as too obscure or as too narrow in scope and coverage and, up to now, the linguistic or non-linguistic(!) community has unfortunately not managed to come up with a term that will exhibit a similar acceptability and wide currency to that of the term 'narrative'. The authors' personal preference is that of 'non-narrative', a term which is increasingly gaining in popularity in discourse analysis. We endorse it here as the lesser evil, the most felicitous of the existing alternatives. The 'non-X' form of the term must not be conceived as having any derogatory overtones or connotations. It simply allows us to use a particularly successful term such as narrative as the basis for a term that captures the other end of the continuum, acknowledging at the same time the fundamental importance of both modes. A preliminary description of the defining characteristics of each mode is given in this chapter. Our presentation in the book is organised and revolves around this constitutive distinction.

2.4 THE NARRATIVE MODE

In very general terms, narrative is the encoding of previous experiences that took place at a specific point or over a specific interval in a past-time story-world (Polanyi 1985: 41). In their narrativisation, experiences are segmented into a sequence of discrete events that are temporally ordered. Though the definitions of an event are numerous and often controversial, an event in its wide sense refers to 'an occurrence in some world which is encoded in a proposition which receives an instantaneous rather than durative interpretation' (Polanyi 1982b: 510). This occurrence breaks into an ongoing activity or state and affects it by destroying its equilibrium. As a result, (at least) one other event or action occurs with the aim of repairing this disruption. This subsequent occurrence is usually goal-based, that is, planned by a (human) actor (e.g. see Quasthoff 1980; Stein and Policastro 1984).

READER ACTIVITY

According to the above description, which of the texts 1.1–1.5 and 2.1–2.4 can be characterised as narrative?

Narratives are generally associated with events that happened in the past. In consequence, grammatically speaking, they are associated with the past tense or with narrative (historic) present, that is, present which refers to past events. This is by no means an unexceptional rule. Generic narratives tell us what usually or habitually happens in the present. Projective narratives tell about events that have not taken place yet (e.g. plans for the future) in the future tense. The latter form part of the elicitation process of life stories in interviews, in which subjects are asked not only to talk about their past experiences but also to map out their future actions, to speculate where they expect to be and what they anticipate doing. Biblical prophecies are also narratives about future events.

READER ACTIVITY

The following narrative is about the plot of a television series. Notice the choice of tense. How would you account for it?

Text 2.18
NYPD Blue 10pm, C4
Life is one big struggle today at the precinct. As Martinez struggles with Lesniak's supposed lesbianism while working with her on a sleazy house burglary, as Sipowitz struggles with the medical side of his wife's pregnancy, and as Medavoy struggles with the station mattress after a bust-up with his wife, Andy and Bobby have a tough case to crack. A young Chinese girl is found stabbed at the family home, and her parents finger her gangster boyfriend, who dumped her a day before the death. A couple of hooker-heavy shakedowns later, Steven Seagal-alike Eddie Wong is in custody. Unusually for a murder suspect, he swears he didn't do it. But even more unusually, the detectives believe him ...
(*Source*: Ross Jones, *Guide*, 16–23 March 1996, p. 76)

Present tense is usually used too for a written synopsis of the major events in the life of somebody. What do you think is the rationale behind the choice of this tense? How does it differ from the choice of the past tense as an indicator of events that happened at a specific point in the past?

According to Fleischman (1990), the use of the present tense in plot summaries or retellings of plots of novels, films, operas, plays etc. suggests that the events narrated are available for repeated viewing and are thus filed in a directory labelled atemporal or timeless.

The use of past tense is related to another point about events in narratives, which is their factuality. Scholars of narrative have puzzled for years over questions such as: do events have to be real to be part of a narrative? If yes, how can we tell real events from fictional events? Also, what relationship does the sequential presentation of events in a story bear with the sequence of the real events in the real world? To a certain extent, these questions gave the first impetus to narrative analysis. As Mischler (1995) claims in his recent attempt at a typology of narrative models, models which focus on issues of reference (i.e. relationship between narrative and real events) and temporal order deserve to form a category of their own. In this book, our focus will be on the other two models in Mischler's typology: those which focus on the textual building, the structure of narratives by means of linguistic strategies; and, to a lesser extent, those which focus on narrative functions.

Let us briefly go back to the issue of narrative reference. Narrative events do not have to be real, if we take into account a major category of narratives, namely fictional narratives, which may recount events that have no existence prior to and independent of the narrative. But what about narratives that purport to be about real events? What is the relationship of their texts with these events? To numerous researchers, this relation needs to be one of correspondence, of an exact match: 'a verbal sequence of clauses matches the sequence of events which (it is inferred) actually happened' (Labov 1972: 359). If this match is not always observed in the text, it can be abstracted from it as the narrative's 'fabula', a sub-stratum that reconstructs the events in their chronological order. Fabula is contrasted to 'sujhet', which originates in the Russian formalists of the 1920s, and refers to the text of narrative that undertakes the telling of events, not necessarily in the order in which they occurred.

Such correspondence views of the relationship between narrative structure and reality structure led to questions of the exact relationship between the two. The priority of one over the other became a long-standing preoccupation of analysts, leading to a lot of controversy. Currently, this relationship is viewed as one of mutual determinism and influence. This view takes into account the role of context in the construction of narratives. The narration of the same events by the same person is not a given and predetermined product but is shifting and subject to changes and revisions as a result of contextual influences. Narratives are produced not in a vacuum but as part of social interactions in specific situations and for specific goals and purposes (Herrnstein-Smith 1981: 228). In view of their contexts of occurrence and their reasons for telling, narratives are presentations of a sequence of events from a particular point of view or perspective. As numerous scholars have claimed, narratives do not just recount temporally-ordered events; they also convey attitudes, feelings and emotions about them. Narratives filter and shape these elements by giving them meaning and structure. In doing so, they make a point about 'the world which teller and story recipients share' (Polanyi 1985: 16).

From this point of view, it does not seem to make sense to look at narratives as accurate representations of past events. They are rather reconstructions and reconstitutions of past events cast in a particular perspective that fits into the narrative's context of occurrence. In very simple terms, this explains how most of us have at different stages of our lives narrated the same events in completely different ways and for different purposes. It also accounts for how we have even attributed to the same events different meaning depending on our experiences, knowledge and mood even at the moment of our telling of the events. This is related to the function of our memory, which, as psychologists have shown, is not a static mechanism. It has an enormously powerful capacity to select the stored material and organise it into meaningful patterns rather than leaving it as raw input, according to intentions and interests presently in play (see Bruner and Weisser 1991: 135).

This view of the relationship between narrative structure and experience or events as an ongoing dialogical process offers a new perspective on the issue of the difference between fictional and non-fictional narrative. Since any recounting of events is bound to be a reconstitution and recreation of them from a particular perspective, distinguishing between fictional and non-fictional or, put in other terms, between literary and non-literary narrative in terms of their factuality of reference is no longer a powerful or helpful criterion.

What is the difference, then? This question has been answered in many different and controversial ways in discourse analysis and other areas. Studies of everyday narrative paved the way towards bridging the seemingly huge gap between literary and non-literary narrative and treating them as structurally and functionally more similar than dissimilar. The complex issue of what constitutes literariness and in what ways it differs from non-literariness are beyond the scope of this discussion (see Eagleton 1983: 1–16; Fish 1980). We will just mention here that one major way of looking at literature has been with reference to either the author's intent to create a fiction, or to the agreement between the text-producer and its receivers to treat it as fiction. Different socio-cultural assumptions and values determine in different ways what is literature. Another way of viewing the relationship of fictional with non-fictional narrative is to focus on the pragmatics of their communication. As Rimmon-Kenan (1983: 3–4) suggested, fictional narration presents a second-level fictional communicative context embedded into the real context of writer–reader (addresser–addressee) which any discourse entails: fictional narrators address a fictional narratee, themselves (first-person narration) or a third person who is a story participant. The voice who speaks the text may not be associated with a story participant.

However, in the area of discourse analysis, it is spoken, non-literary narrative that has been explored most and served as the basis for various theoretical and methodological frameworks. Any research on that inevitably sees the predominance and importance of personal (experience) narratives. These are first-person accounts of pinpointed events from an individual's personal life history which contrast to vicarious narratives, that is, third-person narration of other people's experiences, narration of films and television series, etc. Being 'the most internally consistent interpretation of presently understood past, experienced present, and anticipated future' (Cohler 1982: 207 [quoted in Mischler 1995: 108]), personal stories dominate one's repertoire of narratives. Developmentally, references to personal past experiences appear as early as the age of 2. From then on, as Preece has reported (1987), personal anecdotes are the most frequent form of narration, far more frequent than fictions or fantasies and 'vicarious stories'. Furthermore, they are typically the most 'involved' mode of narration (e.g. see Labov 1972; Shuman 1986). In addition to the narrator's greater degree of attachment and familiarity with the events narrated, they normally present a greater familiarity with the 'realm of conversation' in the sense of lack of distance from the 'taleworld' (Young 1987). The narrators inevitably participate in both worlds as storytellers and characters respectively. This allows for a particularly rich and flexible self-presentation. As such, personal narratives form the most classic example of narrative presentation ways – to be contrasted with non-narrative means of presentation.

A final terminological clarification is necessary. In our everyday lives, we talk a lot about stories but not about narratives. We would tell our friend: 'I want the full story' and not 'the full narrative'. Narrative is recognised as a more technical term. In the literature, these words are often used interchangeably. 'Narrative', however, is as a rule a more inclusive term covering cases such as current reports, generic descriptions, future narration, procedural narratives, plot summaries etc.

2.5 THE NON-NARRATIVE MODE

Whereas the features of temporal ordering, disruption of equilibrium, reconstruction of a taleworld and imposition of a (personal) perspective seem to be universally acknowledged in narrative mode, such criteria are far more difficult to identify in non-narrative discourse. This is partly related to the fact that the distinct school of narratology has succeeded in drawing attention to the unifying threads of different narrative modes. By contrast, while from a cognitive point of view the existence of non-narrative modes has been intensely advocated, linguistic analyses have traditionally focused on separate non-narrative genres rather than on their interrelationships. As a result, the analysts' attention has focused more on their distinct features than on their interdependence.

In our everyday communication, however, it is hardly possible to misconstrue non-narrative discourse as narrative, mainly on the basis of our tacit shared knowledge of the underlying conditions that allow a particular discourse to be used as a kind of action. This knowledge underlies our recognition of a speech act as an offer, a promise, an advice etc.

Non-narrative modes of discourse are uses of language that reflect, construct and participate in a specific kind of knowledge. These uses have to do with putting forward beliefs, views, attitudes, descriptions or arguments. Their focus is less on experiences and more on generic truths or assessments; less on actions and human agents and more on states, processes, opinions, beliefs and different kinds of information. In non-narrative, as speakers or writers, we linguistically express our internal evaluative or externally validated and accepted positions about, among others, problems, circumstances, states, actions and processes.

Whereas narrative discourse focuses on what happened, non-narrative discourse tells us about how something is, needs to be or should be. Non-narrative texts are built around a central entity or subject matter that does not (usually) have a temporal dimension. Therefore, the ordering of non-narrative texts does not follow the temporal sequencing of (real or imagined) events but is dictated either by the structure of the thing (e.g. the landscape, flat, process described) in question or by a basic problem that needs to be addressed (including a question which provokes logical argumentation).

In consequence, non-narrative texts, as a rule, make use of an introduction, a main body (where crucial information is given) and a conclusion or closing. The main body may revolve around a problem (with its related effects and causes), its solution and evaluation (i.e. the assessment of solutions). Or, it may revolve around an argument, which requires explanation, proof, refutation etc. Numerous variants of this pattern occur. For instance, the outline of a position which the author supports may be presented in a succession of positive and negative arguments (a zigzag pattern) or, alternatively, with no refutation (one-sided argument). The common unifying thread among different patterns is the presentation of a generic truth about a specific discourse entity. This truth is commonly presented as (detailed) information about an entity's structure or process, for example in a travel guide, an information leaflet, a scientific essay or an academic article, a manual, a 'do-it-yourself book'. It may also be put forth as a position which needs to be supported or conformed to, for example in a political speech, a sermon, an editorial, a letter of complaints, a TV debate. Finally, the generic truth may take the form of a warning (as e.g. in a street sign) or any other speech act (apologies, thanks, advice etc. in cards, notes, spoken interaction, liturgical texts etc.). There is an overwhelming number of instances in our everyday lives in which we produce and receive non-narrative discourse.

READER ACTIVITY

Do the following texts have the characteristics of non-narrative discourse? If so, could you turn them into narratives?

Text 2.19
Heat up a litre of broth made traditionally or with 1¼ chicken stock cubes. In another saucepan, melt some unsalted butter. Chop a small onion or some shallots finely and fry it lightly in the butter. (You can leave out the onion if you prefer.) Add the rice – about 10 fistfuls for 4 people, stir, add some white wine and stir. When this has all been absorbed start to add the broth a little at a time.

Text 2.20

MUD IS BEING TRAMPLED
INTO THE BUILDING
CAUSING DAMAGE
TO THE CARPET.
THEREFORE, PLEASE
DO NOT WALK
ACROSS THE FLOWER OR
WOODCHIP BEDS.
WE WOULD APPRECIATE
YOUR CO-OPERATION.

In the case of non-narrative texts, we are not concerned with the issue of whether what is presented is factual or fictional, namely the relation between represented and real events. Of more central importance is the verifiability of events, that is, whether we can validate the generic truth presented. Validation here is an issue of conformity – not to the conventions of a reconstructed world but to the 'way things are' in the world. This does not mean that a description of an entity simply reflects the state of the things in the world. Something like that would be an impossibility, since there are two levels of articulation, as shown in section 1.3. It rather means that the criteria of verification do not belong to a taleworld but are dictated by logical necessity. A further consequence of this is that non-narrative texts allow for a much more limited degree of negotiation in different contexts, since they require verifiability as a neutral, universal property. (Imagine what would happen if an instruction manual were to be renegotiated according to the needs of the context!)

For this purpose, the perspective taken by the participants in the two modes is of a different kind. We have claimed that the two modes allow and refer to different encodings of modes of knowledge. This is partly interrelated with the ways in which speakers and writers manage themselves and their relationships with others, including of course their addressees – in other words, with the stances that individuals take with regard to one another and to what is being said. Goffman (1981) uses the term 'footing' for this aspect of discourse.

As we have seen, stories discursively construct and evaluate experience. They encode the storytellers' selection and interpretation of what happened, their subjective views and attitudes towards what is narrated. Subjectivity is less pervasive in non-narratives: there are specific details of categorisation and subjective variation as to how different parts of the world (entities or categories) are perceived, because of the logical processes involved in representation (cf. Bruner's paradigmatic mode). Thus, the two modes are prototypically associated with subjectivity or affectivity and information-giving or analysing, respectively. Narrative touches upon our deep, imaginative processes. Non-narrative relies on rationalisation.

The difference in subjectivity is reflected in the presentation of self in each mode. Goffman (1981) distinguishes between three aspects of self as part of our self-presentation and footing in our everyday discourse: author: the aspect of self which is responsible for the content of talk; figure: a particular image, the aspect of self which is displayed through talk; and principal: somebody whose position is established by the words that are spoken, someone whose beliefs have been told, someone who is committed to what the words say. The complex of these relations between aspects of self defines what is called a participation framework in discourse. In narratives, this is an integral part of the shift in the deictic centre, from the time, place and participants of the present world to the storyworld. Narratives frame an event within a reported reality (the storyworld) which supplements our present purported reality. Storytellers can thus present themselves in a triple capacity: as author, principal and figure. This is particularly characteristic of personal narratives. The narrator can be seen in the conversational world as the animator (a talking machine, the person who produces talk) but also as (the main) character in the story (figure), someone who belongs to the world that is spoken about, not the world in which the speaking occurs. In this case, the narrators can present themselves in the story in as much positive light as they want to; or, they can, generally, choose the image of themselves that they wish to display. Furthermore, they can be the author, that aspect of self responsible for the content of talk, when they quote their prior words. Finally, they can be the principal, that aspect of self whose beliefs and views are encoded in the story and whose commitment to what is said is established.

In the light of the above, self-presentation in storytelling fully exploits subjective, deeply imaginative and affectionate processes to create sympathetic alliances with the audience. The interaction of figure, author and principal as parts of the storytelling self helps transform the person who listens to the story into an audience that vicariously participates in the narrator's experience. This is not an objective process, but is strongly constrained by the sentiments that the speaker holds towards the experience.

In non-narratives, self-presentation misses out on the deictic shifts of the storyworld but can be presented as more objective, tested, universal, holding for all situations and states of affairs, yielding to analysis and argumentation. When individuals make statements about an external world, they are usually seen as displaying a principal. They can manipulate their aspects of self and modify commitment to what is said. Consequently, in non-narrative discourse, speakers/writers modify the display of principal and author: for example, they decrease commitment in opinion-expressing ('that's my opinion') or increase commitment ('everybody thinks so'; for a detailed discussion, see Schiffrin 1990: 241–59; see also section 6.1 of this book and Georgakopoulou 1995a: 466ff.).

READER ACTIVITY

Both texts below aim at convincing their audiences about the truth and validity of what they say using the power of narrative and non-narrative discourse respectively. Analyse how this is done in each case drawing on the above discussion of self-presentation.

Text 2.21

Storyteller: We were on a tour of Scotland, and we dropped then to Loch Ness on the early morning of thirteenth of March nineteen eighty-nine. And we were standing on the shore of Loch Ness, just in front of Urquhart Castle, and being a sailor I was pointing out to Debbie that, you know, perhaps people, because I was very sceptical of all that Loch Ness monster, although some of my relatives had actually seen it themselves, and I was pointing out sort of wee formations, and so forth on the water. And lo and behold I was pointing out something that, as if a submarine was coming to the surface, this hu::ge wake started to er, just off shore from the castle, and it looked like the front of a submarine coming to the surface, and it came to the surface, creating a huge wake in the water. And to the right of it another object appeared, and the two of them were obviously swimming together. They swam along the shore line in front of Urquhart Castle, in parallel with the shore, and I was four or five hundred yards to the right of the water, and there was a motor-launch, coming up the loch, and the two objects were running away obviously from the motor yacht, and they had one large hump each. So then they swam parallel to the shore, and then to the right at ninety degrees, and then swam away from the shore line. The two objects then, to me, looked like a horse's head reared into the water, and the head was turning to the right and left, as if it was looking to see where the noise was coming from.
Judy: Did you have a camera with you?
Storyteller: I was, I mean, I was I was so frightened, the hair just curled in the back of my neck, and I ran to the car to get my camera, in such a panic. I'd recently bought a new long lens, and in my panic and haste, I put the long lens on, and clocked as many shots as I could, but unfortunately nothing came out. I was so frightened.

> (*Source*: 'This morning with Richard and Judy'
> phone-in, 20 February 1996)

Text 2.22

The familiar iconographies of evolution are all directed – sometimes crudely, sometimes subtly – towards reinforcing a comfortable view of human inevitability and superiority. The starkest version, the chain of being or ladder of linear progress, has an ancient, pre-evolutionary pedigree (see A. O. Lovejoy's classic, The Great Chain of Being, 1936). (further down) ... This tradition never vanished even in our more enlightened age. In 1915, Henry Fairfield Osborn celebrated the linear accretion of cognition in a figure full of illuminating errors. Chimps are not ancestors but modern cousins, equally distant in evolutionary terms from the unknown forebear of African great apes and humans. Pithecanthropus (homo erectus in modern terms) is a potential ancestor, and the only legitimate member of the sequence. ... (further down) Nor have we abandoned this iconography in our generation. Consider figure 1.5, from a Dutch translation of one of my own books! The march of progress, single file, could not be more graphic. Lest we think that only Western culture promotes this conceit, I present one example of its spread (figure 1.6) purchased at the bazaar of Agra in 1985.

The march of progress is the canonical representation of evolution – the one picture immediately grasped and understood by all. This may best be appreciated by its prominent use in humour and in advertising. These professions provide our best test of public perceptions. Jokes and ads must click in the fleeting second that our attention grants them. ... (further down) The idea of linear advance goes beyond iconography to the definition of evolution: the word itself becomes a synonym for progress. Nonetheless, life is a copiously branching bush, continually pruned by the grim reaper of extinction, not a ladder of predictable progress. Most people may know this as a phrase to be uttered, but not as a concept brought into the deep interior of understanding. Hence we continually make errors inspired by unconscious allegiance to the ladder of progress, even when we explicitly deny such a view of life.

(Source: Stephen Jay Gould, Wonderful Life
(London: Penguin, 1991), extracts from pp. 28, 29, 31, 32, 35)

As we can see above, the story, with the power of its eye-witness, experiential mode and the dramatisation of the events narrated, aims at luring the audience into an empathetic engagement in it. The storyteller, simultaneously an animator, a principal and a figure, attempts to elicit support for his view that the Loch Ness Monster exists, by appealing to the audience's sympathy towards him as a terrified character in a story of exciting and unexpected events. The non-narrative text, by contrast, aims at objective proof which derives from argumentation, analysis and illustration. Its aim is to gain the readers' support for the views presented by informing them and by appealing to their rationality.

2.6 DEFINING CHARACTERISTICS OF THE TWO MODES

We have briefly presented the general features of narrative and non-narrative discourse by giving an outline of their various aspects. We have mentioned the different options taken by the two modes as regards the question of ordering, the description of particular or general events, the relation to a norm, reference, perspective and context. Table 2.2 summarises their differences (cf. Bruner 1991).

	Narrative discourse	*Non-narrative discourse*
Ordering	temporal sequencing	multiple (logical, temporal etc.)
Particularity	particular events	generic truths
Normativeness	disruption and re-establish-ment of equilibrium	stating (arguing etc,) what the norm is
Reference	reconstructed events	verifiable events
Perspective	personal	impersonal
Context	under negotiation	permanent across contexts

Table 2.2: Defining characteristics of the narrative and non-narrative modes

What seems to be underlying this account of the differences between the two modes is a distinction of prototypical functions. Narrative discourse attempts to sweep narrator and audience into a community of rapport, to enhance intimacy and strengthen the bonds between participants. Non-narrative discourse is, in contrast, concerned with the need to convince, to prove and refute, as well as to present information. Tannen (1989) has distinguished these functions as the requirement to move versus the need to inform. Both kinds of discourse, however, are about sharing and interpreting collectively, reflecting knowledge structures and trying to assess their validity or deconstruct them and construct others through communication. They constitute two different paths for realising the coherence, structure, meaning and value of our internal and external states and actions. They are both concerned with the question of what is accepted as given and familiar and try to deal with the unexpected and the unintelligible.

Different contexts call for different discursive ways of pursuing similar goals. For instance, academic discussions require more non-narrative, while friendly conversations take recourse to narrative more often. Different cultures also capitalise on the two modes in different degrees, as we have seen in relation to Maranhão's research. A lot of cross-cultural stereotyping has to do with the preferred ways of constructing self and approaching others in communication. How much appeal to and use of personal experiences is needed and how much use of analysis and proof can be made are issues of contention between different communities. The same is true about the kinds and legitimacy of the socio-cultural sources of knowledge.

Nevertheless, narrative and non-narrative are far from compartmentalised in the real world. The participation frameworks of both modes are constantly employed in alternation. In conversations, for instance, opinion-expressing and argumentation are commonly strengthened and complemented by stories. Argumentation may lead to a story which will lead back to a conversation. Similarly, a lecturer may strengthen a point by providing a personal anecdote; a news story uses shifts between story and presentation of information as a strategic device. As we will show in Chapter 6, the two poles of narrative and non-narrative must be thought of as points of a continuum that co-exist in complex and fascinating forms of interaction.

FURTHER READING

Schiffrin (1994a: ch. 5) looks into the speech event of an interview in detail (it is not a very easy read though). Scollon and Scollon (1995: ch. 2) provide a user-friendly discussion of speech acts and events in the context of intercultural communication. Hatch (1992) also devotes a chapter (4) to speech acts and events with an extensive discussion of certain speech events (e.g. compliments).

The enquiry into differences between spoken and written language has lent itself to a huge line of tradition. Older, classic references include Halliday (1979), Kroll (1977), O'Donnell (1974) and Olson (1977). The best starting point for a discourse analytic approach to the issue is Tannen (1982), Chafe (1985) and Halliday (1987), summarising the more extended Halliday (1985b). Biber has used multi-factorial analyses of clusters of linguistic features to study the linguistic differences between spoken and written genres (e.g. 1986, 1991, 1992). The broader issues of orality and literacy practices have been studied within broad interdisciplinary frameworks combining sociological, anthropological, psychological and educational models (e.g. Barton 1994; Barton and Ivanic 1991; Gee 1990; Olson and Torrance 1991).

The concept of register has been mainly associated with the name of Douglas Biber and his colleagues who have published extensively (e.g. Biber and Finnegan 1994). In their view, register is viewed as a situationally-defined language variety which presents systematic correlations between clusters of linguistic features and situational factors. Biber, based on large text corpora, has formed sets of co-occurring features for different registers in an attempt to configure similarities and differences between them. His conclusion is that there is no single dimension of variation which defines a register. Biber uses the term 'register' to describe what other linguists would call 'style'. For the notion of style, an unexpected source of information with a comprehensive overview and plethora of references is Chapters 8 and 9 of McMenamin (1993). However, there is still a lot of terminological confusion regarding the terms 'genre-discourse type-register' and 'style'. A useful discussion of the notions can be found in Hatim and Mason (1990) and Swales (1990).

For narrative analyses of life stories, see Linde (1993) and Josselson and Lieblicht (1993). Life stories (or histories) are usually elicited in formal interview contexts, unlike everyday narratives, which are recorded in conversational settings. A growing line of research on life histories as part of psycho-analytic sessions and, on the whole, clinical interviews, contributes to the cross-fertilisation between narrative discourse analysis and sociology. In addition, life stories are of interest to historians, psychologists and ethnographers.

For the role of narrative in the jury, see also Delgado (1989) and Abrams (1991).

Some discussion on the difference between the terms 'narrative' and 'story' can be found in Fleischman (1990: 106) and Polanyi (1982).

For an introduction to literary narrative, see Rimmon-Kenan 1989. Toolan (1988) is a very accessible, classic introduction to (literary and non-literary) narrative.

Oral personal narratives have formed the data of numerous linguistic studies. The tradition is particularly strong in the USA. Polanyi's work is a classic reference (1989). Johnstone (1990) sheds light on the linguistic construction of storytelling in Middle America. Stahl's study (1989) places emphasis mainly on the value and validity of everyday personal stories for the folklorist, serving comparable functions as traditional tales, myths and legends.

The emergence and development of narrative construction in children as well as its interaction with adults' (mainly parents' or caretakers') conversational and narrative styles has been looked into by numerous developmental studies (e.g. Eisenberg 1985; Fivush and Fromhoff 1988; Hausendoff and Quasthoff 1992; Miller and Sperry 1988; Preece 1987; papers in McCabe and Peterson 1991).

Discourse Units and Relations

3.1 NARRATIVE PARTS AND PLOT

It will be clear from our discussion in Chapter 1 that any piece of discourse is not just a string of undifferentiated sentences, but a whole with interrelated parts. This internal structure, consisting of a set of units, has been a major preoccupation in research on narrative discourse. The search for structural units of narrative text characterises most classic work in the field, from Aristotle's *Poetics* to Propp's work on Russian folktales. A central tendency in this work is the identification of narrative units that represent categories of plot. These are combined with definitions of the minimal narrative as a piece of discourse that tells us about a change in an initial state of affairs and its restoration in a new modified version by (one or more) goal-based action(s).

This minimalist definition also underlies more recent attempts to uncover the internal narrative structure. For instance, Stein's (1982) influential scheme of a story's prototypical structure identifies the following constituents:

1. *setting*: the internal or external states and habitual actions that introduce characters and their social and physical environment;
2. *initiating event*: some type of change in the protagonist's environment;
3. (the protagonist's) *response* or *reaction* to the event;
4. *attempt:* a set of overt actions in the service of the protagonist's goal initiated by events or motivating states;
5. *consequence(s)* of the attempt (e.g. success or failure to attain the goal);
6. (the protagonist's) *reaction* to the consequences.

These categories may apply recursively at different (higher and lower) levels of narrative discourse. At the lower level, every single sentence can be parsed into one or more statements corresponding to any of the categories.

At a higher level, the categories can be embedded in one another: for instance, a sequence of events can itself form an event.

Alternatively, categories can be organised into superordinate units, such as *episodes*. In Rumelhart's (1975) definition, a story simply consists of a setting as a statement of time, place and introduction to main characters, followed by (at least one) episode. The episode usually involves the occurrence of some event followed by a character's reaction to it. However, more categories (attempts, consequences etc.) can also be included in an episode, depending on its level of complexity and completeness. For instance, an abbreviated episode may describe aims of a protagonist, but may leave planning in general to be inferred. A complete episode also describes aims but exhibits more evidence of planning. A complex episode elaborates a complete episode by further embedding reactions, repeated attempts, or another complete episode.

READER ACTIVITY

Now try to identify some of the above structural categories in the following passage. You may treat the text as a complex episode and see how the categories apply recursively. How are the categories related to each other?

Text 3.1
After breakfast Burglar Bill plays with his cat by the fire. Suddenly he hears a noise. 'Sounds like a police car' says Burglar Bill. But the noise is coming from the big brown box, and it's getting louder. 'Sounds like TWO police cars!' says Burglar Bill. He creeps up to the box and raises the lid.

'Blow me down' he says. 'It ain't no police cars, it's a … baby!'

Burglar Bill puts the baby on the table. 'What was you doing in that box, baby?' he says. But the baby only keeps on crying.

'All alone', says Burglar Bill. He pats the baby's little hand. 'A orphan!' But the baby only keeps on crying.

Then Burglar Bill says, 'I know what you want – grub!' Burglar Bill gives an apple to the baby. But still the baby cries. He gives a slice of toast and marmalade to the baby. But still the baby cries. He gives a plate of beans and a cup of tea to the baby. The baby eats the beans, throws the cup of tea on the floor and starts to laugh.

'That's better,' says Burglar Bill. 'I like a few beans meself'.

(*Source*: J and A. Ahlberg, *Burglar Bill*, Mammoth)

As with all structural units posited by analysts in texts, the above categories are strongly interrelated. The two main relations exhibited in narrative discourse are the *temporal* and the *causal* relations. Events can be temporally related: one may follow another in time. Alternatively, one event can cause another by presenting the necessary and sufficient conditions for it to happen. In text 3.1 above, the noise coming from the box has a causal relation with Bill's attempt to find out where the noise comes from. In Rumelhart's terms, this is specifically an *initiate* relation, which is not as strong as physical causation, but still causal in nature: an external event causes a wilful reaction to that event. Similarly, once the baby has been found, the baby's crying initiates Bill's attempts to stop it. Bill's attempts are temporally linked: for example, giving him a slice of toast occurs prior in time to giving him a plate of beans. At the same time, the failure of each attempt to stop the baby's crying initiates the next attempt.

Two secondary, but still common, relations are those of *allow* (or *enable*) and *motivate*. *Allow* means 'make possible'. Settings allow all other categories. In our case, Bill's sitting by the fire allows him to hear the noise coming from nearby but does not cause him to hear it. Finally, *motivate* is a relation between an internal response and the actions resulting from it. Bill wants to stop the baby's crying. This motivates him to form a plan for stopping it.

In sum, settings can enable all other categories. Events can cause events, goals and reactions. Goals can motivate goals and attempts. Attempts can enable attempts and cause outcomes. Outcomes can enable attempts and cause goals and reactions.

The narrative categories presented so far are, as a rule, found in models of story grammars. Story grammars set out to account for the structure of a wide range of simple stories such as fairytales and fables. Their major assumption is that there is a universal set of organisational features of stories which are 'consistent with daily modes of comprehension and remembering that are also universal, regardless of type of culture or amount of schooling' (Mandler et al. 1980: 21). These features are to be found in the canonical form or underlying story schema, from which individual stories are generated with the application of a set of syntactic and semantic rules. In Chapter 2, we discussed the concept of a schema and its relevance for our knowledge in discourse encoding and decoding. A story-grammar schema is a goal-based structure, consisting of a protagonist, a set of desired goals, and the means required by the protagonist to achieve them. It is postulated as a conceptual framework that enables the reader to store and retrieve information on story characters and events.

One of the main aims of a story grammar is to account for stories' comprehension processes. To this end, a vast amount of research in the area has attempted to explore the varying ways in which a story's 'surface' corresponds to its underlying form, and in turn how these affect its comprehension and recall. Experiments, mainly conducted with children, provided certain encouraging findings as regards the interaction between story structure and recall. They generally suggested that categories observed in their canonical position are better recalled than those presented out of canonical position. For instance, a reaction occurring after its initiating event would be recalled better than when preceding it. More importantly, stories which do not conform well to the conventional structure, which for example present omissions or inversions of categories, tend to be recalled in a more conventional version. The findings also suggested that a story's setting, beginning and consequences of attempts are more frequently recalled than internal responses and reactions to the outcome of attempts. Furthermore, causal relations were found to be critical for story comprehension and recall. Stories with more causal connections are more likely to be recalled than others (Trabasso and Sperry 1985). In similar vein, propositions on a story's causal chain formed by the causal relations between its events are more likely to be recalled. Causal relations facilitate comprehension and recall not only when they link adjacent events but also when they link events which are quite far apart in a story's surface.

READER ACTIVITY

You may test some of your expectations about narrative structure in the following text. It comprises sentences which are taken from a story's different episodes. What, in your view, is their order in the story? Once you have reordered them, try to label them as story categories (e.g. setting, goal, attempt etc.) and identify the causal relations between them. You may wish to compare your answer with that of friends or fellow students.

Text 3.2
Betty selected a pattern from a magazine.
Betty felt sorry.
Betty really wanted to give her mother a present.
Her mother was excited when she saw the present.
Once there was a girl named Betty.
Several days later, Betty saw her friend knitting.
Betty went to the department store.
Betty could not buy anything.
One day, Betty found that her mother's birthday was coming soon.
Betty was good at knitting.
Betty gave the sweater to her mother.
Betty found that everything was too expensive.
Finally, Betty finished a beautiful sweater.
Betty decided to knit a sweater.

                                        (*Source*: Trabasso and Suh 1993: 7)

On the whole, research has shown that story grammars can adequately represent the structure of some kinds of simple stories. However, there is still a long way to go before they fully account for comprehension processes and model them in terms of artificial intelligence and computer science. The issue of the universal as opposed to the culture-specific elements of storytelling is also far from resolved. While the culture-specificity of story-telling construction has been widely documented, agreement on the particular universals of narrative categories is still lacking in the literature. As a result, criticism against story grammars is more abundant than praise. One point of attack is that they have only been applied to a restricted subset of stories, namely traditional stories, thus failing to capture 'the diversity of story patterns, even within a single culture' (de Beaugrande 1982: 395). Another problem is their mechanistic reliance on the stories' organisational component and the emphasis on story comprehension at the expense of story production. These result, it is argued, in a neglect of the dynamics and functions of everyday narrative communication as a mode of social and cultural interaction. A closely-related critique is that of the lack of interest in the expressive or affective elements of stories as powerful means for encoding attitudes, values and emotions. As de Beaugrande pertinently pointed out, 'a story grammar with the ambition of being only a grammar – composed of left-branchings, right-branchings, embeddings, Chomsky-adjunctions and the like – is not sufficient. We need instead a grammar fully integrated into the larger picture of communication and cognition, in which the telling and enjoying of stories is an enduring component of human activity' (1982: 419). Fifteen years after the above statement was made, surprisingly little has come out of story grammars regarding what makes stories interesting and worth reading or listening to. It has been demonstrated that different story structures produce different patterns of affective response in the reader (e.g. Brewer and Lichtenstein 1981, 1982). However, there is still little consensus as to how a story's point, its tellability, should be incorporated in story grammars.

The shift of interest from the propositional content of stories to their subjective and emotive elements and, subsequently, to their users and contexts was first marked by Labov's model of narrative analysis. By contrast with story grammars, Labov's model has frequently been credited with bringing to the fore 'the often forgotten fact that humans are something more than information processing systems' (Peterson and McCabe 1983: 166). Labov's famous research in the 'Inner City' (1972) and the recording of a corpus of 'danger of death' narratives resulted in the formulation of a particularly influential model for analysing stories, starting from oral personal experience stories. In this model, the main prerequisite for a text to be called a narrative is the criterion of sequentiality. A minimal narrative is defined as a sequence of two clauses that are temporally ordered. The skeleton of a narrative is a series of temporally-ordered clauses called narrative (or free) clauses. These are perfective past tense main clauses in the indicative mood (e.g. *Betty went to the department store, finished the sweater, gave the sweater to her mother* from Text 3.2). By contrast, clauses that present a free range of displacement to other positions in the temporal sequence are treated by Labov as non-narrative clauses.

At a higher level of structural analysis, a fully-formed narrative is built in five parts. It begins with an orientation, proceeds to the complicating action, is suspended at the focus of evaluation before the resolution, concludes with the resolution and returns the listener to the present time with the coda (see Table 3.1).

	Abstract	
Orientation	Complicating action Climax	Evaluation
	Resolution	
	Coda	

Table 3.1: Labov's model of narrative structure

The *abstract* encapsulates the point of the story. It may be a brief summary statement of the substance of the narrative as viewed by the narrator or some kind ofopener signalling transition to the story (e.g. *did I ever tell you about …, you'll never guess what happened …, I had a funny experience the other day* etc.). *Orientation* is the equivalent of the story grammar 'setting'. It identifies time, place, situations and characters, usually before the beginning of the story's action. Much of its material, however, may also be placed at strategic points later on. The *complicating action* answers the question 'and then what happened?' It is the backbone of the narrative formed by the sequence of narrative clauses. The *resolution* normally contains the last of the narrative clauses which began the complicating action, telling us how the complication was resolved. It is followed by the *coda*, which provides the story's ending and attempts to bridge the gap between the narrative time and our (present) time. The coda can take the form of a general observation or a statement about the effects of the events on the narrator, such as *so, there we are, and ever since I …, it was very funny/scary* etc.

Finally, *evaluation* comprises the devices by which the narrator indicates the point of the narrative, or why it is felt to be tellable. As such, it is the narrative part which reveals the narrator's attitudes and emotions towards the events related. Labov and Waletzky (1967) originally claimed that evaluation forms a separate section, which occurs after the complicating action and before the resolution, emphasising thus the break between them. This view was later revised by Labov (1972), who suggested that evaluation can also be spread throughout the narrative, forming a secondary structure. Studies of storytelling have confirmed the latter view, since in numerous cases evaluation is missing as an autonomous narrative unit or section (e.g. Shaul et al. 1987 for Hopi Coyote narratives).

READER ACTIVITY

The following conversational story was told by a young woman (Nadia) in a company of four people (two young men, Alex and Simon, a young woman and a middle-aged woman). One of the two men has witnessed the events narrated. Can you identify Labov's pattern of a fully-formed narrative?

Text 3.3

Nadia: How long do you keep your spices for?

Alexandra: I don't know. Six months?

Nadia: Ah, that's fine. After that. 'Cos your mum ((turning to Alex)) had kept some spices, from when my mum was there, and when we were in their place, your mum wanted me to cook dinner, and use the spices, and I was like oh God! what can I say? Luckily, Tatiana came in and said, that smells horrible, chuck that out mum, and I was off the hook. And then Dan came, and decided he wanted to cook, and he was going on, I'm gonna cook you some pa::sta, and on and on he went about this pasta, pronouncing the pasta pa::sta. Finally he brought this pasta on the table, and there was a friend of your mum's as well, //I can't remember her name//

Alex: //Was that cacciatoree?// ((Alex's mispronunciation of cacciatoray is the cue for Simon's joke)) this is his famous //chicken

Simon: // No, a caccia-Labour

Alex: hh hh

Nadia: It was very funny, because he made the sauce with kidney beans=

Alex: =oh, was that chilli con carne, his other //famous

Nadia: no no, it wasn't con carne, 'cos I'd insisted, I wanted the sauce without the carne. He made this sauce, I mean he used a packet of tomato puree, or something like that, and I don't think he added any sauce. So he had this huge amount of spaghetti, enough for twenty people, and I am not joking, he had that much sauce ((showing, emphasising the fact that the sauce was not enough)) for the five of us. And we just stood there looking at it, and oh my sauce, frightfully good, isn't it? ((audience laugh)) It was really funny, because he made such a big deal=

Simon: ((laughs)) =and all the forks going up in the air, and all the spaghetti=

Nadia: ((laughs)) and then your mum's friend says, oh you've cooked the pasta really well ((ironic tone in view of the disaster

with the sauce)), which really wound him up.
[long digression]
Nadia: But it was very funny. Dan was too concerned with cooking,
and then Simon was also trying to prove that he was domestic,
and decided that he would do the dishes, and this friend of your
mum's walked into the kitchen, and she said to him, really seriously, you're doing the dishes? like this? don't you know that, the
way you're doing them, we'll have a water crisis? ((audience
laugh)) And Dan was going, what do you mean? give the guy a
break, but Simon just stood there looking at her=
Simon: =pathetic, don't remind me.
Nadia: Oh, that was very funny.

(*Source*: Authors' data)

Labov collected his stories in interviews. In other words, the stories did
not occur spontaneously in conversational settings. This context of occurrence is in many ways responsible for their fully-fledged structural pattern.
When we look at non-prompted conversational stories, there are certain
notable differences. Since such stories are triggered by the surrounding
conversational text, they very often dispense with non-obligatory categories
such as abstract and coda. Notice that text 3.3 above lacks an abstract, being
associatively linked with the conversational topic, 'spices'. In addition, the
narrators of conversational stories usually possess a higher degree of familiarity and share more assumptions with their interlocutors than an interviewee does with an interviewer. As a result, they are more likely to dispense
with long orientation sections. Again, in story 3.3, the storyteller does not
need to provide any information about her visit to Alex's mother, since her
interlocutors know the relevant details. They also know the story's characters well, so no introduction to them is necessary.

More importantly, stories in conversational contexts are a joint enterprise.
The audience plays a very active role providing verbal and non-verbal back-
channelling and contributions. This can have a definitive effect on the
story's shaping of structural categories. It may, for instance, force the storyteller to dwell more or less on the story's climax, depending on the audience's uptake. In our story, the effect of the climax is intensified as a result of
Simon's collaboration, who adds '*and all the forks going up in the air, and all the
spaghetti*', emphasising the humour of the scene. Audience reactions may
even force the storytellers to change the climax and the story's point
halfway, or to postpone the telling of certain narrative parts. In story 3.3,
owing to audience interruption, the new complicating act of Simon's washing the dishes (which also provides the story's resolution) and the coda are
narrated long after the climax.

On the whole, research has shown that Labov's classic pattern of narrative presents numerous variants in real-world conversational contexts, depending on the purposes that a story's occurrence serves. A common variant is the existence of more than one climax. As Longacre (1981) has claimed, stories very often reach a peak point or climax, release the tension or slow down their pace, and then mount to another peak point. This can go on at some length so that they present a wave-like movement of ups and downs. A story's peak points (pivotal events) are clearly set off by a conspiracy of linguistic means. Different storytellers and different cultures select from a wide range of devices for peak-marking: they can pack or extend the event-line (i.e. speed up or slow down the action), they can crowd the stage with participants, they can use characters' speech or repetition devices etc (see Chapter 4 for a discussion). On the whole, the peak acts as a zone of turbulence in the otherwise placid flow of a story (Longacre 1981: 351).

Evaluation in particular is very context-sensitive. The degree of evaluation, for instance, depends on numerous textual and situational factors ranging from the story's topic to the storyteller's personal and social attributes (see Chapter 5 for further discussion). Sensational topic stories, that is, stories about violent incidents, burglaries, accidents, deaths and so on, are commonly more fully evaluated than others. Labov reported that evaluation is to be found in stories that narrate the storyteller's own experiences but not in stories that narrate incidents concerning third parties or the plot of films and documentaries. He also distinguished between *external* and *internal* evaluation, and claimed that the former is more frequent in the narration of middle- and upper-class speakers, while the latter is more frequent in that of working-class speakers. When using external evaluation, the narrator breaks the story's flow, that is, suspends the action, and tells the addressee what the story's point is, using statements that explicitly evaluate the experience, for example, *It was the strangest feeling* ..., *It was really quite terrific* etc. Between external and internal evaluation lie a number of intermediate steps that embed the point to a greater or lesser extent in the narrative; these involve quotations of the narrator's and other characters' speech and thoughts. The last technique of dramatising external evaluation before the narrator exploits internal evaluation devices is to tell what people did rather than said (evaluative action). Internal evaluation is in principle signalled by inter- or intra-sentential departures from the basic narrative syntax. Labov distinguished between the following four kinds of internal evaluation devices:

> *Intensifiers*: gestures, expressive phonology, ritual interjections, repetitions and exaggerating quantifiers. Unlike the other three types, they are superimposed or added onto the basic narrative syntax without affecting the unmarked form of the narrative verb phrase.
>
> *Comparators*: marked verbal phrase constructions such as negatives, futures, questions, commands, modals and comparatives. These move away from the line of narrative events to consider unrealised possibilities and compare them with events that did occur.

Correlatives: complex syntax which brings together events in a single independent clause: e.g. progressives, participles (V-ing forms), double appositives and attributes.

Explicatives: appended subordinate clauses introduced by *while*, *(al)though, since* or *because*.

READER ACTIVITY

Analyse story 3.3 above in terms of the category of evaluation. Which evaluative devices does the storyteller mainly rely on?

Story 3.3 demonstrates that the main vehicles of evaluation are usually a closed set of devices comprising intensity markers (e.g. *really, very, that much, huge, frightfully*), repetition (e.g. *cook the pasta, it was funny*), and instances of direct speech (e.g. *I'm gonna cook you some pasta*), thought (e.g. *oh God! what can I say?*), and dialogue (e.g. *you're doing the dishes? ... what do you mean?*). If we add the use of narrative present, which is very common in the narration of numerous cultures, and non-linguistic devices such as expressive sounds, gestures and motions, we get the list of Wolfson's performance features (1979, 1982) characterising dramatised and immediate narratives. Wolfson's attempt belongs to a series of post-Labovian studies that employed alternative concepts (albeit compatible with Labov's) for the stories' expressive level. We will discuss these in more detail in Chapter 5. A second tendency in post-Labovian studies of evaluation has been to refine and extend the notion, and make it more operational depending on the specific type of research and data. This has typically taken the form of breaking down the four categories into numerous more refined ones (e.g. Peterson and McCabe 1983; Polanyi 1985). These devices are intensity markers, narrative or historic present, ellipsis, causal explanations, characters' speech, references to mental states etc. Such studies have also demonstrated that evaluation is particularly text- and context-specific.

The volume of subsequent research stemming from Labov's structural narrative model shows how influential it has been. While primarily designed for oral narratives, it has also been applied to written and literary narratives (e.g. Carter and Simpson 1981). In many ways, it has contributed to the questioning of the traditional gulf between ordinary, everyday narrative and literary narrative. However different, they are both 'display texts': they not only report but also verbally display a state of affairs 'inviting the addressee(s) to join (the narrator) in contemplating them, evaluating them and responding to them' (Pratt 1977: 136). Labov's own rationale for research on natural narrative was that, while most analytical schemes for narrative analysis have been applied to complex traditional or literary narrative forms, 'little will be understood about the structure and function of complex narratives until the simplest and most fundamental narratives have been formally described and related to their social context' (Labov and Waletzky 1967: 12).

READER ACTIVITY

Try to analyse the following text using Labov's structural categories. How does it differ from story 3.3?

Text 3.4
1 H was employed as an Area Supervisor by a contact cleaning company. 2 On 3rd April 1991 H attended a meeting with the director of the company and another employee. 3 During the meeting B, a Manager with the company, came in and said to H 'Hiya big tits'. 4 Neither of the two present heard the remark but they did notice H complaining to B shortly after he had entered the meeting. 5 H found the remark very distressing, particularly as B was the son of the two Company Directors.

6 H complained about B's behaviour. 7 When B was confronted about the incident he became aggressive and denied that he had made the remark. 8 As a result of B's denial the employers decided that, rather speak to B and warn him about his conduct, they would ask H to invoke the Company's grievance procedure. 9 H was reluctant to do this and resigned on 17 April 1991. 10 She complained of unlawful sex discrimination and unfair constructive dismissal.

(*Source*: University of London Newsletter)

3.2 UNITS AS THEMATIC CATEGORIES

The structural categories discussed above are specific to narrative discourse, and in particular to narrative plot: they presuppose definitional features of narratives, such as action, resolution of action, protagonist with a plan etc. A different set of narrative units in the literature stems from a combination of criteria applying across discourse types. These are syntactic, thematic and intonational criteria. (The latter are, of course, only applicable to spoken texts.) Units distinguished by these criteria are very commonly labelled as *paragraphs* and defined as structures with a semantic unity of theme along with certain morphosyntactic features of closure and internal cohesion. These comprise the use of conjunctions, time and location phrases, tense and aspect markers, and, in spoken discourse, suprasegmental features of pause, stress and pitch. In narratives, the main formal markers include time, place and person (characters) markers. Thus, changes of time, place and people tend to cluster at the beginning of paragraphs – although they need not all be present at the same time (for a more detailed discussion, see Chapter 4).

In many ways, a narrative paragraph thus defined would function as an episode. The difference is that an episode is treated as both a linguistic and a cognitive or developmental unit of narrative. By contrast, for the units discussed here, the main concern is with the linguistic devices that demarcate them and secure their internal cohesion. Units with thematic, syntactic and intonational closure are found in the literature under various names, for example act, sentence or extended sentence, scene, verse, stanza etc. Most of these are posited at various intermediate levels, that is, between the lowest unit and the text. Consequently, they can be more or less inclusive than a paragraph. However, the current tendency is to avoid the proliferation of units in favour of only one intermediate, recursive unit (usually called paragraph).

As with Labov's model, the model of thematic narrative segments originated in research on spoken narrative. As such, these segments are based on a combination of syntactic, content and intonational criteria. Pauses play a major role in the identification of these units and in particular of lowest-level units, the spoken rough equivalents of a clause. As Chafe (1980, 1987) observes, spontaneous speech has the property of being produced in spurts. These spurts, which he has labelled *idea units*, are units of intonational and semantic closure. Idea units are usually as long as a clause, having a mean length of two seconds or about six words. Syntactically, however, they may not always be as complete as a clause. Their distinguishing feature is that they are set off from one another by a clause-final intonation, normally a rise in pitch, combined with a slight pause or hesitation. In story 3.3, idea units have been marked by commas. As you can see, the majority of them coincide with the syntactic unit of a clause. However, there are instances where this is not the case, for example *luckily, or something like that, enough for twenty people.*

Idea units are grouped together to form higher-level units, our spoken paragraphs, which are signalled by a distinctive falling contour that gives the impression of completeness. Thematically, paragraphs can range from sections which provide background information about a character to a series of events leading to some kind of conclusion. Their beginning is marked by some kind of shift of perspective or point of view (a shift of focal participants, a change in the place, time or framing of the events). If we go back to story 3.3 and try to identify its thematic units, we can start by forming a unit up to *what can I say?*. Tatiana's entrance onto the narrative stage (marked by the motion verb *came in*) signals a passage to a new scene. The next thematic unit is in turn signalled by Dan's introduction to the narrative action (again marked by the verb *came*: *and then Dan came*). The temporal marker *and then* reinforces the sense of passage to a new event which follows temporally the previous ones.

In terms of the status of spoken paragraphs as cognitive entities, Chafe claimed that they are activated by short-term memory and correspond to the speaker's one mental image or centre of interest. Idea units are, on the other hand, much more restricted in scope than paragraphs and can be processed in one single chunk. They represent a single focus of consciousness.

One of the most influential examples of the combination of features in the identification of narrative units is research on Native American narratives. Systematic work on those narratives led to the discovery of a rhetorical structure that constitutes a form of poetry. This is organised into lines and groupings of lines called stanzas, verses etc. – names chosen to emphasise the stories' poetic quality. Lower- and higher-level units are signalled by intonation, parallelism, patterning of content and formal linguistic features (e.g. time or place markers). These separate components interact strongly in the formation of units. Cases where the syntactic, thematic and intonational components do not pattern with but contradict each other were found to be rare. More significantly, the configuration of form–content in narrative segments presented recurrent formal patterns of organisation. Specifically, sequences of action essentially presented two basic types of formal pattern: they were built up either of pairs and fours (in Zuni, Karok and Tonkawa narratives), or of threes and fives (in Chinookan narratives). These are culturally significant pattern numbers in the respective communities. In consequence, their importance in stories suggests that narrative organisation depends on a culturally-constrained conception of narrative action.

Hymes (1977) made the hypothesis that such interconnections between narrative structure and socio-cultural modes of action would also be found in other cultures that present strong ties with an oral tradition and have a well-developed oral literature. Recent work has confirmed this. Gee's (1989) comparative analysis of narratives produced by black working-class children and white middle-class children in the USA showed that the line-and-stanza poetic structure is very evident in the former but not in the latter. It is not so much insistence on the use of any special number. Rather, segments that concern a single topic (stanzas) are relatively short and quite evenly balanced across the text as a whole. In addition, working-class children's narratives exhibit numerous poetic patterns such as sound play, repetition of sounds, words and phrases, parallelism and generally patterns of rhythm (e.g. changes of rate, loudness and stress). The effect of this stanza structure is an interrelation of narrative segments: stanzas criss-cross and interlock with each other not so much by means of temporal and logical relations as by rhythmic patterns that simultaneously relate stanzas and their lines. We can see this in the following brief extract from a story:

Text 3.5
Stanza 2
I got this thing
MY ear's all bugging me
an everything
MY ear was all bugging me

I was cryin
I was all: oooh, oooh, oooh
I was doin all that
and MY mother put alcohol on

Stanza 4
and then, you know, just all of a sudden
I just got this terrible feelin
after I stopped eatin ice cream,
like, oh short, oh go::d
my ear was killin me
an I was sayin 'ma::ma::'

(Source: Gee 1989)

As we can see above, narrative stanzas are in fact presented on the page as poetic stanzas. As Hymes (1981) suggested, in this way, hidden aspects of their structure become visually evident. Notice how different an extract from our story 3.3 looks when represented in the form of stanzas as below:

'Cos your mum had kept some spices
from when my mum was there
and when we were in their place
your mum wanted me to cook dinner
and use the spices
and I was like oh God!
what can I say?

Luckily Tatiana came in and said
that smells horrible
chuck that out mum
and I was off the hook.

And then Dan came
and decided he wanted to cook
and he was going on
I'm gonna cook you some pa::sta
and on and on he went about this pasta
pronouncing the pasta pa::sta.

READER ACTIVITY

Identify the rest of the stanzas in story 3.3 and rewrite the story as above. How do your stanzas compare with Labov's categories of narrative structure?

Gee employed an intermediate unit between a stanza and the text, that of a 'part', which comprises thematically-related stanzas and is reminiscent of an act in a theatrical play. Gee's parts captured a story's plot development (e.g. complicating action, resolution etc).

If we go back to the stanzas in text 3.5, we can see how stanza 2 and stanza 4 present a common theme, that of 'earache'. They essentially narrate the same states and events in highly similar ways. In this way, they are linked through various repetition and parallelism patterns:

e.g. Stanza 2	Stanza 4
my ear's all bugging me	*my ear was killin me*
Stanza 2	Stanza 4:
I was cryin, I was all: oooh, oooh, oooh	*like, oh short, oh go::d*

In addition, there are numerous pattern-creating devices in text 3.4 based on sound: e.g. *MY ear, MY mother, oooh, oooh, oooh, go::d, ma::ma::*. As Gee suggested, this type of line and stanza structure is very different from American middle-class narration, which is temporally ordered, 'logically' connected and less rhythmic. In Michaels' terms (1981), it is a topic-associat-ing style of narration which contrasts with the topic-centred style. According to her study of children's narratives in American schools, the topic-associating style characterises black children's narratives in classroom while the topic-centred style is employed by middle-class white children and is promoted by schools. The former involves frequent shifts in spatio-temporal or thematic focus across rhythmic stanzas, while the latter presents a tightly-structured discourse with explicit connections between segments.

The above findings suggest that the ways in which experience is put into narrative units are to a major extent dependent on socio-cultural identities and modes of making sense of experience. As a result, different individuals and different social and cultural groups are likely to structure their narra-tives in different ways.

3.3 NARRATIVE UNITS IN SEQUENCE AND HIERARCHY

The narrative units discussed so far can be viewed in two ways: as a *sequence* or as a *hierarchy*. In other words, they can be approached as sequentially emergent and linearly arranged, or as dependent on and included in other units. These are different but not necessarily incompatible points of view. They may both be used in the same analysis but for different analytical purposes. In later chapters, we will discuss specific analytical procedures which are associated with these views. We will also see how they bear on non-narrative discourse as well, starting from section 3.4, where we discuss non-narrative sequential units. Here, we will briefly illustrate them in rela-tion to the narrative units described so far.

When narrative units are viewed in sequence, the emphasis of the analy-sis is on their position in the sequence as first, middle or last, or prior-current-next. For instance, we could be looking at the relations between a current and an upcoming unit in terms of how the storyteller moves from one to the other. To do this, we would have to focus on how the beginning or the end of a unit emerges sequentially. Alternatively, we could be looking at the salient positioning of units in the story: for example, How does the story end? Where does the climax occur? Is evaluation strategically positioned as a unit? Is it clearly set off from other units in the story's sequence? Our discussion has shown that in oral stories, this cannot be defined independently of audience contributions. On the whole, viewing a story as a sequence of units involves moving in it inductively, in the form of predictions as to what comes next on the basis of what the current unit is. This may be called a *bottom-up* approach.

When narrative units are viewed as part of a hierarchy, the emphasis is on the ways in which they are integrated into hierarchical part–whole relations in order to establish and maintain the main theme of the story. The starting point here is conceptual entities that guide a story's overall structure and processing (cf. story-grammar categories). This way of moving in a text from an established whole (theme or point) to the parts which instantiate it is a *top-down* approach. One of its main aims is to establish the ways in which the parts contribute to our understanding of the whole. The parts are hierarchically organised in different levels with different ranks. The difference between them is one of prominence and salience. From an analytical point of view, this no longer involves looking at their relations horizontally; that is, as creating boundaries to the right and left in sequence. It rather involves exploring them vertically, on an implicit axis that establishes how non-adjacent units are mutually implicated to form the narrative whole. Our interest is in how the linear organisation is manipulated to bring some items and events into greater prominence than others.

A very influential line of research on narrative units as hierarchy is that of studies on *foreground–background* (e.g. Hopper 1979; Wallace 1982; Givón 1987). The foreground–background distinction represents an extension into the domain of text-structure of the figure–ground opposition in the visual perception of spatial relations. Its essence is in recognising levels of informational saliency signalled through a particular set of strategies. The primary definition of foreground by Hopper and Thompson is that it is 'the material which supplies the main points of the discourse' and forms the backbone or skeleton of the text. By contrast, background is 'that part of a discourse that merely assists, amplifies, comments on the foreground ... or puts flesh on it' (1980: 280).

Initially, foregrounding was equated with a story's temporally-ordered clauses whose order matches the order of the events reported (cf. Labov's 'narrative clauses'). On this definition, past-tense verbs in main clauses make up the backbone of a narrative which is assisted by subordinate clauses (background). Similarly, verbs and/or clauses reporting punctual or complete events can serve more easily as foreground than reports of durative, repetitive, habitual and/or incomplete events. This qualifies verbs in the perfective (simple) past tense for the foreground, as opposed to verbs in the continuous past tense, pluperfect etc. Reports of alternative modes of narration with negative clauses (e.g. reports of events, states etc. which did not happen) or with modals (reports of events which could/would have happened, might happen etc.) are clearly not part of the narrative skeleton or backbone comprising the 'narrative clauses', so they are backgrounded.

READER ACTIVITY

Go back to stories 3.2 and 3.3 and divide their clauses into fore-grounded and backgrounded. Do you agree that the evaluative clauses (e.g. *it was funny*) should be treated as backgrounded?

Cross-linguistic applications of the above views make it clear that the notions of foreground and background, though useful for capturing narra-tive organisation, need to be relativised. First, they need to be viewed as a continuum rather than as a dichotomy: different languages mark different degrees of salience with the interplay between their semantic and grammat-ical means and their discourse conventions. Second, what is intrinsically important in one language and culture (e.g. transitivity, causality) is not intrinsically important in another and is, therefore, not equated with a story's foreground. Third, while the main grammatical correlates of fore-ground (e.g. sequentiality, main clauses) normally work for oral natural narratives, they are far more difficult to apply in non-literary narratives. Non-literary narratives very often reverse them and their conventional asso-ciations for artistic and stylistic effects. Chvany (1984), for instance, identi-fied numerous cases of subordinate clauses which, contrary to expectations, belonged to the foreground. Finally, the initial views of foreground were based on the assumption that only sequenced elements constitute the main axis of a story's development, while non-sequential elements appeared to be peripheral to the analysis (see Young 1984). As a result, a category like eval-uation, which contributes very significantly to the overall theme or point of a story, was considered as backgrounded and ancillary material. Reinhart (1984) claimed that the problem does not lie in the identification of fore-ground and background, which are indispensable modes of narrative organ-isation, or what transforms a chronicle of events into a story. The problem rather lies in viewing the foreground as necessarily more important and salient than the background. The relation between the two is, in fact, comple-mentary: the background enables us to perceive and understand the fore-ground. In view of the above considerations, the emphasis in the literature has lately moved from intrinsic structural features of foregrounding–back-grounding towards relative saliency. This is determined contextually, in rela-tion to the unpredictability or departure of elements from locally-established textual norms. The position of each unit in the story's hierarchy is assessed on the basis of its relation to its global theme.

The two views of units as a sequence and as a hierarchy are being increasingly integrated in the latest studies of narrative structure, and especially developmental studies (e.g. Karmiloff-Smith 1985; Berman 1988; Slobin 1990). The tendency is to investigate the linearisation of events in a horizontal dimension along with their vertical expansion. The analysis thus presents a dual focus: to 'differentiate between events referentially along the horizontal axis and integrate events into the vertical, hierarchical organisation of the overall theme of the narrative' (Bamberg and Marchman 1991: 277).

3.4 NON-NARRATIVE UNITS IN SEQUENCE

As seen in the case of narratives, discourse is so complex and multi-faceted that it has to be put across to the listeners or readers in instalments, that is, in sequences of utterances laid out in a way that will be easy both to produce and understand. As a result, every text is a chain of utterances (or utterance units like sentences) that are, by virtue of this linearity of discourse, linked by (at least) one kind of relation, that is, *precede–follow*, which distinguishes between prior and subsequent.

The criteria by which units have been identified in non-narrative texts have been predominantly thematic. The emphasis has mainly been on topical or logical relations on which the structure of these texts seems to be based rather than on relations of succession (e.g. Britton and Black 1985). It is usually assumed, for example, that the sentences of text 3.6 below are related to each other exclusively by referring to the same topic or dealing with the same subject.

READER ACTIVITY

Try to identify sections in the following text on the basis of what is being written about (the theme or subject). What problems do you encounter? Could there be alternative segmentations?

Text 3.6

1 In order to talk about the nature of the universe and to discuss questions such as whether it has a beginning or an end, you have to be clear about what a scientific theory is. 2 I shall take the simple-minded view that a theory is just a model of the universe, or a restricted part of it, and a set of rules that relate quantities in the model to observations that we make. 3 It exists only in our minds and does not have any other reality (whatever that may mean). 4 A theory is a good theory if it satisfies two requirements: it must accurately describe a large class of observations on the basis of a model that contains only a few arbitrary elements, and it must make

definite predictions about the results of future observations. 5 For example, Aristotle's theory that everything was made out of four elements, earth, air, fire, and water, was simple enough to qualify, but it did not make any definite predictions. 6 On the other hand, Newton's theory of gravity was based on an even simpler model, in which bodies attracted each other with a force that was proportional to a quantity called their mass and inversely proportional to the square of the distance between them. 7 Yet it predicts the motions of the sun, the moon, and the planets to a high degree of accuracy.

8 Any physical theory is always provisional, in the sense that it is only a hypothesis: you can never prove it. 9 No matter how many times the results of experiments agree with some theory, you can never be sure that the next time the result will not contradict the theory. 10 On the other hand, you can disprove a theory by finding even a single observation that disagrees with the predictions of the theory. 11 As philosopher of science Karl Popper has emphasised, a good theory is characterised by the fact that it makes a number of predictions that could in principle be disproved or falsified by observation. 12 Each time new experiments are observed to agree with the prediction the theory survives, and our confidence in it is increased; but if ever a new observation is found to disagree, we have to abandon or modify the theory. 13 At least that is what is supposed to happen, but you can always question the competence of the person who carried out the observation.

14 In practice, what often happens is that a new theory is devised that is really an extension of the previous theory. 15 For example, very accurate observations of the planet Mercury revealed a small difference between its motion and the predictions of Newton's theory of gravity. 16 Einstein's general theory of relativity predicted a slightly different motion from Newton's theory. 17 The fact that Einstein's predictions matched what was seen, while Newton's did not was one of the crucial confirmations of the new theory.

(*Source*: Stephen Hawking, *A Brief History of Time* (London: Bantam Press, 1988), pp. 5–6)

It is evident that there is no straightforward way of representing the text's internal structure exclusively on the basis of thematic connections. One reason is that we can always discover topical relations between any two parts of the text, since, as Levinson notes, 'for *any* two sets of referents or concepts one can invent a superordinate set that includes them both' (1981: 315). Such entities as 'Aristotle's theory' and 'Newton's theory' are not related *a priori* by some topical connection; their relation, rather, is constructed as such by the text (a relation of *otherwise*, in this case). A further problem with thematic analyses of structure involves the formalisation of what precisely is meant by 'theme' or 'connection'. Theme and especially its near-synonym *topic* are notoriously elusive concepts in linguistics and have been used to refer to a variety of phenomena, ranging from clause constituents to underlying propositions of entire texts. There is, consequently, no widely-accepted definition that could be useful to our purpose of identifying the text's internal structure.

By contrast, we are on much safer ground if we shift our attention from topical structure to criteria of segmentation that rely on formal linguistic devices. This shift would imply looking at the structure of non-narrative texts as a construct of the interaction between discourse participants rather than as a logical necessity that follows from some abstract principle of what is relevant. In dialogical texts, for instance, speakers manipulate shifts in intonation, connective phrases and lexical resources to create jointly a text in sequence. Comparably, in monological texts, like 3.6 above, the writer is responsible for using (and the reader for recognising) signals such as paragraph breaks or linking connectors like *for example* or *on the other hand*, which indicate the succession of text units.

Studies of the ways in which speakers and writers make use of formal linguistic devices to arrange a non-narrative text in sequence have appeared within diverse theoretical frameworks and in different guises. Both major approaches to the study of conversation, namely the Birmingham School approach (Sinclair and Coulthard 1975) and conversational analysis (e.g. Schegloff and Sacks 1973), have regarded the issue of sequencing in discourse as their central concern. The Birmingham School approach describes the sequentiality of conversational utterances in terms of a number of *ranks* realised through *classes* (such as Transaction, Exchange, Move, Act). Conversational analysis, on the other hand, makes use of the notion of *adjacent structures*, sequential pairs of speech acts such as question–answer, compliment–response etc. It also closely analyses phenomena such as topic change, topic shift and so on as instances of sequential relations in text. On the other hand, information about the sequential structure of monological non-narrative texts has been sparse, due to the almost exclusive emphasis on the semantic and logical structure of these texts noted above. Notable exceptions are Longacre's (1979) and Hinds' (1979) description of 'paragraph structure'. This description combines thematic, syntactic and intonational criteria, which define paragraph as a unit with internal closure, thematic unity and structural consistency. Research on paragraph structure has established that many languages are equipped with specialised formal devices such as particles to indicate paragraph closure (see Grimes 1975).

The common thread between all these approaches to sequentiality in non-narrative discourse is the recognition that text units are not simply related by a *precede–follow* relation but can be further linked by the creation of expectations that are later fulfilled in the text. A text is thus seen not as a chain of undifferentiated units but also as a progression of segments with a certain directionality, that is, some beginning and ending. A text is also characterised by a number of breaks in continuity, since some adjacent units are more closely linked than others.

From the perspective of the text-producer, this means that two major tasks need to be accomplished: the indication of continuity of some segments and the signalling of the discontinuity of others. These are the two basic strategies of *continuity* and *shift*, which account for a text's flow or progression. Continuity is, in practice, easier to indicate, being the default case in a text's flow: we usually expect things to remain the same in a text, unless we have an indication to the contrary (cf. Brown and Yule's 1983 principle of 'analogy'). For instance, in the following extract from text 3.6:

> 6 ... Newton's theory of gravity was based on an even simpler model ... 7 Yet it predicts the motions of the sun, the moon, and the planets to a high degree of accuracy 8 Any physical theory is always provisional ...

the two first sentences (6 and 7) are related by continuity, as indicated by the cohesive relations between sentence elements (*theory–it*) as well as by the absence of any signs that would indicate a shift. These signs are found, instead, in the following sentence: a paragraph break and a renominalisation (*any theory* instead of the pronominal *it*) signal that the continuity has been disrupted and a different segment is introduced.

In practice, shift can either be achieved by the opening of a new section as above or by the closing of another section as in line 20 in 3.7, an extract from a conversational text:

Text 3.7

1 A: How are you anyway Danny?
2 B: All right
3 A: You all right
4 B: Uh-huh (mid key)
5 A: Yeah?
6 B: Mm (mid key)
7 A: You got home all right?
8   you weren't too tired?
9 B: Well er (2)
10   I got up pretty late myself
11   I mean I – I was
12   supposed to get up at seven o'clock
13 A: What d'you mean
14   you were supposed to
15 B: Well I had the alarm clock on for seven
16 A: Hah (low key)
17   Well your alarm clock doesn't seem to work

18 B: No it did
19   I think I turned it off
➤ 20 A: Mm (low key)
21   It's you that doesn't work
22   Hey Danny
23 B: Yeah
24 A: You know we bought Ben that helium balloon
25 B: Yeah
26 A: Why doesn't it float any more (1.5)

(*Source*: Francis and Hunston 1992)

Here, the use of a low-key intonation (an intonational move from a higher to a lower point in the speaker's voice) indicates that there is no more information to follow in this section and a new section is expected to begin soon, as happens in line 22, with a new direct address (*Hey Danny*).

The indications of shift mentioned so far separate two units of the same status: the two sections preceding and following line 22 in text 3.7 are equally important and independent of one another (paratactic relation). The opening of new sections, however, can also be specially marked to indicate that one unit is subordinate to (or less important than, dependent on) another, signalling thus a hypotactic relation. For example, in text 3.8, sentence 3 opens a new segment by indicating an aside or digression from the previous section. The following section is marked as subordinate to the previous one. Then, sentence 6 opens the next segment by further indicating a return to the very first section, that is, the resumption of the 'normal' flow of text:

Text 3.8
1 If the cinema were only about acting, the American cinema would be the finest in the world ... 2 That reflection was prompted by ... Gloria Swanson's portrayal of the crazed silent movie diva Norma Desmond ... 3 And before this column gets down to its point I'd like to make a proposal, quite seriously, to Andrew Lloyd Webber ... 4 Dear Mr Lloyd Webber, if you read this, and are looking for a title ... may I suggest 'Swan Song' (or even 'Glorious Swan Song'). 5 Should either title appeal to you, please feel free. 6 Anyway, another reflection that it prompted was ... how few characters we remember by name. 7 Norma Desmond is one ...

(*Source*: *The Guardian*, 30 January 1992)

Different types of aside may be an extended *digression*, an *afterthought*, an *interruption*, or a *correction* (especially in conversations). Most of these are expected to be followed by a technique of *return* (to a prior topic).

To sum up: the basic tasks of continuity and shift are achieved by a number of basic techniques that indicate a succession of sequential relations between segments of a text. These are relations of continuity, opening and closing. Opening relations may be either simple introductions or hypotactic asides and returns. Table 3.2 summarises these relations.

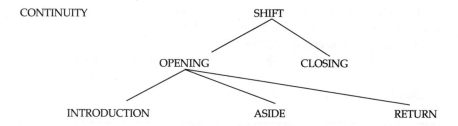

Table 3.2: Sequential relations

READER ACTIVITY

Can you use the basic scheme provided in Table 3.2 to identify sequential relations in texts 3.5 and 3.6? What are the units that can be established in the two texts? What are the linguistic signals of continuity and shift?

As mentioned above, the important shift of focus in establishing sequential relations concerns the emphasis on the formal linguistic devices that indicate continuity or its disruption. These devices may include 'physical' signals (such as paragraph breaks), explicit metalinguistic comments, adjacency structures, conjunctions or cohesive patterns. Paragraph breaks in written texts seem to play a crucial role in signalling sequential relations (Stark 1988; Sinclair 1988). In spoken discourse, their counterpart is intonation. Lehiste (1982), for example, has found that speakers can exploit prosodic patterns to indicate the beginning and end of paragraph-like units. The same finding is borne out in Coulthard's research (1992a), which systematically correlates the occurrence of mid key with opening and the shift to low key with closing strategies, as we can confirm in text 3.7. The use of explicit metalinguistic comments, such as *before this column gets down to its point* in text 3.8 above, is also associated with the signalling of units in sequence. Some common expressions, whose function has been conventionally reserved to indicate sequential relations, include: *to begin with ...*, *to sum up ...*, *as I was saying above ...* etc. Let us note here that whereas such explicit marking is acceptable in written texts, their use in conversation tends to be associated with awkward transitions and problematic situations (see McCarthy 1993 for a detailed discussion).

Adjacency structures are also involved in the indication of sequential relations; a question, for instance, can open up a new segment to which the answer would belong. Conjunctions function as discourse markers (see Chapter 4): they indicate relations of shift or continuity in discourse. See, for instance, the use of *yet* in sentence 7 of text 3.6 (for continuity), *you know* in sentence 24 of 3.7 (for introduction), and *anyway* in sentence 6 of text 3.8 (for return). Finally, cohesive patterns are also basic devices for indicating sequential relations. The occurrence of cohesive links between adjacent sentences (e.g. *it* in sentence 3 of text 3.6 links back to sentence 2 by reference) creates local areas of continuity. On the other hand, a shift to renominalisation after a section in which only pronouns are used for reference indicates an opening relation, as seen above.

READER ACTIVITY

Table 3.3 below lists some signals of sequential relations. By reference to texts 3.6, 3.7 and other non-narrative texts, could you fill in the details missing and add any examples and categories of your own that you find necessary?

Physical signals	intonation:	
	mid key	continuity
	low key	closing
	paragraph breaks	....
	parenthesis	....
Metalinguistic expressions	*to sum up ...*	*closing*
	....	*opening*
	....	*return*
Discourse markers	*now, then, but*	....
	therefore, thus	closing
	and	....
	anyway	....

Table 3.3: Signals of sequential relations

This basic description of sequential relations and units still leaves a lot of important issues to be dealt with. For instance, are secondary hypotactic relations such as aside and return reducible to the primary relation of shift, or not? What happens with cases of gradual transition, where no abrupt shift can be discerned? Do relations remain the same or do they change across discourse genres? Nevertheless, it has been established that non-narrative texts are characterised by an overall sequential structure, which is based on the succession of units linked by relations of continuity or shift. The overall result is a series of periodic patterns of areas of continuity or stability alternating with points of turbulence or shift.

In conversation, continuity and shift are produced by the interactive effort of participants. The units can be minimal adjacent pairs (e.g. question–answer), usually offered by more than one participant. They can also be larger sections (again, created by both interlocutors), marked off from the rest of discourse by the use of intonation. In written texts, the succession of units is indicated by a number of explicit, implicit and conventionalised devices, offered by the writer and dependent on the reader for their interpretation. As a result, non-narrative units can be of a different kind and size, according to the linguistic devices involved. 'Paragraph' is a useful term for many of these, as long as it is not confused with the actual typographic entity. Paragraphs and other intermediate-level units are composed of lower-level units such as utterances or speech acts and are themselves part of the larger internal structure of a text.

3.5 IDEATIONAL ACTS

A first extension of our elementary *precede–follow* relation has been the distinction between *continue* and *shift* in the succession of adjacent text units. However, adjacent units are also linked by some kind of logical relation, which we intuitively seem to recognise in every stretch of text. Logical relations are especially prominent in non-narrative discourse, which is based on acts of information, related to each other in a logical way. These acts can be established on a much lower level than that of paragraph in sequential structure and constitute the building blocks of the semantic content of discourse.

Both the logical acts and their relations can be represented in a general abstract formulation. To give an example from text 3.6, sentences 6 and 7 are not simply related by a continuity relation: their main clauses are also related by the logical relation of *Antithesis* or *Contrast*:

> 6 On the other hand, Newton's theory of gravity was based on an even simpler model, in which bodies attracted each other with a force that was proportional to a quantity called their mass and inversely proportional to the square of the distance between them. 7 Yet it predicts the motions of the sun, the moon, and the planets to a high degree of accuracy.

> ⌐ CONTRAST (Newton's theory was based on an even simpler model)
> ►Yet (it predicts the motions of the planets to a high degree of accuracy)

Similarly, the two first clauses of sentence 4 are related by the logical relation of *Condition*:

> 4 A theory is a good theory if it satisfies two requirements

> ►(a theory is a good theory)
> ⌐ CONDITION if (it satisfies two requirements)

Contrast and *Condition* can be recognised as logical relations because they identify an interpretable connection between two parts of a text. What is related in both cases is the semantic or ideational content of the individual sentences or clauses. To use a different term, the relations of *Contrast* and *Condition* are propositional: they relate propositions, namely minimal units of logic that affirm, deny, question or command something. Propositions are analysable into predicates and arguments. The statement 'Newton's theory was based on an even simpler model' is composed of the predicate 'was based on' and the arguments 'Newton's theory' and 'an even simpler model'. The relations between propositions are analytical, in the sense that they can be expressed in terms of constituent entities, abstracted from the specific context in which they appear. The relation in the first example above can thus be rendered as follows:

> ▶(predicts to a high degree of accuracy (it, the motions))
> └─CONTRAST (was based (Newton's theory, an even simpler model))

Notice that sequential relations cannot be similarly expressed in terms of propositions. This is because they refer to the organisational aspect of a text's flow and do not relate parts of the subject matter, as ideational relations do. Mann and Thompson argue that ideational relations 'do not simply deal with adjacency, textual precedence, and boundaries of parts of texts. ... Instead, they convey essential subject matter' (1986: 77). In other words, they refer to the substance planes of discourse.

Below are a few more ideational relations between sentences and clauses from a variety of non-narrative texts:

REASON: *why*
Follow the manufacturer's instructions on speaker placement. It can make a lot of difference to the sound.
ELABORATION: *tell me some more*
We do everything we can to make our products better. We improve material and add back features and construction details.
PURPOSE: *in order to*
To reproduce high frequencies, the diaphragm must move very rapidly over short distances.
RESULT: *as a result*
In a concert hall, sounds arrive from all directions, so that listeners enjoy better what they hear.
OTHERWISE: *alternatively*
Simply call Freephone with your order. Or ask for our free catalogue.
SOLUTIONHOOD: *how*
Parents can do a great deal to make the first going to school easier, by answering the child's question 'What will it be like?'

Although the list of ideational relations must be finite, not all researchers agree on which and how many these are. The most detailed model of ideational relations is Mann and Thompson's Rhetorical Structure Theory

(RST). Ideational relations in RST hold between two pieces of text, the nucleus and the satellite. In our example above, sentence 7 (*it predicts the motions*) is the nucleus and sentence 6 the satellite.

Rhetorical Structure Theory argues that ideational relations are crucial to the effective functioning of the text as a whole. It has been extensively used in the analysis of whole texts of a wide variety such as advertisements, editorials, fund-raising letters etc. (e.g. Fries 1992; Mann et al. 1992; Abelen et al. 1993). The analysis works by identifying first the nuclei and satellites and then the ideational relations that hold between them. We can try to apply this in the following example:

Text 3.9
1 The first Blacks that came on the scene, were uh – as I say they were uneducated,
2 no one would give 'em a job
3 and they – they started … crime.
4 Now, when other Blacks heard y'know that the – uh what kind of money they were makin' up here, they left,
5 because down South they weren't makin' any kind of money.
6 And then, the Southerners used t'give 'em carfare t'get 'em the hell outa there.
7 So, uh … I'm – I – y – you can't say all Blacks are bad.
8 Just like all Whites are not good either.

(*Source*: Schiffrin 1987)

In text 3.9 we can recognise two nuclei: *they started crime* in 3 and *they left* in 4. The first nucleus is related to a satellite in 2: *nobody would give them a job* (relation: *Reason*), which has its own satellite in 1: *Blacks were uneducated* (relation: *Reason*). The second nucleus has one satellite in 4: *when other Blacks heard* (relation: *Circumstance*) and another two in 5: *they were not making money* and 6: *they were given carfare* (relation: *Cause*). It should be noticed that, although formal linguistic criteria (similar to those concerning sequential relations) may be used to identify ideational relations, they are not necessary for establishing their existence. Their presence in the text, however, helps their identification. We would recognise these relations between parts of the text, even if elements such as *because* or *so* were missing.

READER ACTIVITY

Try to analyse texts 3.5 and 3.6 by using RST. Does the analysis apply recursively? What problems do you encounter?

According to Rhetorical Structure Theory, relations can be identified on more than one level. The prototypical domain of ideational relations is the clause, since clauses are the minimal units in which predicates and their arguments can combine (cf. Winter 1982). RST further claims that its analysis applies recursively to larger units such as sentences or whole parts of the text. For instance, sentence 7 in text 3.9 above (*you can't say all Blacks are bad*) can serve as a nucleus for sentences 1 to 6, which act as its satellite. It should be noted, however, that the relations that hold on this level are essentially of a different kind. In the last example, the relation between 1 to 6, on the one hand, and 7, one the other, is *Justification*. As we will see in the following section, this, like other relations found on higher levels (such as *Justification*, *Evidence* and *Motivation*), presupposes some reference to the author's or speaker's intentions beyond the mere propositional properties of the relation. These two roles have to be clearly distinguished. By including both kinds of relations in the same list, RST has received a great amount of criticism for conflating ideational with intentional aspects of a text's structure (e.g. Moore and Pollack 1992; Moore and Paris 1993).

Another point of contention is the inclusion of such relations as Restatement (*in other words*), Summary (*to sum up*) or List (*first … second …*). These seem to be of a mainly sequential rather than propositional nature. At the beginning of text 3.6, for instance, clauses are precisely related by such non-propositional relations:

2   (a theory is a just a model of a universe, or a restricted part of it)
3   (it exists only in our minds)
    and (does not have any other reality)

We would strain interpretation if we wanted to identify ideational relations between these clauses. Descriptive sections like this are thus less amenable to an RST analysis. Similarly, relations like Attribution (*x is y*), Equivalent (*x equals y*) and Situation (*there is x*) fail the test of analysis into relational propositions, being merely (in propositional terms) arguments of a predicate (see Sanders et al. 1992). For instance, in a constructed sequence like:

A theory exists only in our minds. A theory is a model of the universe.

the second clause, which is in an Equivalent relation to the first (*a theory equals y*) does not relate to the first clause by virtue of this relation but simply adds another predicate (*y: a model*) to the first argument (*x: a theory*). The same is true for Foreground, Background, Circumstance and Setting, which are not propositional relations but seem to cut across the set of other relations. We can see this in a cause–consequence relation, in which both members can be foregrounded or backgrounded depending on which one is the nucleus:

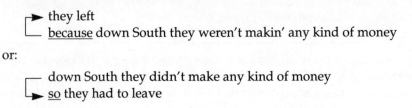

they left
because down South they weren't makin' any kind of money

or:

down South they didn't make any kind of money
so they had to leave

It is interesting that these relations (along with temporal sequence) mostly apply to narrative texts, as seen in previous sections. Again, these relations are determined by the referential content of the segments in which they occur, rather than their propositional properties.

Irrespective of the specific problems of description, models such as Rhetorical Structure Theory are successful in capturing one of the fundamental aspects of text structure, namely the succession of information units. Successive units of semantic content are linked by ideational relations. The distinctive characteristic of these relations is that they can be formalised – in particular, they may be expressed in terms of the individual propositions (predicates plus arguments) which they relate. Ideational relations can be identified between either clauses or adjacent text units. Their role is the semantic connection of individual acts of information, and their overall effect is a hierarchical structure that goes beyond sequential order and dependency. Whereas sequential relations deal with the progression of a text's flow and thus define paragraph-like units, ideational relations concern the building blocks of information content in a text and thus apply on a more fundamental level.

3.6 INTENTIONAL RELATIONS AND ARGUMENTS

We have already mentioned that logical relations between higher-level units are of a different kind from those between lower-level units. This distinction has to do with the semantic or pragmatic nature of relations. In analysing logical relations, we may choose to focus on their propositional content or, alternatively, we may be interested in their effect on the reader, that is, their perlocutionary effect, in Austin's (1962) terms. In the latter case, the emphasis is on the contribution of a certain text unit to a purpose and the underlying intentions of the text-producer. The following comment by a friend of a woman who died leaving a huge amount of money to charity can be viewed in two ways:

> You would never have guessed she had any money ... She was happy in her little two-bedroomed flat.
>
> (*Source: The Independent*, 21 May 1995)

The second sentence can be characterised as a satellite linked to the nucleus of the first one by a relation of *Reason*. Alternatively, the sentence can be viewed as providing *Evidence* for the assertion made in the first sentence. The former aspect refers to what is being talked about, the latter to why the speaker is talking about it (cf. Ford's 1986 analysis of *Solutionhood*). The latter perspective focuses on the speaker's intentions and reveals the persuasive nature of the text on a hearer.

Ideational relations can thus be coupled with pragmatic or intentional counterparts. Thus, in text 3.6 the ideational relation of *Otherwise* and *Contrast* between 5 and 6 and between 6 and 7, respectively, can be paired with an intentional relation of *Exemplification* of 4, as seen below:

> 4   a theory is a good theory if it satisfies two requirements
> 5   For example, Aristotle's theory was simple enough to qualify
> 6   Newton's theory was based on an even simpler model
> 7   it predicts the motions

This pragmatic aspect of the text is indispensable in understanding its internal structure.

As we can see, intentional relations tend to be more prominent on a higher level of analysis. Thus, *Circumstance* and *Elaboration* can be used to support or justify an assertion, as in text 3.9, where the ideational relations in 1 to 6 provide the basis of an intentional relation of *Conclusion* in 7 (*so you can't say all Blacks are bad*). Notice again that *Conclusion* is fundamentally different from *Result*: the former is a consequence of intentional argumentation, whereas the latter is a relational proposition asserted over another proposition. The ideational relations of *Reason*, *Purpose* and *Result* can thus be used for providing *Justification* of a position, while *Cause* can be related to *Evidence* supporting this position and *Contrast* to *Rebuttal* or rejection of the position.

In non-narrative texts, the most basic intentional relation seems to be that between a *Position* and its *Justification* or *Support*. This is, in fact, the basis of argumentation, as has been noticed in traditional treatises of rhetoric. Aristotle was the first to identify these basic parts of a typical syllogism and to found the analysis of intentional effects in a text. A host of models follow his primary distinctions. According to *Ad Herennium*, a complete rhetorical argumentation should consist of five parts: a proposition, a reason, a proof of the reason, an embellishment and a résumé. More recently, Toulmin (1969, et al. 1979) has proposed a model that strongly resembles the classical rhetorical one by distinguishing the following components: a claim, grounds, a warrant, backing, qualifications and possible rebuttals. These parts are variants of the Position–Justification relation (in particular, the five parts correspond to Position, Evidence, Justification and Motivation, Elaboration, Rebuttal). Finally, van Dijk (1987b) also distinguishes between a position statement (consisting of an opinion: *I don't like X*), a usually implicit inference principle (*if X has Y, then X is bad*) and a general or particular fact (*X has Y*) that provides supporting evidence for the position (*that's why I don't like X*).

The common feature of all these models is a tripartite distinction between position, justification and conclusion. Justification deals with the provision of evidence and the presentation of arguments for or against a position. We can further distinguish between the core motivation for stating a position (this is related to van Dijk's inference principle) and its elaboration by reference to something more general or by exemplification. The persuasive effect of justification (cf. Lakoff 1982) leads to the acceptance or rejection of the original position, which constitutes the conclusion. Table 3.4 summarises these intentional relations:

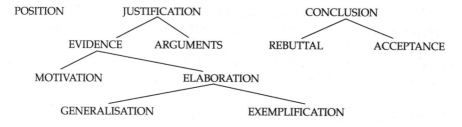

Table 3.4: Intentional relations

READER ACTIVITY

Analyse texts 3.5 and 3.8 in terms of the intentional relations presented in Table 3.4. How does the overall structure compare for the two texts?

It can be seen that the basic intentional relations do not exclusively apply in typical argumentative texts but can also be found in expository texts such as 3.6. The difference is that the former do not anticipate the hearer's or reader's assent, whereas the latter do (Reddick 1992). Hence, in typical argumentative texts we usually have the full development of intentional relations rather than individual couples. Likewise, intentional relations are not restricted to written texts but constitute a basic building block of spoken non-narrative discourse. Both everyday non-narrative speech and formal pieces of rhetoric deal with justifications, motivations, explanations, challenges, confirmations and disagreements. Text 3.9, for instance, is a complex piece of argumentation, starting with position, progressing to evidence for its justification, and ending with a disclaimer about its generalisability. Of course, this does not mean that written and spoken texts have to follow the same conventions. For instance, van Dijk (1987b) notes that the opinion statement is usually first in conversation but last in formal argument (presented in the form of a conclusion). Finally, intentional relations also appear in the narrative mode: *motivation* and *explanation* play a central role in the development of personal actions, while other types of intentional relations also appear in represented characters' speech.

READER ACTIVITY

Going back to your previous analysis of texts 3.5 and 3.8, focus on the linguistic evidence that has guided your decisions. Can you classify the linguistic signals of intentional relations in the texts? (Use table 3.3 as a model.) What is your conclusion with respect to the use of those signals?

By contrast with sequential and ideational relations, the prototypical domain of intentional relations is that of higher units. However, their recognition is based on similar linguistic signals to those mentioned above for sequential and ideational relations. As seen in text 3.6, the metalinguistic expression *for example* indicates an intentional relation, while other common signals include lexical items such as *reason*, *evidence* etc. (Phillips 1989). It is obvious that the signalling of pragmatic effects is much less dependent on physical signals such as paragraphing and is more closely linked to the lexical and semantic properties of text units.

Intentional relations play a central role in argumentation in its broader sense, as the expression of attitudes and opinions organised around contrasts. Van Dijk (1987b) regards opinions, or general evaluative beliefs, as the building blocks of attitudes. Intentional relations are found in the core of our expression of opinions and are thus closely related to shared cognitions and social representations. Our interpretation of texts like 3.6, which may appear independent of evaluative beliefs, crucially depends on interpersonal shared assumptions of an intentional character.

Recent criticism has challenged the view of intentional relations as a well-organised structure in text, especially the one-to-one correspondence between communicative intentions and discourse units (Rambow 1993). It has been claimed that intentionality may be implicit or diffused throughout the structure of a text rather than explicitly expressed in every single discourse segment. At the other extreme, intentional relations have been conflated with either ideational acts or generic patterns of discourse (such as the Problem–Solution pattern: see Chapter 5). Nevertheless, intentional relations seem to be useful in capturing those pragmatic aspects of the text's internal structure that are not accounted for by sequential or ideational relations. Adding a further aspect to this structure, intentional relations refer to the relation of propositions to the purposes for which they are used in text units. As such, they encapsulate the building blocks of information, namely the ideational units on lower levels, into larger argumentation patterns. Their overall effect amounts to the signalling of patterns of argumentation which satisfy the rhetoric requirements of the text,namely the justification of the speaker's or writer's position and the persuasion of an audience.

FURTHER READING
There is a huge literature on story grammars. The classic work includes Black and Bower (1980), Bower (1978), Mandler (1978), Mandler and Johnson (1977), Stein and Glenn (1979), Stein and Policastro (1984). For causal relations and their effect on story comprehension and recall, see Trabasso and Sperry (1985) and Trabasso, van de Broek and Suh (1989). A critique of story grammars can be found in a Special Issue of the *Journal of Pragmatics* 6 (1982). More recent work on story grammar models of comprehension and recall can be found in papers in *Discourse Processes* 16 (1993).

Polanyi (1985) is a classic study of evaluation in everyday spoken stories.

Peterson and McCabe (1983), in addition to extending Labov's model of evaluation, is a very accessible study of narrative structure using both story grammars and Labov in children's narratives. Numerous studies of evaluation have been conducted in children's narratives as part of narrative development research. Kernan (1977) is another useful extension of Labov's model, while more recent studies can be found in Hicks (1990, 1991), Bamberg and Damrad (1991) and Hudson and Shapiro (1991).

Discussions of the combination of the intonational, syntactic and thematic criteria for the identification of spoken narrative paragraphs can be found in Sherzer and Woodbury (1987) and Tedlock (1983). Coulthard and Montgomery (1981) discuss the structural unit of spoken paragraph in conversation, isolated on phonological criteria. General descriptions of paragraph as a semantic unit are abundant in the literature on non-narrative discourse. Different perspectives are given by Koen, Young and Becker (1969), Hinds (1977), Givón (1983) and Bond and Hayes (1984). Stark (1988) remains the best close study available. The line-and-stanza poetic structure has also been found to be evident in oral Greek (Georgakopoulou 1995b) and Japanese narratives (Minami and McCabe 1991: 577–601), mainly in the form of three-line stanzas.

A discussion of narrative foreground–background studies can be found in Dry (1983), Fleischman (1990) and Thompson (1984). Discussions of the bottom-up and top-down approaches to narrative and of how the two can be integrated are found in Bamberg (1987, 1990) and Bamberg and Damrad (1991).

More arguments against structural analyses of texts based on topic or theme can be found in Tyler (1978) and Brown and Yule (1983).

Descriptions of sequential relations appear in many diverse sources. Apart from the references mentioned in the text, see also the discussion in Goutsos (1994). For the study of relevant issues specifically in conversational

Grimes	Longacre	Halliday and Hasan	Hobbs	RST
rhetorical predicates	paragraph types	conjunctive relations	coherence relations	rhetorical relations
collection	coupling	additive		list
alternative	alternation	alternative		otherwise
	temporal	temporal		sequence
	causation	causal	cause	cause
condition	conditionality	conditional		condition
result		result		result
purpose		purpose		purpose
	contrafactuality			concession
adversative	contrast		contrast	contrast
equivalent	paraphrase	apposition	paraphrase	restatement
specifically	illustration		elaboration	elaboration
identification	deixis			
attributive	attribution			
response				solutionhood

Table 3.5: Ideational relations in different theories

discourse, see selectively Craig and Tracy (1983), Button and Casey (1984) and Coulthard (1985).

The terminology used for ideational acts is widely different. Table 3.5 compares the terms used for the most important ideational relations in five major theories, namely Grimes (1975), Longacre (1976), Halliday and Hasan (1976), Hobbs (1979) and Rhetorical Structure Theory (Mann and Thompson 1986).

Other descriptions of ideational structures can be found in Cooper (1983), Fahnestock (1983), Britton and Black (1985) and McKeown (1985). A fuller picture of RST with more details and further references is given in Mann and Thompson (1988). The most thorough critique of RST is found in Sanders et al. (1992).

For issues of intentions and argumentation in discourse, apart from the classic Toulmin (1969), which is still useful, the most comprehensive source is van Eemeren and Kruiger (1987). The introductory chapters of Hirsch (1989) are a fairly accessible introduction, whereas more sophisticated material can be found in van Eemeren and Grootendorst (1982). Descriptions of intentional structures form part of fully-fledged models of discourse relations such as Reichman's (1985) model of context spaces and Grosz and Sidner's (1986) model of focus, though their artificial-intelligence orientation may be discouraging to the non-specialist. A related model with more appeal to linguists is Sinclair's (1985) model of planes, especially as revised in Sinclair (1993).

The best overall description of relations is given by Redeker (1992); but note that the terms used there differ from those in our description. Maier and Hovy (1993) also develop a full taxonomy from an RST point of view and include useful further references. Up-to-date research and criticism can be found in the collective volume on *Intentionality and Structure in Discourse Relations* edited by Rambow (1993).

Discourse Organisation

In Chapter 3 we showed how narrative and non-narrative discourse are not composed of undifferentiated strings of sentences, but constitute wholes with different units or parts. Such units take over the role of the segmentation and presentation of the text's information. As we have seen, units and relations are indicated by a number of devices. These act as the text's signposts that signal the relations between parts and the transition from one part to the other. Reminiscent of road signs on the motorway, they enable the addressees to anticipate what is coming next in the text and to understand how that ties in with what came before. In this way, they provide points of reference so that the addressees can find their way easier through the maze of discourse.

Signals do not operate as individual linguistic elements but usually occur in patterns that constitute a text's organisation. In narrative texts, they usually involve time, space, participants and action. In accordance with the basic characteristics of narrative, they provide information about who did what, when and where. In non-narrative texts, signals further include extended lexical patterning, which satisfies the concerns of presenting information of a non-narrative (impersonal, non-temporal) kind.

READER ACTIVITY

Identify the devices that the author of text 4.1 has chosen in order to signal transition to a new paragraph. Do they relate to the who, what, when and where of the discourse?

Text 4.1
Isaiah is lying with his legs tucked up under him, with his face in the snow and his hands round his head, as if he were shielding himself

from the little spotlight shining on him, as if the snow were a window through which he has caught sight of something deep inside the earth.

Surely the police officer ought to ask me who I am and take down my name and address, and in general prepare the ground for those of his colleagues who will shortly have to start ringing doorbells. But he's a young man with a queasy expression on his face. He avoids looking directly at Isaiah. After assuring himself that I won't step inside the tape, he lets me stand there.

He could have roped off a larger area. But it wouldn't have made any difference. The warehouses are in the process of being partially modernized. People and machines have compacted the snow as hard as a terrazzo floor.

Even in death Isaiah seems to have turned his face away, as if he wants no part of anyone's sympathy.

High overhead, outside the spotlight, a rooftop is barely discernible. The warehouse is high, probably as tall as a seven- or eight-storey housing block. The adjoining building is under construction. It has scaffolding along the gable-end facing Strandgade. That's where I make for as the ambulance works its way across the bridge and then moves in among the buildings.

The scaffolding covers the gable all the way up to the roof. The last ladder is down. The structure seems shakier the higher I go.

They're putting on a new roof. Above me loom the triangular rafters, covered with tarpaulins. They stretch half the length of the building. The other half of the roof, facing the harbour, is a snow-covered surface. On it are Isaiah's tracks.

At the edge of the snow a man is huddled with his arms around his knees, rocking back and forth.

(Peter Hoeg, *Miss Smilla's Feeling for Snow*
(London: Flamingo, 1994), pp. 6–7)

4.1 DISCOURSE MARKERS

In Chapter 1, where we introduced the notion of cohesion, we mentioned that, in Halliday and Hasan's (1976) framework, one of the types of cohesive ties is conjunction. Conjunction involves those tiny linguistic forms that connect clauses and establish various kinds of relations, such as temporal, causal and additive (e.g. *and, but, because* etc.). These connective forms essentially make explicit implicit relations between clauses. Though dispensable, their presence in a text helps the addressees to construct the text's mental representation (see Segal et al. 1991). For many years, connectives served as a point of departure for comparing different texts of the same mode (e.g. narratives told by adults versus narratives told by children, spoken versus written narratives) or narrative with non-narrative texts (e.g. stories versus essays etc.). The focus was on the use of coordinating as opposed to subordinating connectives. Coordinators like *and, or, but, so* tie together two or more clauses of the same status (paratactic linking). Subordinators such as *because, since, although,* on the other hand, signal a non-symmetrical relation holding between two clauses of a different status, a main and a dependent one (hypotactic linking). The main hypothesis of these studies was that the use of subordinating conjunctions constitutes an indicator of a text's difficulty: texts that included more subordinate than coordinate clauses were assumed to be more complex and difficult. From this point of view, non-narrative texts were expected to be more difficult than narrative texts and written narratives more difficult than spoken narratives.

While some of the studies confirmed these hypotheses, others did not. As a result, it has been progressively realised that the categories of coordination and subordination have too many definitional problems to be useful. For instance, the category of subordination does not distinguish between different degrees of integration into the main clause. There are clauses that are so deeply embedded into the main clause as to be a constituent of it (e.g. a complement), for example:

There are clauses <u>that are so deeply embedded into the main clause</u>.
Surely the police ought to ask him <u>who I am</u> (from text 4.1).

Other clauses are relatively more separate from the predicate of the main clause, to which they relate in a circumstantial relation, indicating place, time, reason, manner and so on, for example:

<u>When you come back</u>, we'll have a good time.
I'll certainly stay, <u>if my friends turn up</u>.

Beaman (1984) reported that embedded clauses are more complex and more common in written narratives. Complement clauses, on the other hand, are very common in spoken narratives and do not seem to be associated with structural complexity.

As discourse analysts explored connective forms in conversational and narrative stretches of discourse, they drew attention to their tendency to appear in transitional locations, at the beginnings of discourse units. In these transitional locations, instead of establishing ideational relations between successive clauses, connectives establish a whole range of textual relations between units. For instance, in narratives they signal a transition to a new event or a return to an event after a digression. Notice the use of *but* in the following short extract from a story:

Text 4.2

A: and then she gave me the number of this man, who is Basquan, and I called him up, and he said ((imitating the Spanish accent in English)), as soon as you arrive in Spain, you come and see me straight away,//

V: // when they say it they mean it

A: <u>he</u> does, apparently he has lots of contacts, I'm sure he'll sort us out, once we get there. <u>But</u> he was very very positive, and very welcoming.

(*Source*: Authors' data)

In text 4.2, *but* does not seem to establish an adversative relation between two successive clauses. The narrator, on the contrary, wishes to emphasise that his contact in Spain is going to be very helpful. *But* occurs after the narrator's digression from the narrative line in order to uphold the listener's suggestion that 'when they say it they mean it'. Its occurrence essentially signals a return to the narrative event line that was interrupted, that is, the scene of the phone call. *But* thus makes the event line available for continuation by marking the speaker's concluding remark regarding his contact in Spain.

In numerous cases, the use of conjunctions as signals of textual relations bears little or no affinity with their original propositional meaning. The textual use of *because*, for instance, may establish coordinate rather than subordinate relations. Instead of creating a relationship of causal dependency between clauses, *because* very frequently signals continuation or elaboration of previous statements in conversational or narrative discourse, for example:

Nadia: How long do you keep your spices for?

Alexandra: I don't know. Six months?

Nadia: Ah, that's fine. After that. <u>'Cos</u> your mum ((turning to Alex)) had kept some spices, from when my mum was there, and when we were in their place, your mum wanted me to cook dinner …

As we can see in the above extract from our – by now – familiar story 3.3, *because* is employed as a signal of a passage from the conversational topic of 'spices' to a story. It is thus a signal of a paratactic discourse relationship rather than a subordinator marking causality (see Schleppegrell 1990 for further discussion).

In cases like the above, the speakers do not seem to employ conjunctions on the basis of their propositional meaning. In other words, the strongest relation which conjunctions establish between two units is not ideational, one that would entail the speakers' commitment to the existence of the relation in the world which the discourse describes. Instead, the strongest relation is between discourse spans in terms of their illocutionary force (not their propositional meaning). In this way, conjunctions are signals of textual relations as well as indicators of the speakers' orientation and attitudes towards what is being said and towards their addressees.

READER ACTIVITY

Compare the use of *but* in the following two extracts. Does it signal more than one type of relation?

Text 4.3
so I started to write that book and, um, well, I published that myself and uh, as a result got, got into a lot of other publishing stuff, unrelated to that. I mean, somebody called me up asking me to do a jazz guitar book, on the basis that I had published this banjo book, this bluegrass banjo book (laughs) and wh– which I couldn't see, you know, I couldn't see that, how that followed all that.
➤   But it was, it was just a fortunate accident really, because when I got into doing a lot of other, projects like that, that were a lot of fun.
(*Source*: Linde 1993: 150)

Text 4.4
the south had come to negotiate a very complex bill of goods – or so they thought. If the north wanted to safeguard the planet, they would have to pay the south to protect their forests and forgo cheap and dirty technology, and help on poverty and population.
➤   But that is where the common perception of the south ended. For the newly industrialised world, it was not only a matter of a green dividend. For this group, the unfettered ability to industrialise was essential, pollution an unavoidable consequence.
(*Source*: *New Statesman and Society*, 23 January 1993)

The function of signalling a range of textual relations between units is shared by a wide and heterogeneous set of linguistic elements. Chafe (1986: 21) observes that markers such as *in fact*, *rather* etc., which are found in written texts, 'help the reader appreciate the flow of information from one unit to the next by making explicit the relations that in speaking might be signalled by the context, prosody and gesture' (cf. Sinclair's 1993 'logical operators'). As mentioned above, detailed studies (e.g. Beaman 1984; Grabe 1987) have established that spoken genres favour coordinating conjunctions and interjections like *I mean, y'know*, whereas adverbial conjunctions (such as *consequently, specifically* etc.) are usually restricted in the domain of writing. We can, then, distinguish between three different word classes with similar textual functions but different preferred contexts of occurrence: interjections (*oh, y'know*) and comment clauses (*I mean, mind you*), which are common in speech; conjunctions (*and, but*), which are common in both speech and writing; and descriptive adverbials (*firstly, namely* etc.), which are mainly found in written texts.

The standardised term for all these items that share a range of textual functions is *discourse markers*. Notice though that other terms such as *cue phrases* and *pragmatic connectives* are also common in the literature. The term 'discourse markers' originates in Schiffrin's classic work (1987) on how connectives function not just as cohesive devices but also as coherence devices, which establish relations on all levels of discourse, between what is said, meant and done. A simple definition of discourse markers is that they are sequentially dependent elements that bracket units of talk and exhibit multiple functions, usually a primary (more dominant) one and various secondary ones. To account for this multi-functionality, Schiffrin postulated the following *planes of talk* (1987: 35ff.) in operation in conversations:

- the ideational level (plane), covering the propositional content of speech
- the level of exchange structures, covering the turn-taking mechanisms
- the level of action structures, coordinating speech acts
- the level of information states, covering the participants' knowledge and metaknowledge regarding the ongoing discourse
- the level of participation framework that marks the speaker–hearer roles and relations (i.e. interpersonal) during the conversational event.

The above planes have been amply criticised for their limited validity and explanatory power. Similarly, Schiffrin's identification of certain functions for certain discourse markers has been questioned and revised (see Redeker 1991). There is a general consensus though among discourse analysts on the main ideas which underlie Schiffrin's framework. First, they agree on the *anisomorphism* and multiplicity or non-exclusivity in the relationship between discourse markers (as forms) and their functions: this means that a single discourse marker can exhibit more than one function in that it can convey meanings and relationships in more than one discoursal component. The opposite is also valid: the same function may be realised by more than one discourse marker. This idea is widely accepted in relation to all discourse forms. Second, discourse markers are viewed as forms which establish textual as well as interactional or interpersonal relations. The standardised scheme employed to account for their functions is essentially traceable to Halliday's tripartite division of language functions into ideational, textual and interpersonal. The textual function covers the stringing-together and segmenting of units (e.g. the signalling of topic shifts and continuities, the return to topics after digressions etc). The interpersonal function covers the relation between addresser and addressee(s) and the expression of the subjective elements of linguistic communication (e.g. feelings, attitudes, stances etc).

The above broad functions of discourse markers have varying realisations in the two discourse modes. In narratives, it is very common to find discourse markers as part of the text's temporal strategy, that is, of the presentation of new events as occurring later in time than those already narrated. This relationship is commonly conveyed by *then* (temporal sequencer) but also by temporal adverbial phrases (anchorage markers) such as *at that point, after a while, the next day, at ten o'clock, that morning* etc.

One of the conjunctive forms, *and*, which is a less explicit indicator than temporal adverbials, is a very common minimal signal of presentation of new events (additivity), the default norm of connection, in particular in spoken narratives. It has also been found to be the commonest means of linking two time-line events in children's narratives. In addition to temporality and additivity, *and* can signal various relations ranging from contrast to expansion, elaboration, return to an event after a digression etc. Its role is thus not restricted to the beginning of 'spoken' paragraphs, but extends to the beginning and ending of plot categories such as orientation, evaluation and action (see Peterson and McCabe 1991).

READER ACTIVITY

Look at the role of the underlined discourse forms in the following story. Where do most of them occur and for what purposes? Why does *and* repeatedly occur at the beginning of segments?

Text 4.5
Alexandra: but this is how it goes, people drift apart you know,//
Phil:// <u>well</u>, I was terribly upset when I met last of David Glasgow,
Viv: <u>cause</u> you were at school together, right?
Phil: well, not just at school together, <u>I mean</u> we were closer than brothers, and <u>you know</u>, we did absolutely everything together, and we were as close as two boys can be. <u>And</u> I lost touch with David, and then we met again, and we had this lunch together, and in fact I didn't realise
Alexandra: when he'd become a helicopter pilot?
Phil: he'd become a helicopter pilot, and we actually, I do remember now, funnily enough, little that I realised, we were actually eating in the ANC restaurant, we were eating in Judith Marcus's, Judith Marcus was the spokesperson for the ANC for a little while, and we just had absolutely nothing in common. <u>And</u> he was saying, that was fifteen years ago, and I haven't seen him since//
Alexandra: You're joking!
Phil: there's no point, we just have totally different agendas. <u>So anyway</u>, I remember saying, this was just after the time when, some elements of British business were beginning to disengage with South Africa whe:n, this was around about the time, when

> the Midland Bank, eh ..., the Midland Bank was the first of the
> high street banks which was disengaged. And I remember saying
> something like, you know, there are good business reasons,
> being political, there are good business reasons for being
> extremely careful about South Africa. And I remember David
> saying, it's extremely profitable right now ...
>
> (*Source*: Authors' data)

    In spoken narratives like 4.5, the occurrence of connectives at transitional locations can be used to buy time for the narrator, who is not only trying to organise the narrative on-line but also has to adjust to the audience's contributions at the same time. As a result, *and* is commonly found at the beginning of paragraphs as a filler that covers up for the narrator's hesitation before a new segment. This is normally not the case in written narratives, which are, as a rule, the product of more planning and deliberation. Similarly, the physical presence of the addressee in spoken narratives calls for numerous interactional uses of discourse markers. Interjections and comment phrases such as *well, you know, I mean* establish or reinforce a rapport between addresser and addressees. They also signal to the addressee the speaker's attitudes towards what is talked about. In story 4.3, for instance, the occurrence of *well* right at the beginning signals that the speaker is going to embark on the telling of a story. In other words, *well* frames the story that follows.

    In non-narrative texts, discourse markers have a similar function of bracketing. For instance, Sinclair and Coulthard (1975) have found that the segmentation of lessons in English is typically marked by a framing technique. This involves the use of five markers (*OK, well, right, now, good*) in combination with strong stress, high falling intonation and an accompanying short pause (cf. Coulthard 1985). Teachers may vary in the particular word which they favour, but framing almost always occurs at discourse boundaries such as the beginning of a lesson or a new section within a lesson, as in the following:

Text 4.6
Teacher: So we get energy from petrol and we get energy from food. Two kinds of energy. Now then, I want you to take your pen and rub it as hard as you can on something woolen.

(*Source*: Coulthard 1992: 3)

These markers are similar to those found in conversation. Similar techniques can also be observed in written genres such as academic prose:

Text 4.7
We do not yet have such a theory, and we may still be a long way from having one, but we do know many of the properties that it must have. And we shall see, in later chapters, that we already know a fair amount

about the predictions a quantum theory of gravity must make.

Now, if you believe that the universe is not arbitrary, but is governed by definite laws, you ultimately have to combine the partial theories into a complete unified theory ...

(*Source*: Stephen Hawking, *A Brief History of Time*
(London: Bantam Press, 1988), p. 10)

Here, *now* acts as a framing device to shift the discussion into a new aspect of the topic. The use of *and* in the previous sentence plays a similar role; it functions at the global level of text organisation and not (or rather not simply) at the level of linking the two first sentences of the extract locally. *And* here does not signal a propositional (ideational) relation between the two sentences but primarily indicates that there is a supplementary (and perhaps final) comment to be made by the author. The multiple functions of discourse markers are also crucial in non-academic argumentative texts, in which the large-scale articulation of relations and units in the text may be dependent on their use.

READER ACTIVITY

Which of the items underlined in the following text function as discourse markers? What is their role in signalling the texts internal structure?

Text 4.8
Quietly nested in the lush landscapes of Northamptonshire, lies the sleepy village of Silverstone. Every now and again <u>however</u> this wooded heaven is woken by the ear-splitting roar of its less tranquil neighbour. The famous Silverstone Circuit.

<u>Yet</u> for Saab, both provide the perfect surroundings for its latest green generation car. The new Saab 9000S 2.3. Out on the track the long-legged new 2.3 litre engine is able to flex its 150 bhp muscle. The car can demonstrate its controlled cornering, its swift, smooth and much safer overtaking, its higher torque. A powerful argument, the Saab 9000S 2.3.

<u>But</u> with power comes responsibility.

<u>So</u> the car leaves the circuit, and begins to weave its way more conservatively through the country lanes. This is where the ultimate green machine really begins to blossom. ...

Can you now compare this with the use of discourse markers in text 3.8 from the previous chapter?

Discourse markers seem to clarify a text's structural relations for the reader. Despite any differences in their use in different genres, these items share a number of formal and textual features. The former can be summed up in the following: they do not belong to the sentence elements proper (subject, verb, complements); they are typically found in utterance initial position or, on the whole, in transitional locations (beginning and end of units); they do not always have a clear propositional (semantic) meaning or their propositional meaning is superseded by their discoursal functions (cf. Fraser 1990; van Dijk 1979); they exhibit multiple roles in signalling relations (ideational, textual, interpersonal) between units at different levels.

4.2 PARTICIPANT CHAINS

Reference forms have also been included among the basic cohesive devices of a text. Their use and patterning function as a main signpost in both discourse modes. In narratives, chains of reference allow us to trace characters, entities and events. The set of referential patterns by which a story's characters are introduced and reidentified has been called participant tracking. Reference forms are frequently employed as a measure of a narrative's density of cohesive ties. However, as with discourse markers, the emphasis has gradually shifted from their role as links between successive clauses to their role as signals of discourse units. This was partly motivated by occurrences of referential forms that were contrary to any predictions about the role of distance (number of clauses between a given anaphor and its antecedent) in referential choice.

According to the cognitive view of distance as a determinant of referential choice, when a character is introduced in a narrative the most likely form to be used is nominal reference (see Givón 1983). Subsequent mentions are to be made by non-explicit forms, that is, pronouns, for languages like English, or ellipsis, for languages like Japanese, in which the subject of a clause can be deleted. This should be the case as long as there is no ambiguity in the 'who is who' of the story, which could confuse the addressees. However, this is not always the case in narratives. As Clancy has observed, the theory of distance 'cannot account for cases in which something like eleven clauses separate the two mentions of a character and yet the second mention is done with a pronoun' (1980: 161), or, comparably, cases in which only two sentences separate the two mentions of a character and yet the second mention is done with a noun.

The explanations for such unpredictable choices lie in narrative organisation. The segmentation of narrative units is a very common reason for the use of explicit reference forms such as nominal phrases for characters when a pronoun would suffice. Research by Fox (1987) on participant tracking in written popular narratives called for the complementation of cognitive factors by discourse structure factors in accounting for referential choices. The study confirmed the role that a story's hierarchical organisation plays in the choice of reference forms for the reintroduction of characters. It was found that a crucial factor for the choice of nominal reference is the transition at higher-level categories from an initiating event to the character's reactions to it. On the whole, explicit forms are frequently employed in narratives as signals of world shifts: for example, shifts from narrative action to characters' speech or from digressions and background comments (off-event line) back to the event line. This can be illustrated in story 4.5 above. When the narrator moves from the segment of the background information about his friendship with David to the new segment of the story's complicating action (resumption of the event line), the narrator's friend is referred to nominally (*David*), where the form *him* would be adequate.

> well, not just at school together, I mean we were closer than brothers, and you know, we did absolutely everything together, and we were as close as two boys can be. <u>And</u> I lost touch with <u>David</u>, and then we met again, and we had this lunch together, and in fact I didn't realise …

As we can see above, the passage to the new segment is signalled by the orchestration of the marker *and* with the character renominalisation. Comparably, in the following example, the beginning of a typographic (this time) paragraph is emphasised by an explicit referential form and a temporal adverbial:

Text 4.9
While <u>Franklin</u> felt burdened by what he knew … (same paragraph) He ((Franklin)) should get down to see her more often. Perhaps he could take her with him when they filmed the next series. She could watch his famous walking shot in the Forum; she'd like that. Now where could he place the camera? Or perhaps a tracking shot. And some extras in toga and sandals – yes, he liked it …
  Next morning <u>Franklin</u> was taken to the purser's office.
(*Source*: Julian Barnes, *A History of the World in 10½ Chapters* (London: Picador, 1989), p. 50)

The case of unit demarcation with an explicit referential form illustrates the interaction between discourse structure factors with cognitive constraints. According to the 'attention' model of referential choices (see Chafe 1987; Tomlin 1987), while narrative units (i.e. episodes) represent sustained attentional effort in the decoding of discourse, their boundaries constitute attention-shift points. There, the occurrence of explicit reference helps to redivert the addressees' attention from the prior to the upcoming discourse unit.

The centrality of characters in the narrative plot is another factor that influences participant tracking choices in narrative. A common strategy is to use pronominal reference or ellipsis (depending on which of the two forms of reference is allowed in the language in question) for the central character or protagonist. In this case, secondary characters are explicitly referred to. This is a hero-centred strategy and promotes a sense of empathy with the protagonist (Clancy 1992; Hinds 1983; Karmiloff-Smith 1985). Alternatively, all characters may be nominalised independently of their centrality in the plot. Fox (1987) has suggested that this happens when two characters are on stage but do not interact with each other in terms of actions and goals. If they are involved in fast-paced confrontations and/or interaction, they are normally pronominalised as in the example below:

Text 4.10

He took a step towards her, reached out helpfully. She bolted, ducking just beneath his clutching fingers. Then she was out in the corridor, sprinting for the bridge. Then she was too busy to scream for help, and she needed the wind. There was no one on the bridge. Somehow she got around him again …

(Source: Alien, p. 244, quoted in Fox 1987: 165)

However, even in that case, other discourse factors such as the demarcation of narrative units may block pronominalisation and trigger an explicit referential form. Fox also reported that when two characters of the same gender are involved in the same action, a full nominal reference seems to be the norm for the character who becomes the grammatical subject of a clause:

Text 4.11

She placed the transparent mask over Ripley's mouth and nose and opened the valve. Ripley inhaled …

(Source: Alien, p. 238, quoted in Fox 1987: 171)

Explicit reference in cases of character interaction can also function as a means of emphasising the characters' contrast and disagreement or solidarity and cooperation (see Flaschner 1987). Story 4.5 again provides us with an example:

And I remember saying something like, you know there are good business reasons, being political, there are good business reasons for being extremely careful about South Africa. And I remember David saying, it's extremely profitable right now …

In this case too, the shorter form *him* (*I remember him saying*) would not cause any ambiguity problems. The explicit form *David* is chosen, however, to emphasise the contrast between his view and the narrator's view about the situation in South Africa. Furthermore, this form succeeds in drawing attention to the camera shift from the speech of one participant to the speech of the other. The shift to characters' speech has been found to be an important factor in eliciting explicit reference, for example:

Text 4.12

Spike gently took her hand and didn't release it until he was on his feet and about to speak.
'It's nice to be back' said Spike, and looked around the room …

(Source: Julian Barnes, A History of the World in
10½ Chapters (London: Picador, 1989), p. 263)

READER ACTIVITY

Look at the nominal reference forms underlined in the extracts below. How do you account for them from the point of view of narrative organisation?

Text 4.13

Peter Dutton stood in the darkness of the kitchen, gripping the edge of the sink. He wrestled with his temper. His face flushed and his left eyelid flickered. Releasing a hand he tried to calm the eye but the lid agitated beneath his finger tips.

Dutton moaned in incoherent agony. In the next room the television talked at a woman he knew was not watching it. ...

> (*Source*: Lesley Grant-Adamson, *The Face of Death*
> (London: Faber and Faber, 1985), p. 71)

Text 4.14

Kien approached the well. It seemed in good order, the lid fitted snugly and around its base a gutter had been dug, to drain away muddy water during heavy rains. The silence was unnerving.

Kien left the others and on a hunch turned towards the stream and noted the girls' tiny toilet built over the stream, almost totally hidden from the view behind bamboo. The narrow track from well to toilet was gravelled, weed-free.

Kien approached not by the path, but circuitously, by stepping quietly into the water and wading upstream.

> (*Source*: Bao Ninh, *The Sorrow of War*
> (London: Minerva, 1994), p. 29)

The following extracts present two characters on stage. What are the organisational strategies of participant tracking adopted in each of them?

Text 4.15

One morning in early 1947 my mother was stopped at the school gate by the old porter. He handed her a note and told her that Kang had gone. What my mother did not know was that Kang had been tipped off, as some of the Kuomitang intelligence agents were secretly working for the Communists. At the time, my mother did not know much about communists or that Kang was one of them. All she knew was the teacher she most admired had had to flee because he was about to be arrested.

The note was from Kang, and consisted of only one word: 'Silence'. My mother saw two possible meanings in this word. It could refer to a line from a poem <u>Kang</u> had written in memory of his girlfriend, 'Silence – in which our strength is gathering', in which case it might be an appeal not to lose heart. But the note could also be a warning against doing something impetuous. <u>My mother</u> had by then established quite a reputation for fearlessness.

(*Source*: Jung Chang, *Wild Swans*
(London: Flamingo, 1994), pp. 121–2)

Text 4.16
And <u>Richard</u> was alone.

As <u>he</u> looked down the vista into which they would soon disappear, towards Ladbroke Grove and its circus horses of traffic, <u>Richard</u> saw his son Marco – <u>Marco</u> a long way away, and on the fair side of the street, but with <u>Marco's</u> unmistakably brittle and defeatist stride. There was something terribly wrong with <u>Marco</u>: there was nobody at <u>his</u> side. And yet <u>the child's</u> solitude, his isolation, unlike <u>the father's</u>, was due to an unforgivable error not <u>his</u> own. There was always somebody at <u>Marco's</u> side. In all <u>his</u> seven years there had always been somebody at <u>his</u> side.

A drama, thought <u>Richard</u>. And a diversion: at least this will get me up the goddamned stairs. <u>He</u> realised that he still had the vacuum cleaner: in <u>his</u> arms, across his body, round his neck. <u>Richard</u> was still Laocoon, engulfed in coils and loops. That too <u>he</u> would have to hump, all the way up to 49E. That too.

<u>Father</u> and <u>son</u> started hurrying towards each other. <u>Marco</u> wasn't crying but <u>Richard</u> had never seen him looking so unhappy: the unhappiness that has always made for <u>Marco</u>; the unhappiness that was all <u>his</u> own. <u>Richard</u> knelt like a knight, and held <u>him</u>.

'Who was with you?'
<u>Marco</u> told <u>him</u>: Lizzette.
'And you were lost?'

(*Source*: Martin Amis, *The Information*
(London: HarperCollins, 1995), p. 492)

Since the role of participants is much less important in non-narrative texts, we would expect participant tracking to be less prominent. Indeed, non-narrative texts, in contrast to narratives, do not seem to favour long reference chains (see Francis' 1989b findings). As we will see below, this tendency is compensated (and, partly, accounted) for by the use of lexical patterning such as encapsulation, which is more frequent in non-narrative discourse. Descriptive texts or sections in exposition, such as text 4.17, are an exception to this general tendency:

Text 4.17

In the past 20 years <u>transnational corporations</u> (TNCS) have grown in size and influence. Through mergers and takeovers <u>their</u> power has reached the point where many now control larger budgets than the least developed countries. In many cases <u>they</u> control or influence whole industrial processes from demand to extraction of raw materials, through to manufacturing, finance and end use. By definition <u>they</u> control the pollution and poverty that go with these processes.

<u>The world's largest 500 companies</u> now control at least 70 per cent of world trade, 80 per cent of foreign investment and 30 per cent of global GDP. <u>They</u> control the way countries develop. <u>They</u> are key actors in channelling and fostering consumer tastes, patterns of production and lifestyles. <u>They</u> are the most important players in the science and technology leap taking place throughout the rich world with enormous research and development capability. And <u>they</u> directly and indirectly influence the economic and social performance of the countries they operate in.

(*Source*: *The Guardian*, 1 June 1992)

We can see that in text 4.17 both reference chains begin and finish within the boundaries of a single written paragraph. As Hofmann (1989) has observed, paragraphs are barriers to anaphora, that is, they do not allow for pronominal references to items outside their boundaries. As a result, the introduction of a new participant is usually associated with a new paragraph break and renominalisation after successive pronominal references.

READER ACTIVITY

How do you explain the appearance of a pronominal at the very beginning of the following text? (The text is an editorial referring to the events of the 1991 Gulf War.)

Text 4.18
A last chance and the tragedy
And so, at the last gasp, he sought to wriggle free. In the afternoon, another speech to his people talking of martyrdom and the 19th province; as Tariq Aziz reported back to Mikhail Gorbachev, the clearest signal yet that, in fact, Iraq will quit Kuwait; that, in fact there need be no ground war.

It is infinitely too early for celebration. The Iraqi regime has come perilously late to a realisation that it has no cards left and only the neck of its leadership to save. Just as the Americans were wreathed in smiles earlier yesterday when they thought Saddam would fight on after his broadcast speech, so there will be many frowns this

morning over a formula which would save Baghdad and seems to leave Saddam as an irritant for years to come. ...
(*Source*: *The Guardian*, 22 February 1991)

In what other kinds of text do you find this strategy? (You might like to consult Halliday and Hasan (1976: 297) for a description of this phenomenon.)

A second important organisational technique in non-narrative texts involves the interplay of a three-item contrast: *it*, *this* and *that*. In her study of apartment layout descriptions, Linde (1979) found that *it* was used for unmarked reference to the current focus of attention, *this* for shift to a new focus of attention and *that* for a more radical shift to a non-current, non-central entity. Compare the following two extracts from her data, which describe first a single room and then more than one room in a house:

Text 4.19
And then through a doorway into the living room, which sort of curves itself around so that it's not really a square room. It's maybe ten, twelve feet, but the width of it varies.

At the end of the long hallway there's a door which is the entrance to my room, which is about seven by eleven and has a window facing the door. Next to that is a room which is about the same depth, about eleven feet, but about twice as wide. And next to that is another room which is about the same size as the one next to it.
(*Source*: Linde 1979)

A similar strategy is followed in other kinds of non-narrative text, as can be seen in the following extracts, where *that* is used to refer back to a chunk of discourse rather than an item in the immediately preceding sentence:

Text 4.20
American hopes centre on a successful Labour campaign leading to a coalition with a chastened Likud. In coalition Likud would create obstacles to peace talks but could be dragged along for a while; in opposition it would be more troublesome.

That, at least, is the theory.
(*Source*: *The Guardian*, 29 February 1992)

Text 4.21
Rules aren't rules; there is no longer, for this Government, a book of rectitude. Concrete mixers in marginal seats whir into life. This is just another bunch of politicians in a jam, making it up as they go along.

That may, in truth, always have been the case.
(*Source*: *The Guardian*, 29 February 1992)

As we will see below, *that* can also be combined with a set of lexical items to label further the cohesive relation to the preceding text. What this strategy achieves is to make a whole stretch of text an entity, which can thus become part of a participant chain.

The choice of reference forms and the occurrence of pronominalisation have been two main foci of research in both linguistic and cognitive models of the previous decade. Linguistic models have focused on the role of 'givenness' and implied knowledge in the understanding of reference (Clark and Haviland 1977; Prince 1981). This line of research has brought to the fore the notion of mental representations in the construction of participant chains. Thus, shifts between different forms of reference have been viewed as signals of shifts in frames, namely mental constructs of entities and their relations (cf. Brown and Yule 1983). Artificial intelligence approaches have also challenged a static, 'surface' view of reference, by closely studying patterns of pronominalisation along with phenomena such as interruption, digression etc. (see Sidner 1983; Reichman 1985; Grosz and Sidner 1986, among others). In their view, the selection and use of participant forms is guided by a focusing strategy followed by the producer and the receiver of discourse. Focus refers to the priority and the overall importance of some entity in terms of the ongoing discourse. It corresponds to the focus of attention of the discourse participants as the discourse progresses. Successive shifts of focus influence the selection of reference forms. The outcome of research within artificial intelligence has been that participant chains are viewed as more than surface phenomena or simple concatenations of items. They are, instead, indicative of discourse organisation (units and their relations) and their corresponding mental structures.

4.3 TIME CHAINS

We have already noted on a number of occasions that a story's temporal strategy is very important to its organisation. Devices of signalling temporality in narratives include temporal adverbials, which commonly appear at transitional locations, the discourse marker *and*, as well as the shift in the tenses used. A tense shift that has captured the attention of linguists, in oral narratives in particular, is the shift from the past tense to the historic or narrative present. The vehicle of any narrative is normally the perfective past tense. Nevertheless, the narrative present also refers to events that happened in the past. As a tense, it is specific to narratives. Traditionally, its use was treated as a dramatic device that bases its effect on removing the events out of their past frame and into the time of speaking. As a result, the audience feels as if it was present at the time of the experience.

This view was seriously challenged by Wolfson (1979, 1982). Wolfson's spoken data of American English narratives suggested that it is not the use of historic present *per se* that is significant in narration but the switch from the past to the historic present and vice versa. The main function of this switch is organisational: it segments a story and groups the otherwise indistinct series of its acts into units that constitute events. As we will see in Chapter 5, the more widely-held view nowadays is that narrative present exhibits other functions too. However, it is also a well-recognised signal of narrative segmentation. As such, it commonly co-occurs with other segmentation signals (e.g. temporal adverbials). Fleischman (1990), for example, reported that, in medieval French narratives and in natural narratives, shifts to narrative present correlate with shifts in participant focus. The two devices together foreground the passage to specific events.

Switches to narrative present as a rule occur at episode-initial points to mark the turn of events, in particular, climactic ones. Switches out of it and into the past (imperfective or perfective) as a rule mark the transition to the outcome (resolution) of events, the insertion of orientation, background comments or evaluative remarks, or references to characters' physical or internal states (cf. Fludernik 1991). The function of time chains can be seen in the following extract from a story analysed by Schiffrin (1981) for its shifts to narrative present.

Text 4.22

So we were in this car, an' we were in Allentown, it's real dinky, an' it's like real hick town off o' Allentown, right around there in this factory. We just pulled into this lot, it was just in this lot, <u>and all of a sudden the buzzer sounds, and all these guys come out</u>, and we didn't know what t' do, cause we were stuck. So we asked some guy, t' come over an' help us. <u>So he opens the car, and everyone gets out except me and my girl-friend</u>. We were in the front, we just didn't feel like getting out. <u>And all of a sudden all these sparks start t' fly. So the girl says</u>, 'look, do you know what you're doing? Because y' know um ... this is not my car, an' if you don't know what you're doing, just don't DO it'. <u>And he says</u>, 'Yeh, I have t' do it from inside'. <u>And all of a sudden he gets in the car, sits down, and starts t' turn on the motor</u>. We thought he was taking off with us. We really thought he was, he was like rea – with all tattoos and smelled, an' we thought that was it! But he got out after a while.

(*Source*: Schiffrin 1981)

In text 4.22, we can see how the first shift into the narrative present (... *the buzzer sounds*) marks a turn in the complicating action that is emphasised by the occurrence of *all of a sudden*. *All of a sudden* and *suddenly* very frequently join forces with narrative present in highlighting the passage to an experientially significant event. The subsequent switch into the past marks the result of this turn of events (*and we didn't know what t' do*) and the attempt to react to it (*so we asked some guy ...*). The new event referring to the 'guy' offering help is underscored by a new switch into narrative present (*So he opens the car ...*). This shifts back into the past for insertion of background comment (*We were in the front ...*). A new switch into the narrative present, again preceded by *all of a sudden*, signals passage to a new segment of action (*all these sparks start t' fly*). The use of narrative present for the quotative verb in characters' (direct) speech (*so the girl says*) is well documented in the literature as a means of highlighting the shift (e.g. Schiffrin 1981; Fludernik 1991). The final shift out of the narrative present and into the past tense encodes evaluative remarks (*he gets in the car*).

As a rule of thumb, switches to narrative present cover one third of a story's action verbs. However, this is not without exception, since, as happens with other segmentation signals, stories of different languages employ narrative present in different degrees. For instance, the figure is much higher for Greek oral narratives (Georgakopoulou 1994) or Scottish folktales (Leith 1995).

Irrespective of the proportion of verbs in narrative present, the device's segmentational power lies in the strategic switches to it at the endpoints of segments to mark the turn of events and to emphasise their experiential significance. This is not the case in literary narratives where the device on the whole does not present the same organisational edge. Its use in modern English literary narration is historically the outcome of its migration from medieval popular literature in Romance languages (see Fleischman 1990). There, the dynamic pattern of rapid alternations with the past started to dismantle gradually until it took the form of sustained sequences that portray static situations instead of pushing forwards the narrative action. This is called the visualising or scenic narrative present. In terms of *Aktionsart* (i.e. inherent aspect of the verbs, manner of verbal action), it involves the use of atelic verbs, that is, verbs whose action goes on in time with no set terminal point (activities), or which involve time periods in an indefinite and non-unique sense (states). By contrast, the narrative present of oral stories almost without exception involves telic verbs, namely instantaneous occurrences of actions at a single moment (achievements) or, in any case, with specific endpoints (accomplishments; see Vendler's scheme of verbs classification, 1967: 97–121). This is confirmed in text 4.22 above: its narrative present verbs denote telic, instantaneous action (e.g. *come out, get out, open*) whose initial endpoints are in places emphasised by the occurrence of the punctual time adverb *all of a sudden* and by the ingressive auxiliary *start* (*start to fly, start to turn*). By contrast, text 4.1 from a literary narrative illustrates the sustained use of scenic narrative present realised mainly by atelic verbs: for example, *is lying, he is, are in the process of, seems to have turned, is barely discernible, are putting on* etc.

Narrative present is not the only tense that has been explored as a foregrounding device in a story's organisation. On the whole, shifts in tense and aspect (i.e. the internal constituency of verbal action: see Comrie 1976) have been studied as signals of narrative segmentation into events of different degrees of salience. Different languages have their systems of tense and aspect verbal forms for expressing main and secondary lines of narrative development. As a rule, the main event line is the line of sequential, punctiliar and perfective verbs (see Longacre 1989). In English, this means the use of perfective past-tense verbs (mostly achievements and accomplishments). As we saw above, shifts out of it and into the narrative present act as devices for highlighting and foregrounding the pivotal events of the main event line. Past progressive is normally the tense for non-punctiliar, non-sequential activities and states, orientation information and (externally) evaluative comments. Pluperfects are normally for flashbacks and events which are out of sequence. Finally, the irrealis line of narration (Longacre) which encodes alternative, possible narrative worlds is realised by various modals (e.g. may, might, could, would) and future tense. The above do not automatically apply to other languages with different tense and aspect systems. Even in English narratives, we should always bear in mind that the salience (foreground vs background) of tense and aspect forms in narrative organisation can only be judged relatively within the norms of a text, by assigning varying degrees of importance to them and their switches.

READER ACTIVITY

The following is an oral story translated from Greek. Look at the shifts into and out of the narrative present. Do they observe the patterns of segmentational use discussed here?

Text 4.23
E: have you ever been to an officer's wedding?
P: no//
E: //you haven't? with the sabres? well you're missing something. I'll tell you about Sakis' wedding. They really gave him a hard time at the end, when he came out of the church with Katerina–, as they came out of the church, they had to go under the sabres, clack clack clack the guys there went. They get to the end, now go back the last one tells them, go back and kiss your colleagues one by one, and you do the same too they tell the bride. When they kissed them all, they go back there, to the same guy, that guy who was at the entrance of the church. He tells him, kiss the bride ten times, one two three four five six seven eight, nine nine nine. (hh hh) Then they walked a bit further towards the door, the last one in row was Spiros, this rascal from Piraeus//
A: //Spiros? who's Spiros? a short and chubby guy?
E: no, no, tall and well-built, very nice bloke. I thought that Spiros would be the one that'd tease them most, I had this impression right? probably because I know that he's a rascal from Piraeus. But when they reached the guy before the last, it was Vassilakis who was down there dressed in civilian clothes, and he had a champagne. So Vassilakis opens the champagne like this, and they tell the bride take off your shoe. She takes it off, they fill it in

> with champagne, now drink it <u>they tell</u> Sakis. <u>Sakis drinks</u> it, poor
> Sakis wouldn't say no. <u>But they fill it</u> once again, <u>they give</u>
> Katerina as well, and she drank it down in one go. <u>So they finally</u>
> <u>reach</u> Spiros, who we thought would tease them most, free to go
> Spiros <u>tells</u> them, the rascal from Piraeus, off you go. hh hh
> (*Source*: Georgakopoulou 1993: 413)

As expected, the significance of tense shifts seems to be much less prominent in non-narrative texts. Polanyi and Scha (1983), Hoey (1979) and
Sinclair (1988) all include tense in the segmentation signals of non-narrative
discourse, but the actual choice of tense forms seems to depend on the text's
genre. As we will see below, many non-narrative texts such as instructions
of procedure (e.g. recipes) or descriptions of place and time (e.g. travel
brochures) are organised on the basis of time-chain patterns. The difference
with narrative texts is that here what counts is not shift into a specific tense
but tense continuity and repetition (e.g. *Wash* three apples. *Peel* them and *put*
them in the oven ...).

A different genre, in which time chains are important, is that of newspaper editorials. Bolivar (1994) reported that editorials are very sensitive to the
time dimension. Shifts from the past into the present and vice versa are
accompanied here by temporal adverbials such as *last year*, *this year* etc. or
by discourse markers like *but, however, indeed* etc. These shifts indicate major
points of transition between discourse units. More important is the use of
modality for similar purposes, as can be seen in the following extract from
an editorial discussing multilingualism in international business:

Text 4.24
The notion of the perceived disadvantage <u>is</u> very important. The use of
German in negotiation between a Stuttgart and a Copenhagen firm
<u>may</u> be efficient and perfectly logical where the Danes concerned are
fluent in German. But, perhaps without the Germans noticing, the
Danes <u>may</u> well feel that they are on less than a comfortable equal
footing and <u>may</u> harbour some silent resentment. And this, of course,
<u>can</u> hardly make for the most satisfactory outcome on either side!
    As a result, it <u>is</u> precisely the native speakers of the 'major'
languages, such as German and English, who have to be most assidu-
ous in foreign language training and most sensitive about the choice of
language in negotiation.

(*Source*: *The European*, 1 June 1990)

Here, the chain of modals (*may–may–can*) is framed by shifts from and into
the use of verbs without modality (*is–is*). Bolivar (1994) found that modality
selection is one of the main devices of unit segmentation in editorials and
has established that the normal progression is from actual (*is*) to possible

(*may be*) to desirable (*should be*) events. However, this progression is not sufficient to indicate text segmentation on its own but functions in conjunction with other signals.

4.4 LEXICAL PATTERNING (1)

In the three previous sections, we have dealt with patterns of organisation that mainly involve grammatical items: conjunctions, pronouns, verb tenses. However, texts are also organised through their lexical vocabulary resources. The distinction between lexical and grammatical (or function) words divides a language's (and thus a text's) vocabulary into two sets according to whether a word functions to indicate grammatical relations or not. Roughly, pronouns, articles, auxiliary verbs, prepositions and conjunctions are grammatical words, whereas nouns, adjectives, verbs and adverbs are lexical. What is particularly significant, from a textual point of view, is that grammatical words form a closed set to which no new items can be added. It is impossible to create a new article or a new verb tense. As a consequence, a text develops by adding new words drawn from the open set of lexical items. The latter are syntactically related to each other by items selected from the set of grammatical words.

The ratio of grammatical to lexical words in a text as a whole can be measured by the indicator of lexical density. The mean lexical density of a text is estimated as the ratio of the number of lexical items (types) to the total number of running words (tokens) or as a ratio of the number of clauses in a text. It has been argued that written language has a higher degree of lexical density than spoken language. In other words, there are more lexical words compared to grammatical words in written text when compared to spoken text (Ure 1971; Halliday 1985b).

A much more important measure for discourse organisation concerns the relative distribution of vocabulary within parts of the same text. A first indicator is the type–token ratio for successive chunks of text. As the vocabulary of a text can only be renewed through lexical items, the number of new words as a ratio of the number of total words tends to decline as the text progresses: words that have been mentioned tend to be repeated and not very many new words are added.

A more sophisticated measure is the notion of vocabulary flow (Youmans 1990, 1991), which expresses the distribution of old and new vocabulary in successive segments. This consists in counting the number of new vocabulary words (types) introduced into a text over an interval of a specified number of words (tokens). For example, in the first thirty-five words of a text, there might be ten new ones, in the next thirty-five words six new etc. The resulting picture is a regular alternation between peaks and valleys in type–token ratio curves, which reflects the alternation of new and repeated vocabulary. It is significant that this alternation follows closely the structural segmentation of the text into paragraphs, episodes or other discourse units. In other words, a peak in the type–token ratio curve coincides with transition into a new unit, whereas a valley corresponds to unit maintenance. It seems thus that the distribution of a tex's vocabulary correlates with its structural organisation.

The distinction between lexical and grammatical words is also reflected in the type of cohesive tie that can be established between them. Whereas participant or time chains (consisting of grammatical words) are mainly based on co-reference or reiteration, lexical items can also be related by collocation, in Halliday and Hasan's (1976) terms, that is, through semantic relations of paraphrase, synonymy, antonymy etc. This results in a different kind of patterning in a text that complements that of reference chains. For instance, to go back to text 4.17, along with the established participant chains, we have lexical items related by repetition (*control–control*), synonymy (*control–influence*), paraphrase (*actors–players*) and metonymy (*world–countries*), as shown below:

> **Text 4.25**
> In the past 20 years <u>transnational corporations</u> (TNCS) have grown in size and influence. Through mergers and takeovers <u>their</u> power has reached the point where many now control larger budgets than the least developed countries. In many cases <u>they</u> control or influence whole industrial processes from demand to extraction of raw materials, through to manufacturing, finance and end use. By definition <u>they</u> control the pollution and poverty that go with these processes.
>
> <u>The world's largest 500 companies</u> now control at least 70 per cent of world trade, 80 per cent of foreign investment and 30 per cent of global GDP. <u>They</u> control the way countries develop. <u>They</u> are key actors in channelling and fostering consumer tastes, patterns of production and lifestyles. <u>They</u> are the most important players in the science and technology leap taking place throughout the rich world with enormous research and development capability. And <u>they</u> directly and indirectly influence the economic and social performance of the countries they operate in.
>
> (*Source: The Guardian*, 1 June 1992)

The two kinds of patterning have been distinguished as identity and similarity chains by Hasan (1984). Identity and similarity chains organise the whole of the text in different ways: the former provide a backbone of organisation, while the latter exploit the text's lexical resources. The degree of interaction between the two kinds of chains is expressed by the notion of cohesive harmony (Hasan 1984). For instance, in text 4.17 the reference chain *TNC–they–they* interacts with the similarity chain *control– influence–control*, because the words involved are in an actor–action relation, respectively. Cohesive harmony is estimated as the percentage of those words that participate in chains versus those that do not (relevant vs peripheral tokens). Alternatively, it can be measured as the percentage of those items in chains that interact with items in other chains versus those that do not

(central vs non-central tokens). Hasan (1984) further claims that the greater
the degree of cohesive harmony in a text, the more coherent this text is.

READER ACTIVITY

Test Hasan's claim by measuring the degree of cohesive harmony in
text 4.1, 4.2 and 4.3. Can we conclude that one text is more coherent
than another? What other factors should be taken into account to
explain the degree of difference between the three texts?

Hoey (1991) broadens the picture by presenting a more radical hypothesis about text organisation through lexical patterning. According to this,
links established between words of a text are significant for the text as a
whole because they define a number of bonds between sentences. Cohesive
ties or links do not simply relate individual words but also create a bond
between the sentences in which they occur. In this way, we can distinguish
between marginal and central sentences, according to the number of bonds
that they exhibit with other sentences. For instance, in text 4.26 a partial
identification of links would show that sentences 4 and 12 are marginal,
while sentences 13, 15 and 16 are central. Hoey (1991) further argues that the
set of interconnecting bonds between sentences in a text defines an overall
net. This net can always be used to produce a meaningful or interpretable
paraphrase of the whole text, either by omitting marginal sentences or by
bringing central sentences together.

Text 4.26
Skin deep
1 The idea that humanity was once divided into a series of biologically
distinct races which differed in quality has had a disastrous impact.
2 Everyone knows of the Nazi experiment, but the ties between politics and race extended to many other countries. 3 The latest genetics
research has undermined this concept of race.

  4 Dr. Steve Jones, a geneticist at University College London, who is
delivering this year's Reith Lectures, explains how this turnaround is
coming about.

  5 New technology allows us to look at the structure of genes in
many ways. 6 As so much of modern medicine depends on genetics
– blood transfusions, tissue transplants, the treatment of in-born
disease – we have suddenly arrived at the position of knowing more
about the patterns of genetics in humans than about those in any other
animal.   7 Hundreds of different genes – blood groups, proteins and
variants in the structure of DNA – have now been mapped across the
world.

8 Most of them, like skin colour, blood groups or alcohol tolerance, do vary from place to place. 9 The picture of human diversity which emerges when we consider all the genetic trends together is quite different from that supported by those who believe we are divided into distinct races.

10 The trends in skin colour are not accompanied by those in other genes. 11 Instead, the patterns of variation in blood groups, proteins or DNA are largely independent of each other and of the patterns in the way we look. 12 Our genetic gradients do not overlap.

13 Using information from blood groups, enzymes, and proteins, the analysis shows that around 85 per cent of total human genetic diversity comes from the differences between individuals from the same country: two randomly chosen Englishmen, say, or two Nigerians.

14 Another five to 10 per cent is due to the differences between nations, for example the people of England and the Spain; of Nigeria and Kenya. 15 The overall genetic differences between 'races' – Africans and Europeans, say – is no greater than that between different countries within Europe or within Africa. 16 Individuals – not nations and not races – are the main repository of human variation.

17 The idea that humanity is divided up into a series of distinct groups is quite wrong. 18 Genetics shows that the ancient homeland in the Caucasus – the cradle of the white Caucasian race – was just a myth.

19 This means that if, after a global disaster, only one group – the Albanians, the Papuans or the Senegalese – survived, most of the world's genetic diversity for functional genes would be preserved. 20 For these genes, humans are a remarkably homogeneous species; perhaps because we evolved so recently.

21 Much of the story of the genetics of race – a field promoted by some of the most eminent scientists of their day – turns out to have been prejudice dressed up as science; a classic example of the way that biology should not be used to help us understand ourselves. 22 Most geneticists are genuinely ashamed of the early history of their subject, and make every effort to distance themselves from it.

(*Source*: *The Guardian – World Media*, 13 December 1991)

READER ACTIVITY

Complete the identification of links in text 4.26 and define a net according to Hoey's (1991) model. What problems do you come across? Can you derive a meaningful paraphrase of the whole text, by following Hoey's suggestion?

Phillips' (1989) findings concur with Hoey's approach on lexical pattern-ing. By developing a sophisticated statistical method to identify collocates of any given words in a text, Phillips has established that lexical items often intercollocate in text, forming a network of connections. In other words, items that co-occur at a certain point in the text tend to also co-occur in other parts of the text. More importantly, it was found that collocation is text-sensitive: lexical networks of collocates correspond to major divisions in the text's planes of content. The network of collocations thus correlates with the large-scale organisation of subject matter.

Hoey's (1991) model is not intended to apply to all non-narrative texts and certainly does not apply to narrative texts. If we tried to analyse texts 4.1 or 4.3 by this model, we would find that only a few sentences are bonded and no meaningful paraphrases can be identified. This is revealing of the kinds of organisation preferred by the two modes: narrative discourse puts emphasis on the succession of shifts in the time, participant etc. configuration, whereas non-narrative discourse allows for long-distance lexical patterning, indepen-dent of adjacent succession.

4.5 LEXICAL PATTERNING (2)

The relations between lexical and grammatical items discussed so far are not binding: items can be linked freely wherever they might be in a text and their occurrence does not predict or anticipate a link with another item later in the text. (This is a reason why these links are susceptible to statistical analysis, which is not sensitive to position in the text.) By contrast, there is a degree of prediction in the use of certain 'descriptive' discourse markers such as *firstly, first of all* and *on the one hand*, which clearly anticipate a subsequent part of the text (*second, then, on the other hand*). These markers show strong similari-ties with another type of signal, namely metadiscourse items. Metadiscourse items are lexical units (expressions, phrases or sentences) used to make explicit metalinguistic comments on the organisation of the text. These include expressions like *to begin with, in other words, to sum up, as I was saying above* etc. We have already used in our presentation many of these phrases to direct the reader to prior or following text (e.g. *as shown in the example above, as we will see in the next section* etc.). Metalinguistic expressions are generally favoured in non-narrative written texts but are not absent from spoken non-narrative texts (see Schiffrin 1980) or from narratives (see Fleischman 1991). We have already noted their role in text segmentation (Chapter 3). Their functions are also easily adaptable to the specific requirements of the text, as we can see in the following example:

> **Text 4.27**
> Now, <u>before I try to offer a somewhat more positive conclusion</u>, I want
> to sketch the analysis of a full-blown postmodern building ...
> *(Source: New Left Review 146: 80)*

The underlined lexis of the example above creates certain expectations in the reader that a specific part of a text will follow. At the same time, it indicates the role of the current part of the text and evaluates the contribution of each part of the text. The metalinguistic expression thus has a multiplicity of functions.

READER ACTIVITY

Can you identify or invent metalinguistic expressions to march some of the relations discussed in Chapter 3 (e.g. temporal, causal, solution-hood, otherwise etc.)? Do you expect these expressions to occur in all genres or to be exclusive to some?

It should be noted that, by contrast to discourse markers, metalinguistic expressions are an open class: there is freedom to create new ones for a wide range of purposes. In more general terms, their function is performative, in Austin's (1962) terms: by explicitly stating a relation at a certain point in the text, they manage to introduce it in discourse. Although there is a broad scope of creativity, Fleischman (1991) has observed that speech favours expressions of time, whereas written discourse prefers expressions of space. Thus in the oral delivery of lectures we might have *I'll come back to this point shortly, as I mentioned earlier*, while in written versions of the same lecture we could have *see below, section 4*, or *as mentioned in the preceding section*.

Non-narrative texts are also characterised by another type of binding lexical patterning, the use of anaphoric nouns (Francis 1986). These include words such as *assertion, answer, assumption, belief, idea, aspect, issue* etc. (cf. Winters 1982 Vocabulary 3 items), which have the property of encapsulating a preceding stretch of discourse (retrospective labels) or anticipating a subsequent one (advance labels) (Francis 1989). In many cases, anaphoric nouns may have both backward- (anaphoric) and forward-looking (cataphoric) properties, as we can see in the following example:

Text 4.28
Mr. Baker has already discounted any idea that his tour will produce significant results. 'You are not going to make progress on Arab–Israeli peace', he said, 'unless the parties themselves really want to make progress'. The problem is twofold. The Palestinians are depressed and in disarray. ... Israel, which can only take joy from the PLO's confusion, constitutes the second problem.

(*Source*: *The Guardian* 1 March 1991)

The nominal containing the anaphoric noun here (*the problem*) encapsulates and characterises what has been previously described and, at the same time, anticipates a further comment on what follows (*what the problem is like*). In this way, non-narrative texts can step on a level up from simple cohesive

chains, which link individual words or sentences, by introducing an item
that summarises and thus links entire stretches of text:

Text 4.29
Faceless masters continue to inflect the economic strategies which
constrain our existences, but no longer need to impose their speech (or
are henceforth unable to); and the postliteracy of the late capitalist
world reflects, not only the absence of any great collective project, but
also the unavailability of the older national language itself.
    In <u>this situation</u>, parody finds itself without a vocation; ...
                                        (*Source: New Left Review* 146: 65)

The anaphoric noun here sums up what has been described before as a *situation*, and this encapsulation allows for the following stretch of text to refer
to the previous one. Argumentative and other non-narrative texts prefer this
strategy of 'stepping back' in order to make a claim. The grammatical means
used is nominalisation, which allows the writer to turn a part of the text into
an entity to be discussed and commented upon.

The use of anaphoric nouns is, in fact, a special technique of a more
general strategy in text, that of prediction. Acts of prediction involve binding pairs of a predictive and a predicted member, where the occurrence of
the former predicts the occurrence of the latter. When the predicted member
of the act occurs, the text-producer is under the obligation to offer the
predicted member, fulfilling thus the prediction. We have already found a
type of prediction pairs, when mentioning adjacency structures as signals of
sequential relations in Chapter 3. Question–answer, compliment–response
and other so-called dialogical pairs obviously involve acts of prediction: the
occurrence of a question, for example, anticipates an answer. Tadros (1994),
who closely studied prediction, has identified six kinds of prediction pairs in
expository texts:

> *advance labelling*: the use of anaphoric nouns as advance labels
> mentioned above (the occurrence of the anaphoric noun predicts what
> is to follow).

> *enumeration*: the use of numerals, which commits the writer to enum-
> erate:
> I want to propose <u>two ways</u> of reading this painting ...
> I first want to suggest ... There is a second reading ...
>   (*Source: New Left Review* 146: 58–9)

> *reporting*: the detachment of the writer from propositions attributed to
> others, requiring that the writer will come back and declare his/her
> own position:

> **Text 4.30**
> <u>It has proved fruitful to think</u> such experience in terms of what
> Susan Sontag once, in an influential statement, isolated as 'camp'. I

propose a somewhat different cross-light on it, drawing on the
equally fashionable current theme of the sublime.

(*Source: New Left Review* 146: 44)

recapitulation: the use of metalinguistic expressions or anaphoric nouns
as retrospective labels, presented as information that is recalled:
As I have said, however, I want to avoid the implication that ....
Rather, I want to suggest that ...

(*Source: New Left Review* 146: 79)

hypotheticality: the writer's detachment from the world of actuality by
referring to another conceptual world:

Text 4.31
Consider, for example, the powerful alternative position that post-
modernism is itself little more than one more stage of modernism
proper ...; it may indeed be conceded that all of the features of post-
modernism ... can be detected, full-blown, in this or that preceding
modernism .... What has not been taken into account by this view is,
however, the social position of the older modernism ...

(*Source: New Left Review* 146: 56)

question–answer: the pair involves 'offering an incomplete proposition
presented to the reader for completion through an answer' (Schiffrin
1988: 270)

Text 4.32
What then is the advantage which we may hope to derive from a
study of the political writers of the past? A view prevalent in earlier
ages would have provided a simple answer to this question.

(*Source*: Goutsos 1994)

This last kind of prediction pair is prevalent in conversation, known as adjacency pairs. Adjacency pairs consist of two utterance sequences, produced
by different speakers in a specific, non-reversible (binding) order.
Conversational analysts, who first identified adjacency pairs, also included
among them greetings, challenges, offers, requests, complaints, invitations
and announcements (Schegloff and Sacks 1973).

READER ACTIVITY

Analyse a complete section of the text by F. Jameson in the *New Left
Review*, where the above examples come from. Where and why do
prediction pairs occur? How do they contribute to structuring Jameson's
discourse?

It is certain that prediction acts have a central role in conversation. Their function shows how vocabulary is constitutive of text organisation, in this case by predicting part of the text. Sinclair (1993) considers the predictive function an instance of the interactive quality of language and uses the term 'prospection' to identify it as a general text-organising strategy. Prospection includes all cases in which 'the phrasing of a sentence leads the addressee to expect something specific in the next sentence' (12). This type of lexical patterning, which involves an interactive relation between addresser and addressee, is at the core of discourse construction and constitutes an indispensable complement of other types of organisation.

4.6 SENTENCE STRUCTURE PATTERNING

Cohesive ties between individual items may constitute reference chains or create lexical networks in a text. Other more complex patterns of cohesion may involve more than two individual lexical items. For instance, relations between segments may be unmarked by morphosyntactic means, but marked by a form of repetition. In Halliday and Hasan's (1976) model of cohesion, repetition belongs to the lexical means of cohesion. In Gee's terms (1989), instead, it establishes an expressive type of linkage as opposed to a temporal or logical linkage in narrative discourse. Similarly, in Silverstein's terms (1984), it constitutes a form of poetic organisation. As with the rest of the cohesive devices, research on repetition in narratives has gradually shifted from a local cohesion view to a global marker view. The latter involves looking into the role of repetition in a story's hierarchical ordering of events, the stringing-together and segmenting of units. There, repetition exhibits a salient role in that it shows how different text parts are held together, how new utterances are linked to earlier ones and how all of them contribute to the meaning of discourse, its coherence. In this way, it links surface patterns of discourse with the interactional goals of discourse participants. It mediates between a hierarchical organisation of discourse units and the real-time enactment of discourse (Silverstein 1984). We will discuss the contribution of repetition to interpersonal and expressive relations in Chapter 5. Here, we will mainly focus on its organisational role.

Instances of repetition may range from exact repetition or repetition with variation to paraphrase (similar meaning in different words) and parallelism (different words in the same syntactic and rhythmic paradigm as a preceding utterance, frequently reinforced by repetition: e.g. we get energy from petrol – we get energy from food). These forms can be immediate (adjacent to each other) or non-immediate (see Tannen 1989: ch. 3). We can look at some of their instantiation in the following extracts from the play *My Night with Reg* by K. Elyot (Nick Hern Books, 1994).

Text 4.33
Immediate repetition
John: <u>The worst thing</u>, Eric ... <u>the worst thing</u> of all. (p. 76)

Daniel: I'm loving <u>the people I can talk to</u>.
John: <u>You can talk to me</u>. p. 76)

Repetition with variation
Daniel: <u>I got it in my head</u> that <u>he was being unfaithful</u>. Not the odd bit on the side – <u>I don't think</u> there was and I never asked because I didn't want to know – but that <u>he was actually having an affair</u>. And it got to the point where <u>I'd convinced myself</u> <u>he was in love with somebody else</u>. The stupid thing is – and this is what I regret – <u>I couldn't confront him</u> about it, I suppose because <u>I couldn't face it</u> and was hoping <u>he wouldn't do that to me</u>. Then when he was dying and the things he was saying to me, I felt ashamed. <u>He wouldn't have done that to me</u>, would he? <u>You don't think</u> <u>he was having an affair</u>, do you, John? ... <u>I couldn't stop myself thinking about it</u>, wondering <u>if he'd cheated</u>. (pp. 46–7) ...

Non-immediate paraphrase
1. I got it in my head – I convinced myself – I couldn't stop myself thinking about it
2. he was being unfaithful – he was actually having an affair – he was in love with somebody else – he'd cheated

Non-immediate repetition with variation
1. he was actually having an affair – he was having an affair
2. I don't think – you don't think
3. he wouldn't do that to me – he wouldn't have done that to me

Parallelism
I couldn't confront him – I couldn't face it

READER ACTIVITY

Identify the different forms of repetition in Text 4.5 and comment on their positioning in the story.

All the above forms of repetition have been widely documented as common devices for demarcating narrative episodes by appearing at their endpoints (linking repetition in Tannen's terms) or for creating internal patterns of similarity between them. In oral narratives in particular, repetition makes the task of on-line, unplanned production less energy-draining, by buying time for the narrator. Similarly, it facilitates comprehension by uniquely emphasising relationships between narrative parts and intensifying the story's point. As Tannen (1989) suggested, it establishes a frame, a paradigm with slots for insertion of new information. Repeating the frame succeeds in foregrounding and intensifying not only the part repeated but also the part that is different.

READER ACTIVITY

Explore the contribution of the underlined repetition to narrative organisation in the oral narrative below.

Text 4.34
B: and this was definitely the best summer in England
C: I was saying to John that <u>I was clearing my email yesterday</u>, before I went away, <u>and I discovered a letter</u> and <u>I was laughing with it</u>, cause I'd been to see the people who were saying, well there is a lot of subsidy by the council, for heating and –, and there is a big boiler for a whole block of flats, so somebody has to take the decision <u>when it will be off</u>, and <u>when it will stay on</u>. And basically the assumption is, that <u>it goes off</u> for three months a year, <u>it goes off</u> at the end of May, <u>it's off</u> for June, July and August, and then <u>goes on</u> in September, except for when the weather is particularly bad. And when <u>I was clearing my email, I found a letter</u> I sent somebody on the 15th of June, saying I'd been to a meeting about it, and basically it's possible to override it. Because it was June and we thought <u>it would be warm</u>, <u>the heating was off</u>, but their pleading was that <u>the heating should come back</u>. And someone said we'd like to look at it again, after the weekend, because the weather forecast was saying that <u>it was going to be warmer</u>. I mean obviously the whole issue was forgotten, cause it was after that–, that <u>the weather became warm</u>. And I was reading this, and <u>I was laughing</u>, thinking, <u>this was really only two months ago, this was really in the middle of June</u>, and we were saying we think <u>the radiators should be on</u>, cause <u>it's not warm</u> yet.

(*Source*: Authors data)

As with the rest of the organisational signals, it is quite difficult to invoke a notion of universal use of repetition. Its degree, type and forms differ significantly with cultural and individual style. Different languages and communities provide a range of cultural patterns from which speakers choose the repetition strategies which make up their individual style. For instance, the amount of repetition, in particular reduplication (e.g. *slowly slowly*), which Indian speakers habitually use, has been found to be a source of miscommunication in Indian–British interactions, sounding redundant and pointless to British speakers (see Gumperz 1982). In Arabic non-narrative (argumentative) discourse, paraphrase in the form of paratactically-connected couplets is a rhetorical strategy of persuasion which reinforces the presentation of proof (Koch 1983).

With respect to Anglophone speech communities, several varieties of

American English (e.g. New York Jewish, Black American English etc.) have been found to use repetition more extensively than others (e.g. Erickson 1984, Tannen 1989). In such cases, repetition, in conjunction with other linguistic and paralinguistic signals, underlies the creation of rhythmic segments that criss-cross and are interlocked with each other. As we discussed in Chapter 3, this type of connection relies on a very evident, poetic line-and-stanza structure of narration and is characteristic of an oral-based narrative style. The predominance of intricate repetition forms, in cooperation with rich variations in pitch and pause, makes up for the use of more explicit signals of narrative progression such as discourse markers. Different narrative anecdotes are stitched together by an underlying similarity of point.

On the whole, structures of repetition are more in evidence in oral narrative traditions than in highly literate narrative forms. Grimes (1983) has documented a particular narrative protocol of repetition in a number of unrelated languages of Brazil (Bororo) and New Guinea (Chuave, Angaataha, Pidgin), for which he coined the term *overlay*. This is a particular type of linkage that moves the narrative time forwards by drawing attention to the novel elements, while nearly repeating relatively long stretches so that certain elements in one stretch recur in the other. Here is an illustration of the technique from a narrative extract translated from Godie (an Ivory Coast language).

Text 4.35

they <u>entered the canoe</u>. Now <u>having entered the canoe</u>, they paddled until the middle of the river and there the genie of the river <u>came out</u>. His <u>having come out</u>, he grabbed the canoe ...

(*Source*: Marchese 1988)

This technique was also found in operation in medieval French epic poetry (Fleischman 1989). Longacre (1976) also refers to it as 'tail-to-head' linkage.

A similar type of symmetrical patterning with which we are more familiar in the western world is that of narrative jokes (see Chiaro 1992). In their case, repetition first creates a matching pattern between certain segments and then breaks it in the climax or resolution. This achieves the effect of intensifying and foregrounding by means of juxtaposition. A comparable pattern is found in traditional folktales and children's stories. If we go back to our familiar text of 'Burglar Bill', we will notice that this technique is employed extensively throughout the text:

Text 4.36

a. Then Burglar Bill says, 'I know what you want – grub!' Burglar Bill gives an apple to the baby. But still the baby cries. He gives a slice of toast and marmalade to the baby. But still the baby cries. He gives a plate of beans and a cup of tea to the baby. The baby eats the beans, throws the cup of tea on the floor and starts to laugh. 'That's better', says Burglar Bill, 'I like a few beans meself'.

b. Burglar Bill creeps to the top of the stairs. Down below a torch is shining and a voice says, 'That's a nice umbrella – I'll have that!'

Burglar Bill creeps down the stairs. The voice says, 'That's a nice tin of beans – I'll have that!'

Burglar Bill creeps along the hall and into the kitchen. The voice says, 'That's a nice date and walnut cake with buttercream filling and icing on the top – I'll have that!'

BURGLAR BILL PUTS ON THE LIGHT.

(*Source*: J. and A. Ahlberg, *Burglar Bill*, Mammoth)

In both extracts above, the use of repetition and parallelism establish a frame, a pattern of similarity which is then broken for the action to move forwards. In this way, both what is constant and what is variable are foregrounded. In the first extract, the pattern involves the technique of application of plans, of which the third is successful (it stops the baby from crying). This tripartite pattern is very common in jokes and in narratives of many cultures: it involves three events, attempts etc. of which the third breaks the established pattern of similarity and marks the resolution. In the second extract, we also get a tripartite pattern of a different kind though: three similar event-schemas lead to the breaking of the matching pattern by a completely different event-schema (*Burglar Bill puts on the light*). Such patterns contribute not just to the organisation of a story but also to its tellability (see Chapter 5 for a discussion).

In view of the above, we can now safely argue that repetition establishes patterns that involves whole utterances (and units higher than utterances) rather than their individual constituents. This is a device of organisation that narratives share with non-narrative texts. Sentence structure repetition may be used in the latter to indicate continuity, as in the following instance of parallelism:

Three years ago it was Panama, to overthrow a dictator. Two years ago it was the Gulf, to liberate Kuwait. This year it will be the horn of Africa, to help to get food to masses of starving Somalis.

(*Source*: *The Independent on Sunday*, 6 December 1992)

Different patterns of matching sentence arrangements have also been described in the model of thematic progression developed by Daneš (1974). Although the model can be unnecessarily perplexing because of the technicalities of identifying 'theme' and 'rheme', we can take advantage of its insights if we follow a clear and workable definition of the terms involved. Such a definition would be to identify theme with the initial, pre-verbal position and rheme with the rest of the sentence. We can thus describe the three patterns observed by Daneš (1974) as follows.

Linear progression: the rheme of a sentence becomes the theme of the immediately succeeding sentence, as in the following extract from text 4.8:

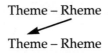

Text 4.37
Quietly nested in the lush landscapes of Northamptonshire, lies <u>the sleepy village of Silverstone</u>. Every now and again however <u>this wooded heaven</u> is woken by the ear-splitting roar of its less tranquil neighbour. The famous Silverstone Circuit.

Progression with constant theme: the same theme is repeated, as in the example from *The Independent* above and the following extract from text 4.17:

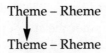

Text 4.38
<u>The world's largest 500 companies</u> now control at least 70 per cent of world trade, 80 per cent of foreign investment and 30 per cent of global GDP. <u>They</u> control the way countries develop. <u>They</u> are key actors in channelling and fostering consumer tastes, patterns of production and lifestyles.

Progression with derived theme: subsequent themes are derived from a superordinate item at the beginning of the text:

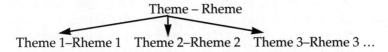

Text 4.39
Replies were divided into <u>three groups</u>. <u>Group 1</u> consisted of men with no reported history of CHD who were negative to WHO chest pain questionnaire. <u>Group 2</u> consisted of men with no reported history of CHD who were positive to WHO chest pain questionnaire; and <u>group 3</u> consisted of men with a reported history of CHD, either MI or AP.

(*Source*: Nwogu 1990)

In practice, these patterns are rarely found in a simple, straightforward way. In most cases, there are combinations or variants of them. Furthermore, they are more frequent in simple narratives due to the relatively long participant chains. In non-narrative texts, by contrast, they are usually found in restricted stretches of text, for example in descriptive sequences.

Finally, arrangements of sentence patterns are exploited for text-organising purposes such as the introduction of new entities in discourse. First, sentence-initial adverbials and clauses are related to the framing of the discourse that follows. It has been observed, for example, that these syntactic patterns consistently occupy the thematic position in texts like the following:

Text 4.40

<u>As you open the door</u>, you are in a small five-by-five room which is a small closet. <u>When you get past there</u>, you're in what we call the foyer, which is about a twelve-by-twelve room which has a telephone and a desk. <u>If you keep walking in that same direction</u>, you're confronted by two rooms in front of you.

(*Source*: Linde and Labov 1975: 929)

Descriptive texts organised around time or location are well known for this kind of patterning (Virtanen 1992). It is doubtful, however, whether we can generalise this technique to a topic development strategy for all non-narrative texts, as seems to be implied by Winter (1982) and Fries (1983). What seems to be involved here is rather the creation of a local context for what follows (Chafe 1984; Thompson and Longacre 1985). In other words, we have to do with a technique used for demarcating boundaries and preparing the introduction of a discourse entity.

A second means of exploiting sentence structure arrangements concerns the use of light-thematic or rheme-focused patterns – again, to be defined as empty or near-empty initial positions and heavy final or post-verbal positions, respectively. Illustrations of this are sentences with *there, it* or a *wh-* item in pre-verbal position:

Text 4.41

To illustrate some of the similarities and differences between these new industrial spaces, let us briefly consider a few empirical examples drawn from Italy, Britain, France and the United States.

In the so-called 'Third Italy', <u>there has been a great expansion</u> of localised production complexes based on highly flexible kinds ...

(*Source*: Goutsos 1994)

Text 4.42

Revulsion and hatred followed in train. So did many lawyers brandishing the Geneva Convention.

<u>It is necessary</u>, at such a moment, to cling to rationality. ...

(*Source*: *The Guardian*, 22 January 1991)

Text 4.43

but if ever a new observation is found to disagree, we have to abandon or modify the theory. At least that is what is supposed to happen, but you can always question the competence of the person who carried out the observation.

In practice, <u>what often happens</u> is that a new theory is devised that is really an extension of the previous theory. ...

(*Source*: S. Hawking *A Brief History of Time*.
London (Bantam Press, 1988), p. 9)

The three examples above share the presence of a 'dummy' element in initial or thematic position, which has as a result to shift the focus on the rhematic or sentence-final position. At the same time, these structures signal a boundary in the text's organisation in the form of a major shift in continuity. This shift is related to the introduction of new entities in discourse (cf. Chafe 1980; Kies 1988; Williams 1988). Sentences with indefinite or context-independent subjects are also used for the introduction of a new entity and display the same functions.

4.7 THE SYNERGY OF SIGNALS

Let us remind ourselves once again of the basic tasks which the organisational signals discussed in this chapter perform: these are the tasks of continuity and shift in the overall sequential structure of a text. Continuity matches more closely a hearer's expectations in the process of his or her mental representation of a text. In narrative for instance, one expects a transition from one event to another in a sequence. Discontinuity (shift) is more marked (i.e. unexpected) and requires more attentional effort, cognitively speaking. The building of any text inevitably makes use of both continuity and discontinuity even within the same unit. Comparably, continuity and discontinuity are not an all-or-nothing matter: for example, we can have a minor or a major break in continuity. As we have seen, discontinuity is mainly achieved by the opening or closing of units.

Let us now summarise the role of signals in relation to the two strategies of continuity and shift. First, not all signals have the same potential for establishing a topic strategy. Different signals mark continuity or discontinuity in different degrees. For instance, we saw how 'and' is primarily a marker of continuity. Of the temporal adverbials which play a vital role in narrative organisation, it has been found that anchorage markers (e.g. at three o'clock) mark discontinuity more effectively than sequencers (e.g. then; see Bestgen and Vonk 1995). Second, the same signal may mark continuity or discontinuity depending on its positioning in a text and on its cooperation with other signals. With respect to textual positioning, we saw how the occurrence of signals at unit endpoints is a device for rendering discontinuity more salient. With respect to the cooperation of signals, we saw that signals do not work in isolation from each other but in synergy or orchestration: they may co-occur and cooperate in establishing a specific sequential strategy. For instance, discourse markers and cohesive devices are not always unequivocal in the identification of a sequential technique and need corroborating evidence from other signals. A discourse marker combined with a paragraph break, a metadiscourse item or a prediction pair may signal discontinuity more effectively or may succeed in signalling a major instead of a minor continuity break. The above leads us to another important point about the textual occurrence of signals: since signals co-occur and cooperate with each other, then signals of topic shift may occur alongside signals of topic continuity. You may now ask: how is the resulting conflict resolved in these cases? A simple answer is that it is in principle resolved in favour of topic shift signals.

The specific role of a signal in a text's sequential strategies cannot be accurately established *a priori* for every text but varies with respect to discourse modes, or is set anew for individual texts and even individual addressers and addressees. With respect to narrative and non-narrative modes, we saw how signals such as temporal markers and participant tracking chains (via nominalisation and pronominalisation) are more prominent markers of segmentation in narrative texts. Non-narrative texts favour more explicit conventional devices (e.g. paragraphing, metalinguistic expressions, encapsulating cohesion).

While the role of signals has been looked into systematically in the literature, there is still plenty of room for research on the forms and functions of their synergy in different text-types as well as on the effect of this synergy on discourse processing. One relatively easy way to study the correlation of signals is by looking at the beginnings of paragraphs (or other units) where most signals of topic shift tend to occur. Different categories can be distinguished according to the type of paragraph-initial items, namely elements in the thematic position of the first sentence of each paragraph. To this end, large-scale analyses of corpora could be employed to indicate the relative probabilities of occurrence in initial position.

FURTHER READING
For signalling in general, see Hoey (1979).

The most extensive description of discourse markers in conversation is the classic Schiffrin (1987), which, however, has to be read in conjunction with Redeker's (1991) review. Basic references also include Schourup (1985) and Fraser (1990). For the use of discourse markers in different genres, see Smith and Frawley (1983). There is also a rich bibliography on the function of discourse markers in specific genres; some of the most interesting studies include Bäcklund (1988) for expository text, Berman (1988) and Payne (1992) for narratives in languages other than English, Bäcklund (1992) for telephone conversation, Maschler (1994) for bilingual discourse and Bazzanella (1990) and Miller and Weinert (1995) for conversation. Developmental studies of discourse markers can be found in Peterson and McCabe (1991), Bestgen and Costermans (1994) and Heritage and Sorgonen (1994). Basic studies on discourse markers and comprehension are Vonk et al. (1992) and Bestgen and Vonk (1995).

Analysis of metalinguistic elements can be found in Harris (1980), Schiffrin (1980), Kurzon (1985), Bäcklund (1988), Fleishman (1991) and Crismore et al. (1993). Traugott (1982) gives the wider picture by bringing in diachronic considerations.

One of the basic theories on participant chains is that of topic continuity as developed by Givón (1983) and the plethora of research which it has promoted. One of the most recent studies in this line of research is Payne

(1993). On the other hand, purely semantic models include Ariel (1991) and Reinhart (1983), and AI approaches range from Sidners (1983) model of focus to Webber (1981), Reichman (1985) and Grosz and Sidner (1986). The main drawback of these two lines of research concerns their isolated, constructed data. Fox (1987) provides a synthesis of their views with authentic data but is slightly dated now. Current tendencies emphasise the collaborative nature of reference (Clark and Wilkes-Gibbs 1986) and, more generally, the role of both discourse pragmatic factors and cognitive constraints in triggering referential forms (e.g. Pu 1995). Refreshing approaches to the same issues include Redeker (1987), which focuses on types rather than forms of intro- duction in narrative texts, Myers and Hartley (1990), which explores the intricacies of scientific text, and McCarthy (1994) on *it*, *this* and *that* in non- narrative text.

For the use of the narrative (historic) present as an internal evaluative device, see Fleischman (1990), Schiffrin (1981), Silva-Corvalan (1983) and Georgakopoulou (1994). Centineo (1991) also studies tense switching as an evaluative device. For the use of direct quotes as internal evaluative devices, see Dubois (1989) and Johnstone (1990).

The general introductory book on lexical patterning is Carter (1987). Especially, on anaphoric nouns, see Francis (1989a); and on paraphrase and other types of repetition, see Hoey (1991).

The starting point of research on repetition should be Tannen (1987), which includes an extensive review of studies of repetition in various cultures and languages. Tannen (1989) provides a thorough typology of forms and functions of repetition. More recently, Johnstone (1994a and b) provides a wide variety of studies of repetition in narrative and non-narra- tive genres.

Some of the most useful different approaches to thematic progression include Dubois (1987), Lautamatti (1987), Hatim and Mason (1990), Nwogu (1990) and Nwogu and Bloor (1992). For pedagogical applications of the cohesive harmony analysis, see Yang (1989) and Parsons (1992).

Structures and Functions

The previous two chapters focused on relations and organisational patterns in discourse. We focused on *how* units and relations compose the text's internal structure and on *what* devices are used for holding together and segmenting a text at different levels. What has not been discussed at length yet is *why* structure and organisation are present in text and how they collaborate with discourse functions. As already mentioned, any piece of discourse, apart from being a meaningful construction of part–whole relations, serves a range of functions. Both individual linguistic elements of the text and its overall structures are tuned to these functions. This form–function interaction accounts for the subjective component of discourse: the expression of attitudes, feelings, judgements, beliefs and, on the whole, the addressers' emotional interest and engagement in the content and the participants of discourse. The linguistic realisations or displays of subjectivity (i.e. interpersonal, expressive functions) have been a major preoccupation in the analyses of different discourse types. There is already a vast amount of research, a proliferation of relevant terms and a considerable heterogeneity in the approaches, sometimes even in the definitions of the same concept. Here, we will selectively present the major unifying threads of different approaches, thus avoiding a forbiddingly diverse domain. Our focus will be on the ways in which narrative and non-narrative structures are fashioned to serve textual functions and meet the needs of communication.

5.1 EVALUATION AND TELLABILITY IN NARRATIVE

The encoding of subjectivity is a central concern of narrative discourse. Narratives are generally treated as high in affectivity and expressivity. The narration of personal stories in particular is an affective device *per se*. Specific, linguistic displays of expressivity within a story have long been viewed through the lens of the Labovian evaluation and a story's point. Evaluation was introduced in Chapter 3 as a part of the structural categories of narrative, along with orientation, complicating action etc. The notion of evaluation is essentially an inspired systematisation of an old concern of narratology with metastructures that go beyond the story's referential content. These aspects of the text are not concerned with reporting what happened but with conveying the narrator's attitudes and feelings towards the sequence of events narrated (see the distinction between fabula and sujhet or the French structuralists' *histoire* and *discours*, i.e. story and discourse). In addition, evaluation involves the set of devices that make a story reportable or tellable. Tellability ensures the audience's engagement in it.

Numerous studies after Labov attempted to establish the validity and generalisability of the evaluative devices which he first identified. In many cases, these devices were broken down into more refined categories to suit specific data (e.g. Polanyi 1985). The following story entitled 'Eating on the New York Thruway' by Polanyi (1985) exemplifies some of these categories:

Text 5.1

Carol: I went, I always drink coke, right?

Livia: Right.

Carol: So, Livia is thr … walking around with this gallon of spring water and I can't understand why she is walking around with this gallon of spring water. And she keeps talk … She keeps telling me these … vague making these vague remarks about the restaurants on the New York Thruway and at least we have this spring water and I don't … I don't know what she's talking about. So we go to this restaurant and I order a coke and I ordered some sort of sandwich. Now, I don't think you ordered anything.

Livia: I didn't order anything.

Carol: Right

Livia: I sat there making faces.

Carol: Well, one thing about this restaurant was that every person in it was retarded. ((laughter)) that's all. The people who worked there they were one after the other of the weirdest looking people I've ever ((laughter)) either they were retarded or they were let out for the day from the mental hospital. I … you know.

Livia: They didn't seem to be able to distinguish between washing the floor and making a hamburger. Both things were done in the same way ((laughter)).

Carol: So, this coke appears. I was very thirsty. And I went this ((demonstrates)) straw in took a sip of this coke and I started screaming 'I've been poisoned' and Livia very calmly handed me this spring water. I mean I have never in my life tasted anything so bad. ((laughter))

(*Source*: Polanyi 1985: 51–2)

Some of the evaluative devices that Polanyi notes in this story are negative encoding (e.g. *I can't understand, I don't know*), hyperbole or exaggeration (e.g. *every person, one after the other of the weirdest looking people, I have never in my life*), repetition (e.g. *she's walking around, this spring water, this coke*), direct speech (*I've been poisoned*) and collapse of the storyworld and narrating world (*this coke, this straw*). Peterson and McCabe's study (1983) of children's narratives also identified a broad set of evaluative devices. Some of them are common with those found in other studies of narrative development. These include gratuitous or aggravated signals (e.g. *very, just, really*), marked emphasis in voice, negation, repetition, causal explanations, characters' speech and references to characters' mental and emotive states (e.g. *I don't know what she's talking about, the weirdest looking people, Livia very calmly* etc. from text 5.1 above).

READER ACTIVITY

Read the following story told by a 6-year-old boy. Can you identify any of the above devices used for making the story more interesting and tellable?

Text 5.2
M: But, you know, once we were over at Jack's, cause we were studying there for the day, cause Mommy and Daddy had to go to work, that's where they took us every day, cause they have to go to work, we were over there, and they have lots of sheep and stuff, and he took me back there on his mini-bike, and we saw this sheep stuff, and it was just bones.
E: it was just bones?
M: And I was getting off and he said, don't be foolish. And Lenny was trying to scare me, cause there was haunts back there, and he was trying to scare me and saying, are they gonna haunt us.
E: Are they going to haunt you?
M: So he went back there and said, mo, you wanna have a ride? And they know he was gonna run out of gas, so he went back there ((laughingly)) and was pulling it back.

                              (*Source*: Peterson and McCabe 1983)

As you can see, organisationally the story does not qualify for the classic pattern. This is not surprising for a story recounted by a 6-year-old. What would you expect about the development of evaluative devices in the child's stories?

Labov's research suggested that the use of all four major types of evaluatives increases with age. Lately, developmental studies have shown that along with the number and variety of evaluative devices, the ways of employing evaluation also change with age. Younger children have been found to lack the skill of strategically using evaluation to signal globally important events and the story's coherence. They, instead, tend to evaluate locally specific events and to ascribe meaning to individual events and actions. In Bamberg and Damrad-Frye's (1991) research, the subjects were asked to narrate a picture book (*Frog, where are you?*) that referred to a boy and dog's search for their lost frog. Despite various obstacles, the search is finally successful. The aim of the research was to establish the developmental pattern of the occurrence of evaluative devices. Bamberg and Damrad-Frye found out that one particular picture attracted many more references to 'frames of mind' or emotive states (in this case, anger) from children than adults. Young children seemed to be tied to the pictorial information of the boy's facial frustration with the dog, who has just shattered a jar. By emphasising the boy's anger, children adopted a perspective that was restricted to a purely local outcome. By contrast, in their references, adults were found to consider anger just an obstacle that is overcome for the global theme of the joint search to be reinstantiated. In this way, they revealed a more global perspective, in which evaluative devices were governed by an awareness of the story's overall plot structure. These findings have confirmed the important role of evaluation in a story's discourse coherence. Despite what Labov's and older narratological models seem to suggest, expressive devices are currently not treated as embellishing metastructures that are superimposed on a story's organisational backbone. These devices are not intrusive or backgrounded with respect to action. By contrast, they are recognised as vital devices for pointing to the implicit hierarchical order of the events in the organisation of the whole.

In addition to redefining the role of evaluation, post-Labovian research has also emphasised its context-sensitivity, its variation across cultures, situations and story participants. Contextual variation affects and shapes not only the ways in which a story is evaluated, but also the story's point. That too is not static or predetermined but is discovered and negotiated through the telling of a story in different settings and to different audiences (Sacks 1972, 1974; Robinson 1981; Young 1987). This context-dependence was not fully captured and expressed in Labov's model. Labov argued that evaluative devices 'say to us that this was terrifying, dangerous, weird, wild, crazy, or amusing, hilarious, wonderful, more generally that it was strange, uncommon or unusual, that is, worth reporting' (1972: 371). How is this unexpectedness of events defined, though? Is it only intrinsic? Systematic research on the telling of stories has demonstrated that what is reportable ultimately depends on what is thought to be interesting or appropriate in certain social and cultural contexts, on certain occasions and for certain storytellers and audiences. As Polanyi has aptly suggested, 'what stories can be about is to a very significant extent culturally constrained: stories ... can have as their point culturally salient material generally agreed upon by

members of the producer's culture to be self-evidently important and true'
(1979: 207).

Polanyi's study of American storytelling identified general tellable
themes in it and derived, on their basis, a system of cultural values, attitudes
and beliefs, a cultural 'world'. For instance, the analysis of text 5.1 can yield,
among others, the following basic cultural construct: food is supposed to be
reliable, safe and predictable, especially in the USA and especially in relation
to the quintessential American coke. Hence, the unexpectedness (and
reportability) of the story's events. Another major value underlying the plot
of text 5.1 is that of friendship. Livia behaved as a true friend of the narrator.
She tried to protect and warn her, to be honest for her good. At the same
time, we could easily imagine contexts in which this story would not be
tellable. In addition to its culture-specific elements, its tellability would vary
across contexts, tellers and audiences.

This context-dependence of tellability casts doubt on the validity of unexpectedness as its criterial feature. In numerous cases, a story's point may not
arise at all from the content of the events narrated but from the importance
attributed to the story's telling in particular circumstances. Shuman (1986)
has postulated a distinction between a story's intrinsic point (storyability)
and its contextual point (tellability). She has further argued that an experience may be storyable in its being remarkable and yet not tellable in a
particular context and vice versa. We can put this more simply by saying
that events are not only tellable in themselves (intrinsically tellable) but also
tellable on occasions (contextually tellable). Since tellability is not only a
matter of narrative reference (i.e. real-world events) or of narrative text, we
can also suggest that a story can be very tellable without being very evaluated with specific linguistic devices and the converse.

READER ACTIVITY

A. The following brief story was told (in Greek) in a conversation about
nudism on Greek beaches in a group of three men and four women.
The storyteller, who supports nudism, relates the following incident
before she expresses any of her views. Where, in your view, does the
story's tellability lie and how does it interact with its evaluative devices?

Text 5.3
This happened in Folegandros ((a small and not very developed
Greek island)), the locals were up in arms, because of the nude
tourists, and on the beach, there was a large water tank, for showers,
and it said, don't drink this water, they had it for watering their plants,
or I don't know what. So we used some to wash, and there was this
tourist, probably Dutch, blond guy, long hair, he pulls down his

trunks to wash. So they start yelling, from a balcony opposite, oy put your pants on, put your pants on, put your pants on, hh hh. How could he understand? And someone threatening him with his walking stick, put your pants on, shame on you, and the others shouting at him//hh hh. At some point he says, why are they yelling at me, do they want to save the water? ((whispers)) it's your trunks, somebody tells him, it's your trunks, oh my trunks. And he finally pulled them back on.

(*Source*: Georgakopoulou 1994c: 26)

B. You may wish to apply a similar analysis to the following story that was jointly told by Ira and Jan, a lower-middle-class, middle-aged Jewish couple. Note that, unlike the story above, this story is part of a sociolinguistic interview. Ira and Jan are explaining their position against intermarriage between Jews and Gentiles to their interviewer, Deborah Schiffrin:

Text 5.4

Ira: Now my daughter went out with eh– she went out with a couple Gentile kids, and she said that=

Jan: //she wouldn't go out with them=

Ira: =she wouldn't go out with them again.

Jan: = again.//She// said they're too different.

Ira: She said that uh ... they're just eh–the–

Jan: //they're// different.

Jan: She says, 'It's not what I'm used to'.

Ira: So em ... s–she

Jan: //One// was a, his father was a friend of my husband's. And when I heard she was goin' out with him, I said, 'You're goin' out with him', I said, 'You're goin' out with a Gentile boy?' She says, 'Well Daddy knows his father'. I said, 'I don't care'. So she introduced him, and they went out, and she came home early, and I said, 'Well, y' goin' out with him again?' She says, 'Nope.' I said, 'Did he get fresh?' She said, 'No!' She says, 'But he's different!' She says, 'I'm not used t' Gentile boys!' That cured her! She'd never go out with one again.

(*Source*: Schiffrin 1990: 250–1)

Can you think of contexts in which the above stories would not be tellable?

5.2 STRATEGIES OF INVOLVEMENT

Studies of expressivity in storytelling have frequently employed alternative but comparable concepts to evaluation. These are intended to capture the ways in which stories express their tellers' inner states and degrees of emotional interest and engagement in the various elements of the story-world. They are also intended to describe the ways in which stories shape their audiences' interest and engagement in them. Specific linguistic strategies and techniques used for these purposes are frequently called in the literature 'involvement strategies'. Involvement was initially proposed as a strategy of any type of discourse and was contrasted to detachment, which comprises devices for encoding distancing from the elements of discourse. Chafe (1982), who introduced the distinction, suggested that the list of involvement features mainly comprises the following features:

- details and images (tendency towards concreteness, imageability and particularity)
- first- and second-person pronouns
- actions and agents (emphasis on people and relationships rather than states and objects)
- hedges (e.g. just, sort of, kind of, somewhat)
- aggravated signals (e.g. really, so, very)
- direct speech and dialogues.

Detachment, on the other hand, comprises features of complex syntax such as relative and complement clauses, sequences of prepositional phrases, nominalisations, passive voice, attributive adjectives, etc.

Chafe claimed that the degrees of involvement or detachment differ according to discourse type. In his research, conversations and narratives were found to draw more on involvement strategies than academic essays and other non-narrative texts which integrate their ideas by means of complex syntax in order to convince their addressees of their arguments.

READER ACTIVITY

Compare story 5.3 above with the following text in terms of their involvement and detachment devices. Which of the two draws on detachment features more?

Text 5.5

Once one has gained some familiarity with constructing simple Turing machines, it becomes easy to satisfy oneself that the various basic arithmetical operations, such as adding two numbers together, or multiplying them, or raising one number to the power of another, can indeed all be effected by specific Turing machines. It would not

---

be too cumbersome to give such machines explicitly, but I shall not bother to do that here. Operations where the result is a pair of natural numbers, such as division with a remainder, can also be provided – or where the result is an arbitrarily large finite set of numbers. Moreover, Turing machines can be constructed for which it is not specified ahead of time which arithmetical operation it is that needs to be performed, but the instructions for this are fed in on the tape.

(*Source*: Roger Penrose, *The Emperor's New Mind*
(Oxford: Oxford University Press, 1989), p. 47)

Chafe did not posit involvement and detachment as the two poles of a strict dichotomy. He rather viewed them as a continuum, in which there are different degrees of relative focus on involvement. As Tannen has claimed, these grow out of communicative purposes, social and cultural conventions and discourse-type norms. The prototypical spoken discourse is expected to be characterised by involvement, while the prototypical written discourse by integration and detachment. Comparably, narrative discourse is prototypically more involved. In fact, conversational and literary narratives prove to be more similar than they are usually thought of as being, from the point of view of their involvement strategies (Tannen 1986). Ultimately, both discourse types seek to encode feelings more than information and, in doing so, to move rather than convince their audiences. Storytelling about personal experiences in particular has been found to be very high in involvement and to occur more frequently in high-involvement conversations that exhibit numerous instances of overlapping talk and interruptions between the participants (Tannen 1989).

In Tannen's (1989) terms, there are two major categories of involvement strategies. The first work primarily on sound; they involve the audience with the speaker or writer and the discourse by sweeping them up in what Scollon and Scollon (1995) call 'rhythmic ensemble', much as one is swept up by music and finds oneself moving to its rhythm. This category mainly comprises patterns based on various forms of repetition (see chapter 4). Repetition succeeds in giving discourse a character of familiarity and creating the impression of a shared universe of discourse between the participants. By contributing to the connectedness and coherence in discourse, repetition also contributes to the emotional experience of connectedness between the discourse participants. This is its essence as an involvement strategy.

According to Tannen, the other category of involvement strategies aims at engaging the audience in the discourse through participation in its sense-making. It comprises *ellipsis, imagery and detail, tropes* and *constructed dialogue*. Tropes cover four figures of speech: metaphor (speaking of one thing in terms of another), metonymy (speaking of a thing in terms of something associated with it), synecdoche (a part for the whole) and irony (saying the opposite of what one means). Constructed dialogue refers to the representation of characters' speech as direct quotation rather than as a report (indirect speech) or as dialogue with other characters or with oneself (direct thought presentation). Tannen coined this term to emphasise the fact that 'when speech uttered in one context is repeated in another, it is fundamentally changed even if "reported" accurately' (1989: 110). In numerous cases, much of what appears as reported speech in discourse was never uttered in this form: for example, when a character's inner speech is represented, when speech is represented as choral, that is, attributed to many people in unison, etc. (for details see Tannen 1989: pp. 111–18). Its occurrence in these cases serves as a means of dramatisation and authenticity.

All the above devices bring the discourse alive by creating a sense of concreteness, particularity and familiarity. The speakers communicate their meaning and emotions through the power of evoking specific scenes. In this way, they send messages of rapport and intimacy to the audience inviting their involvement with them and with the events which are so vividly recreated.

Numerous studies have looked into the vital role of speech presentation in narratives as a device for vividness and involvement (e.g. Polanyi 1985; Dubois 1989; Mayes 1990). The animation of voices adds to the immediacy of the narration and creates the illusion that both teller and audience co-witness the events. In story 5.3 above, constructed dialogue occurs in the peak event to emphasise its point:

> So they start yelling, from a balcony opposite, oy put your pants on, put your pants on, put your pants on ((audience laughs)). How could he understand? And someone threatening him with his walking stick, put your pants on, shame on you, and the others shouting at him ((audience laughs)).

The repetition of the speech renders it more salient as an involvement strategy. In addition, the narrator imitates the male voices with the effect of enhancing the dramatic evocation. The story finishes on a high point with a dialogue:

> At some point he says, why are they yelling at me, do they want to save the water? ((whispers)) it's your trunks, somebody tells him, it's your trunks, oh my trunks.

Constructed dialogue has been reported as a major involvement strategy in conversational narratives of cultures that are very close to oral styles (such as Brazilian, Greek or American Indian communities). As we will see below, it is an integral part of performed (i.e. highly dramatised) narratives.

READER ACTIVITY

Identify the involvement strategies of the following text. How would you account for the use of the underlined items?

Text 5.6
Amy and I went to see An Inspector Calls at the National. <u>Brilliant</u> production on a stunning surrealist set, played without a break, like a <u>perfectly</u> remembered dream. I never rated Priestley before, but tonight he seemed <u>as good as bloody</u> Sophocles. Even Amy was swept away – she didn't attempt to recast the play once over supper. We ate in Ovations, a selection of starters – they're always better than the main courses. Amy had two and I had three. And a bottle of Sancerre between us. We had a lot to talk about besides the play: my trouble with Heartland and Amy's latest crisis over Zelda. Amy found a pill in Zelda's school blouse pocket when she was doing the laundry, and she was afraid it was either Ecstasy or a contraceptive. She couldn't decide which would be worse, but she didn't dare to ask the girl about it for fear of being accused of spying on her. She fished the pill, sealed inside an airmail envelope, out of her <u>great swollen</u> bladder of a handbag, and tipped it on to my side-plate for inspection. I said it looked like an Amplex tablet to me, and offered to suck it and see. I did, and it was. Amy was <u>hugely</u> relieved at first. Then she said, with a frown, 'Why is she worried about bad breath? She must be kissing boys'. I said 'Weren't you at her age?' She said 'Yes, but not with our tongues down each other's throats like they do now'. 'We used to' I said, 'it was called French kissing'. 'Well, you can get Aids from it nowadays' said Amy. I said I didn't think you could, though I don't really know. Then I told her about clause fourteen. She said it was <u>outrageous</u> and I should sack Jack ...

(*Source*: D. Lodge, *Therapy* (London:
Secker and Warburg 1995), p. 113.)

In addition to the involvement strategies discussed above, Text 5.6 also exhibits instances of affective (expressive) devices which are often labelled in the literature as *intensity markers*. As we have seen, in Labov's model, the evaluative category of intensifiers comprises a range of items from repetition and details to markers such as *certainly, really, very, absolutely*. The category of intensity markers is as a rule less embracing and covers only lexical elements that express the speaker's positioning, attitudes, emotions and degrees of certainty towards the proposition. In Quirk et al.'s (1985) terms intensity markers can be divided into the following three classes:

- emphasisers (also referred to as qualifiers: e.g. *certainly, mainly, only*)
- amplifiers (also referred to as quantifiers: e.g. *very, too, absolutely, extremely, completely*)
- downtoners or hedges (e.g. *rather, sort of, maybe*).

Intensity markers also include verbs, adjectives and adverbials that encode the speaker's emotions, feelings, moods and general dispositions. These can be classified as positive (e.g. *fortunate, amazing, happily, luckily, conveniently*) or negative (e.g. *shocked, sadly, alarmingly*) depending on the emotion encoded. Although the proliferation of terms may be confusing, what is important to remember is that intensity markers, when occurring in stories, are vital clues for the narrator's subjective orientation towards the message. Let us look at them more closely in the following extract from a personal letter:

Text 5.7
The big news is ... I might be moving to Minneapolis Minnesota! See, this is the situation: recently I have been in contact with an old ex-boyfriend. His name is Alan. He's the guy I broke up with while I was in Scotland. At any rate I had spoken with him maybe four times in the four years since then. Each time I saw/talked to him I was totally attracted to him. I saw him while I was at home at Christmas and I really felt passionate toward him (nothing happened between us because at that time we were both seeing other people). Anyway in the six months since then I spoke with him more regularly – once a month, once a week and eventually quite often. He's a PhD student at the University of Minnesota. So eventually he started asking me to come visit him in Minneapolis. Originally, I thought to myself 'It'll never happen', but as things with Kevin became apparent I came to the conclusion that I needed to make a decision ... So I decided to go to visit him for the first week of July. And it was absolutely wonderful. I felt totally head and heels in love. We spoke about all sorts of serious things like the M-word, religion, children etc. etc. He asked me to move to Minneapolis to live with him and I think I just might go! The real question is timing. It has all happened so fast that I can't believe it myself. My biggest reservation is leaving my job ...

(Source: Authors' data)

As can be seen, the narrator draws on a series of intensity markers to evaluate the tellable experience, which is her relationship with and feelings towards Alan (*big news, totally attracted, really passionate, totally heads and heels in love, all sorts of serious things*). At the same time, she highlights her emotional dilemma about leaving her job and going to live with Alan with quantifiers and hedges (*I just might go, the real question, all so fast, biggest reservation*). Furthermore, the intensification of the events narrated is put forward by verbs that denote feelings, thoughts and beliefs (*I thought to myself, came to the conclusion, decided, felt, I think, I can't believe*).

READER ACTIVITY

The following short narrative is from a film review. How do intensity markers contribute to the text's involvement strategies?

Text 5.8
On first meeting the gay writer Lytton Strachey during a visit to Vanessa Bell's south coast cottage in 1915, the virginal young painter Dora Carrington feels such antipathy that she decides to cut off his beard as he sleeps. His awakening however coincides with the sudden, secret awakening of her love for him; only later does she manage to convince Strachey to share a country home with her. Inevitably, given his preferences, the relationship is rarely untroubled, so that after a while both look elsewhere for sexual gratification; so deep is Carrington's love however that to the end she'll stay true to him in her fashion.

(*Source*: Geoff Andrew, *Time Out*, 13–20 December 1995)

Intensity markers are prototypically associated with the affective component of written discourse as more explicit cues. Compared to Tannen's categories of involvement strategies, they are more overt, less internalised ways of encoding attitudes and emotions (Tannen 1982a). Oral narratives as a rule draw more on involvement strategies which are deeply embedded in the narrative action and owe their emotive effects to the creation of drama, reminiscent of that in a play: the events are acted out on stage in front of the audience's eyes. Appropriately, the term used for such a narrative style is 'performance'.

5.3 NARRATIVE PERFORMANCES

The overall discourse style of performance is prototypically associated with oral narratives and their interactional dynamics. This involves the construction of highly dramatised and animated storytelling that calls forth special attention to the act of its expression and to its teller. From a psychological point of view, performance is an act of personal communication, of total engagement and emotional identification (Havelock 1982). At a linguistic level, it constitutes a form of verbal artistry. According to Bauman (1986, 1993), the essence of oral narrative performances is the storyteller's assumption of responsibility to display communicative skill and efficiency, thus creating a story which will sweep the audience off their feet.

Bauman also claimed that the specific set of devices for signalling performances is not fixed and predetermined but is expected to vary cross-culturally and needs to be discovered empirically. Each community conventionally makes use of a structured set of distinctive communicative means among its resources to key the performance features. However, certain features have been widely attested as an integral part of narrative performances. Some of them are found in Wolfson's (1979, 1982) list of performance features:

- expressive sounds and sound effects
- motions and gestures
- repetition
- direct speech
- historic present
- asides (the narrator's suspension of the action to explain what is going on behind the scenes).

We have already seen how these devices form part of Labov's evaluative categories and Tannen's involvement strategies.

Recurrent performance features in the narratives of numerous cultures include historic or narrative present and direct speech (frequently introduced by a verb in narrative present). In Chapter 4, we discussed how switches to narrative present contribute to a story's organisation by separating discourse units and events, in particular the pivotal or peak events. In this way, they set off and highlight the experientially significant moments of storytelling. Combined with the characters' animation of voices, tense shifts function as a means of abolishing the distance between the past taleworld and the immediate situation of telling. Conveying this sense of proximity has significant implications for the relation between teller and listeners: the teller is presented as recording the experiences as if they were happening at the moment of their telling and, by implication, the listeners become 'eyewitnesses' of the events.

READER ACTIVITY

Do you agree that the oral narratives used in this chapter draw more on performance devices than the written narratives? If yes, how would you account for this difference?

Narrative performances are not an all-or-nothing affair. Stories may exhibit rapid breakthroughs into performance or may constitute more sustained, fully-fledged performances. The latter are based on an orchestration of performance devices: sustained repetition patterns, repeated switches to narrative present, animation of voices accompanied by shifts in prosodics and imitation, numerous gestures, deictics which abolish the distance between the taleworld and the immediate storytelling situation (e.g. *now* for *then*, *this* for *that*) etc. In this way, a narrative becomes a kind of multi-media show of dramatic evocation combining visual and auditory resources.

READER ACTIVITY

Ask a friend to tell you a story on a specific topic and record it. Then, try and record a story that occurs spontaneously in a conversation. Are there any differences in their degree of performance? What, in your view, are the contextual features (e.g. setting, participants, themes, functions etc.) that favour narrative performances?

5.4 SUMMARY

Our discussion so far has introduced a rather long list of terms designed to capture the linguistic means by which discourse, narrative in particular, encodes subjectivity and realises its interpersonal functions. These terms are: evaluation devices, involvement features or strategies, intensity markers and performance devices. Evaluation and performance devices are to a major extent narrative-specific, since they have grown out of research on narrative structures and functions (for evaluation in non-narrative, see section 5.6). Involvement strategies and intensity markers have been applied to both narrative and non-narrative texts, sometimes with the aim of comparing different text-types (cf. Chafe's work on involvement).

The terms discussed here are only a small selection from a proliferation of terms in the relevant literature, for example affect keys, affect specifiers, loaded terms etc. (for a detailed discussion, see Caffi and Janney 1994). On numerous occasions, even the same term means different things within different paradigms. Involvement, for instance, has been used to refer to specific linguistic strategies, to speakers' preconditions (inner states) and to the effects of these strategies and states (i.e. 'metamessages' of rapport, shared feelings; again see Caffi and Janney 1994).

This profuse terminology is at times confusing and exasperating. The upshot, however, is that the topic of subjectivity in discourse, albeit over-looked and under-researched in the past, is currently at the heart of attention in various discourse analyses. There are already numerous unifying principles in the different, seemingly chaotic research strands. First, we have seen how certain devices are recurrent: for instance, repetition forms, narrative present and characters' (direct) speech and dialogues are well-established expressive devices in narrative. Second, we discussed the concept of context-dependence of expressive devices, mainly in relation to evaluation. Studies of involvement in particular have cast significant doubt on the cross-cultural validity and applicability of devices postulated for English discourse. It is nowadays apparent that the concepts of expressivity or subjectivity need to be relativised to be of use in cross-cultural investigations. Instead of being defined as lists of signs *a priori* of discourse analyses, they are linked to different discourse types and contexts (see Besnier 1994).

Third, all the different subjectivity concepts (e.g. evaluation, involvement, intensity) are not necessarily incompatible. They can be brought together by certain linguistic categories of subjective (i.e. emotive, expressive) communication. One such category is related to positive or negative orientation towards discourse. Biber and Finnegan's positive and negative affect markers are immediately classifiable as its instantiations. The same applies to Labov's external evaluation which encodes the narrator's explicit, positive or negative evaluation of events. Intensity is another dominant category of emotive communication: it is related to more or less intense orientations and is clearly the point of departure for intensity markers. There are numerous other categories (Caffi and Janney 1994: 340–2), among which is that of proximity.

Proximity is related to far/near orientations, the speaker's positioning towards the discourse and its participants. All discourse, narrative in particular, is capable of signalling different degrees of proximity to or distancing from its message and its participants. This is an indispensable means of encoding subjectivity. Most of the devices discussed in this chapter can be brought together through their function of signalling proximity. Chafe's involvement and detachment are nothing more than a scheme for capturing the linguistic means by which different degrees of proximity are marked in discourse. Proximity also underlies the use of narrative present, which owes its expressive function to its shift from the distant and reminiscing mode of the past tense to the proximal visualising (Fleischman 1990: 42) mode of the here and now of storytelling. In this mode, the narrator presents the events as if witnessed and experienced at the moment of their telling. The animation of characters' voices is also a means of signalling the abolition of distance between the taleworld and the immediate situation of telling. Combined with various intonational variations, it adds an auditory element to the visual mode of immediacy. We could argue that the essence of (oral) narrative performance devices is the signalling of proximity between the teller and the tale and, by implication, between teller, tale and audience. In this way, the displays of subjectivity are not overt and explicit but deeply embedded in the story's drama. In the discussion which follows, we will see how non-narrative discourse normally draws on devices which make explicit references to feelings and attitudes.

5.5 NON-NARRATIVE RHETORICAL PATTERNS AND FUNCTIONS
Narrative is an inescapably fundamental mode for encoding subjectivity, since it is the ideal site for registering and making sense of our experiences. We showed how this major function of subjectivity is realised by specific linguistic devices. These devices are well suited to the prototypical purposes of sharing experiences in narrative form. We tell stories to create or enhance intimacy and rapport with our interlocutors, to entertain, move and invite them to partake in our emotional life, to express and at the same time comprehend our personal, social and cultural reality. Proximity devices which dramatise and animate are favoured more for achieving these purposes.

On the basis of the fundamental definitional differences between narrative and non-narrative, we can expect the linguistic encodings of subjectivity to differ in non-narrative. The ways in which they will differ will correspond intelligibly with the non-narrative purposes of communication. The rhetoric of expressivity in non-narratives has been developed in accord with some basic concerns of their discourse. These concerns are the solution of a problem, the answer to a question, the identification of what really happens (instead of what might be the case) and the establishment of resemblances or contrasts. Their pursuit links fundamental non-narrative functions with general rhetorical patterns.

First, the structure and development of a non-narrative text may be based on the identification of a problem (that needs to be solved) and on the suggestion of a solution. For this function, one of the most prominent structures is the *Problem–Solution* pattern (Grimes 1975; van Dijk 1977; Hoey 1983). Characteristic types of Problem, according to Jordan (1984), include a deficiency or lack, something unusual or different, a break or failure, the need to know something, an aim or requirement, a decision or dilemma. This problem is the basic component of a *situation*: this comprises a general description of the conditions in which the problem arises. The suggested solution is usually accompanied by *evaluation*: this component deals with the assessment of how good or bad the solution is.

Hoey (1983) has suggested that these basic parts of the pattern can be identified in a text by asking the following questions: What was the situation? What happened? What was the response? What was the result? How successful was this? By applying this method to text 5.9 below, for instance, we find that the first paragraph states the problem, the second describes the solution and the third evaluates this solution.

Text 5.9

The post-war explosion in the use of detergents was a prime cause for the deteriorating condition of the Thames twenty-five years ago. Between 1951 and 1961, detergent use increased threefold. A tragic example of the results of this was when a man drowned because, though salvation was at hand, the would-be rescuers could not see him through the mass of foam.

The menace became so serious that in 1975 the Standing Committee on Synthetic Detergents held talks with government representatives, river authorities and manufacturers. Friendly persuasion was the order of the day, and it worked. Manufacturers voluntarily agreed to phase out 'hard' detergents in favour of biodegradable ones which could be broken down during sewage treatment.

A very marked improvement to the Thames, and some other rivers, swiftly came on the heels of this application of co-operative common sense. As we read in the next chapter, this has been by no means industry's only contribution to the river.

(*Source*: *The Living Thames* (London: Hutchinson, 1982))

The use of lexical items is another means of identifying the basic parts of the pattern, and, as such, an important signal used by the text-producer. For instance, in text 5.9, Problem is signalled by *deteriorating condition, tragic, menace*; Solution is indicated by *held talks, friendly persuasion*; and Evaluation is marked by *it worked, very marked improvement, swiftly*. Some other markers of the pattern's parts include words like *danger, difficulty, dilemma, problem, smelly, unpleasant, destroy, fear* for Problem; *advancement, completion, precaution, counteract, overcome, prevent* for Solution; and *confidence, failure, success, bad, excellent, quick, unique* for Evaluation (cf. Bäcklund 1988). The relation of the parts may also be made explicit by the use of discourse markers. For example, *but* may indicate that what follows is a negative evaluation of the solution suggested in the previous text.

In certain cases, only some of the components of the pattern may appear, allowing for a variation from the basic pattern. Further variation is based on the recursive application of parts like evaluation. For instance, a negative evaluation may constitute itself a signal of Problem (see Table 5.1, from Hoey 1983: 83):

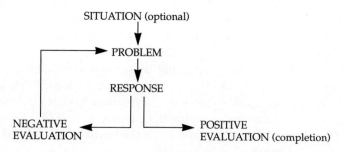

Table 5.1: Recursivity in the Problem–Solution pattern

Some variations of the pattern which make use of recursivity are: chained patterning, in which each Response results in a different Problem; spiral patterning, in which each Response leaves the same Problem unsolved; and progressive patterning, in which each Response solves part of the Problem but leaves another part of it unsolved (see Hoey 1983).

The Problem–Solution pattern is found in a range of texts with wide rhetorical functions. It plays a prominent role in the exposition parts of scientific or academic texts, which essentially address a need to be covered or a gap to be filled. It may also support the argumentation structure of a text, as for example in the case of advertisements, where a (real or imagined) problem is usually solved by the product:

Text 5.10
When a work of creation is gone, there is no way to bring it back.
We can never bring back the Carolina parakeet or any of those birds and animals that have vanished forever from the face of the earth.

The Japanese crested ibis, an elegant bird that used to be found in Japan, Korea and parts of China, is in danger of going the way the last Carolina parakeet went. It lives under the spectre of total extinction.

Should it vanish forever, it would be very sad indeed. But sadder still would it be, were we to be left with no records of it all.

And that's where Canon comes in. With Canon the Japanese crested ibis and all of wildlife can be recorded for posterity.

It would be a photographic heritage worthy to be handed down from generation to generation.

(*Source*: advertisement for Canon, 1981)

As in the following appeal for money, the Problem–Solution pattern is frequently employed as a device for enhancing a text's persuasive power:

Text 5.11

THE HUMAN FACE OF WAR TOUCHES US ALL

Hospitals operating without electricity. surgeons without anaesthetics; reports of up to 50 children a day dying due to disease, nutritional deficiencies and inadequate medical facilities … Whatever one's views on the war in the Gulf, it is impossible to remain unmoved by the scenes of destruction and civilian casualties brought about as a consequence of that conflict and its aftermath.

In an effort to alleviate this suffering, Medical Aid for Iraq has been launched. If you can help in any way, please fill out the coupon below, and return it to: … If you wish to offer help call our 24 hr ansaphone …

MEDICAL AID FOR IRAQ

(*Source*: magazine advertisement, 1991)

READER ACTIVITY

Try to analyse texts 5.10 and 5.11 by applying the Problem–Solution pattern. Why are some components missing and how are they replaced?

It must be noted here that the rhetorical pattern of Problem–Solution is built upon ideational acts and relations. First, the presentation of the Problem occurs quite commonly within the Problem–Solution pattern as a cause–consequence chain – note the lexical item *cause* that signals the upcoming problem in text 5.10. Second, a means–achievement relation may indicate a division between a Response and its specific Result – note, again, the relation between *persuasion* and *it worked* in 5.10. Besides ideational relations, the cohesive and thematic development patterns of a text are influenced by and interact with its division in parts of Problem, Solution etc. For instance, paragraph breaks, which we have found to define the limits of pronominalisation and thematic development patterns, may also be signals of component parts.

Two other culturally-accepted rhetorical patterns have been described for English (Hoey and Winter 1986). The Question–Answer pattern is typically found in sermons and is employed when an aspect of situation requires a verbal response. The Hypothetical–Real pattern is used when another person's view is first presented and then rejected or affirmed by the author. One of its most widely-found variants is the Denial–Correction pattern. This is frequently found in newspaper letters columns, where rejections of another's opinions or disclaimers are common. Its component parts include a Denial, followed by a Basis or a Correction (also optionally followed by a basis).

READER ACTIVITY

Identify the Denial–Correction pattern in the following letter. Is any part missing and how does this serve the rhetorical purposes of the text?

Text 5.12
I am quoted (Guardian, September 6) as saying – in a letter to staff – that the confidentiality of tax records might be at risk under government proposals to privatise key parts of the Inland Revenue. I said nothing of the sort.

That is annoying enough, but my main concern is that you repeat the frequent assertion made by the Inland Revenue Staff Federation that confidential tax data could be held or processed outside the UK. That is quite false.

The arrangements being made by the Inland Revenue for all its market testing and particularly for the selection of a strategic partner for handling information technology support of the department's business expressly forbid confidential and personal tax data being held or processed outside the UK.
Steve Matheson
Deputy Chairman, Board of Inland Revenue,
Somerset House, London WC2
(*Source*: *The Guardian*, 7 September 1992)

There are obvious parallels between the three patterns discussed so far. As Hoey and Winter (1986) point out, the basic parts of the three structures are parallel: a question or problem receives a response by another person. This response is denied or negatively evaluated. Subsequently, the author's response gives the final solution. This similarity underlies the fundamental common concern of all non-narrative texts to verify events and states of affairs, provide accurate information and state the norm. The three patterns may differ with regard to their underlying ideational relations. As Hoey (1986a) has observed, in the Question–Answer pattern, there is no cause–consequence or other logical relation holding between the component parts, in contrast to the Problem–Solution patterns.

Another major purpose in non-narrative discourse is to establish basic similarities or differences between two entities or categories. For this purpose, the simplest overall rhetorical pattern is Matching Contrast or Matching Compatibility, depending on whether the matched elements are contrasted or compared. We can see an instance of Matching Contrast in the following text:

Text 5.13
1982
Britain had just one major phone company, businesses faced huge phone bills and MERCURY was the stuff you got in a thermometer.
Well, 1982 was a bit of a dull year anyway.

1993
There are TWO major phone companies and Mercury is known by thousands of businesses, large and small, as the one who helped them REDUCE their phone bills.
Which makes 1993 much more exciting.
Mercury Communications
'Really jolly good'

(*Source*: newspaper advertisement, 1994).

This text's cohesive and thematic development patterns serve the signalling of the antithesis between the two parts of the text. Note also the use of discourse markers and typography (the original text was printed in two columns on two successive pages), as well as the articulation of ideational relations.

The rhetorical patterns discussed above can be viewed as large-scale extensions of elementary ideational acts, rhetorical relations and organisational devices. The Problem–Solution pattern is clearly related to the relation of Solutionhood, which organises ideational acts between clauses or sentences. The Question–Answer and the Hypothetical–Real pattern are an extension of prediction acts: the two patterns apply to whole texts while prediction acts apply to sections of texts. Finally, the two Matching patterns are systematic forms of parallelism used to structure a text from beginning to end (and not just in a section). In this way, rhetorical patterns meet macro-organisational demands and generalised functions.

Hoey (1983) views these patterns as culturally-approved configurations that simplify the reader's task in seeking a linear path through the non-linear network of discourse. We could add to this view that both this kind of rhetorical organisation and the network of the total set of relations (described in Chapter 4) are necessary to produce a coherent and rhetorically apt text. The significance of rhetorical patterns is that they override subject-matter boundaries and do not depend on substance configurations. Although they are more common in fields like science, they also occur in a large variety of texts (see Harris 1986). Their widespread use is indicative of their significance in serving non-narrative functions. A consequence of this is that components of the patterns play a vital role in the part–whole articulation of non-narrative texts and interact with their sequential relations. For instance, they correspond to non-narrative units (a narrative unit may coincide with the presentation of a problem or the evaluation of solution etc.).

5.6 EVALUATION IN NON-NARRATIVE DISCOURSE

As we have seen, research on the expressive or interpersonal functions of discourse is characterised by a proliferation of terms, most of which are employed in widely different ways within different paradigms. Evaluation is a classic example of this tendency. We have discussed in detail its role and forms in narrative discourse. In studies of non-narrative, it figures as a separate component part in the Problem–Solution pattern. Whereas the rest of the parts are concerned with facts, evaluation is concerned with the expression of opinions and of the evidence or the expert knowledge on which these opinions are based. As in studies of narrative texts, non-narrative evaluation is a concept with an interpersonal orientation: it encodes the speaker's or writer's stance towards the information presented, the participants and the communicative value of the discourse itself. Its expression attempts to create a shared point of view between addresser and addressee (Hunston 1994). In texts like book reviews or editorials, evaluation seems to concentrate in a separate section. This is, certainly, related to the function of the genre. In text 5.14, for instance, the final paragraph can be characterised as the text's evaluation section.

Text 5.14

FLORIDA SLUDGE

Good Intentions Joy Fielding (MacDonald, £12.95)

Joy Fielding's budding best seller is set in Delray Beach, Florida – a suburban paradise where the sun always shines, where career women put in long hours and their men sneak home at lunch-time to sleep with clients and secretaries.

In long summers of such discontent, divorce is rife. This book is littered with discarded wives and spurned husbands.

Lynn Schuster, a social worker (in this Florida, social workers have schedules, secretaries and the occasional posh lunch in town) is one such cheated woman. Distraught and confused she embarks on an affair with the handsome Marc. Their liaison is, however, complex: her husband and his wife have just run off together.

Meanwhile, Lynn's high-flying divorce lawyer, Reene, has a weight problem, an unfaithful husband problem, a wicked step-daughter and a suicidal sister – not to mention cruel and unloving parents.

<u>Fielding's attempts to incorporate the stifling nature of family ties and issues such as child abuse into the fast pace of the working woman's best seller is trite, to say the least. As a pulp novel this book hasn't enough thrills; as an attempt to deal with trauma and pressures of women's family lives, it is merely ridiculous.</u>

(*Source: The List*, 12–25 January 1990)

Book reviews like text 5.14 usually have a clearly-signalled discrete section of evaluation. However, as in narrative texts too, in most non-narrative texts, evaluation is spread out over long stretches in the whole of the text. In 5.14, for instance, the author of the book review expresses her attitudes and judgements by means of specific lexical choices in the purely descriptive section. These include items such as *budding, littered with* or the insertion of metacomments (*in this Florida …, not to mention …*).

In addition, evaluation may appear on an intermediate and a micro-level. It is in fact included in the list of ideational relations by approaches such as RST or Grimes's (1975) model. It also appears in the role of anaphoric nouns and prediction pairs. For instance, a retrospective label, in addition to encapsulating a previous stretch of discourse, may evaluate it, that is, express the text-producer's opinion on what is described in the stretch. Similarly, the predictive member of Report anticipates the evaluation of the reported opinion in the predicted part.

Hoey (1983) also concurs with the view that evaluation operates at a number of levels. He distinguishes between its function as an element in the overall discourse pattern (macro-level) and its role as an element at lower levels, including the sentence level. This latter function of evaluation is crucial to the effective function of a text as communication. At the sentence level, evaluation is typically expressed through the system of modality. Modality is responsible for expressing the text's orientation towards the participants and the proposition expressed. It concerns the assessment of certainty, probability, possibility of proposition and the degree of speaker (or writer) commitment. Halliday (1985a) has analysed the system of modality as the interaction of two pairs of choices: that between subjective and objective modality, on the one hand, and that between implicit and explicit modality, on the other. The two pairs of choices are realised through different selections of linguistic forms, as shown in the following:

subjective implicit: modal auxiliary: *a piece of evidence that <u>could</u> make a difference …*
modal verb: *which <u>appears</u> to be most successful …*

subjective explicit: subjective projecting clause: <u>*I'm sure*</u> *everybody here is interested …*

objective implicit: modal adjunct: <u>*Perhaps*</u>, *he was promoted because …*

	nominalised phrase: *Another factor is* <u>*the fact*</u> *that ...*
	likely to: *Nothing less than that is* <u>*likely*</u> *to serve the case ...*
objective explicit:	modal projecting clause: <u>*It is unlikely*</u> *that such data ...*
	objective projecting clause: <u>*His remarks do not suggest*</u> *that he has ...*
	reported projecting clause: <u>*Piaget showed that*</u> *children ·are ...*

(Notice that most of the above forms (e.g. *I'm sure, perhaps, likely*) would be classified as intensity markers in other paradigms.) In text 5.15 below, there is a gradual progression from subjective explicit (*I must say*) to objective implicit (*obviously*) and then back to subjective explicit (*I think*) in the first paragraph. The text is an extract from an interview with Clare Short MP; here, the interviewee answers the question of whether Mrs Thatcher has improved the position of women in Britain or not.

Text 5.15

1 The answer to that is both and I'll explain why both. 2 First of all I must say in all honesty that Mrs Thatcher's prime ministership laid to rest for ever the argument that women couldn't take tough decisions, that they couldn't be warriors, that they couldn't decide about war and peace. 3 Nobody will ever say that again. 4 Mrs Thatcher's obviously one of the toughest politicians in the post-war world. 5 On the other hand she did absolutely nothing for women. 6 She did nothing to help single mothers, she did nothing to help the many women who look after elderly patients because many of the support services were diminished in her time, and she did nothing to encourage women in politics because she had as the prime minister the ability to extend her hand to other able women, and it's quite notable that she didn't do so. 7 So I think the answer has to be that the scales rest evenly but if you're a woman in this country then she didn't do very much for you.

8 But finally I mean the real indictment of Mrs Thatcher is not that she didn't do anything for women I represent in the inner-city area you know poor women, black women. 9 The real indictment of her as a woman that supported other women is she'd achieved absolutely nothing for women in her party and she's one of the few post-war prime ministers who for most of her time had no women in her cabinet whatsoever. 10 I think the one woman she did have until she kicked her out was Baroness Young. 11 And when people complain about Major not appointing women what was he to do? 12 Mrs Thatcher had done nothing to help women even in her own party and I think in some ways that's the most telling comment on Mrs Thatcher as a supporter of other women.

(*Source*: Authors' data)

Modality is only one of the factors that contribute to non-narrative evaluation. Hunston (1994) has developed an elaborate model of analysing evaluation in non-narrative discourse by referring to a complex of factors. In her model, evaluation is seen as the interplay of three distinct functions, Status, Value and Relevance. Status concerns the degree of certainty and commitment towards the propositions expressed in the sentences and the ascribed source of the facts. It generally shows the speaker's or writer's perception of the relation between a specific proposition and the world. Four different elements compose Status:

- activity, referring to the activity described by the proposition, for example *assess, recommend, generalise, project, compare, interpret* etc.;
- source of the information: for example, is it the writer(s) or a citation from others? (text averral, in Sinclair's 1993 terms);
- modification, involving the use of modal verbs, report verbs (*show, report, suggest, find*) and metalinguistic labelling;
- certainty, namely whether the proposition is certain, known or possible. On the basis of these clues, each clause is assigned a Status.

In text 5.15, for instance, Status is conveyed through the progression from subjective to objective modality mentioned above and the concomitant variation of certainty (*I must say – obviously – absolutely nothing – I think – I mean – absolutely nothing – I think*). As a result, evaluation in the text as a whole is cumulatively assessed by the contribution of clauses with a certain Status.

Value is assigned on a scale of good–bad, which assesses the usefulness of a piece of information and encodes the text-producer's attitudes to it. It is not confined to a single sentence but arises from an accumulation of items over several sentences. In particular, a key item is shown to be gradually collecting positive or negative Value. In text 5.15, Value is based on the judgement of the effect of the policies *for women*. This central item accumulates a negative Value in the text passing from *she did absolutely nothing* to *she didn't do very much* and so on. According to Hunston (1994), Value operates on a paragraph level in contrast to Status, which changes from clause to clause. As a consequence, Value serves to bind a section together by referring to a single item.

Relevance shows the significance of the information given and is expressed through markers, at the beginnings or ends of units (typically coinciding with the beginnings or ends of paragraphs). Relevance markers are scaled from important to unimportant, and can be prospective or retrospective (i.e. cataphoric, pointing forwards, or anaphoric, pointing backwards). For instance, in text 5.15, Relevance is expressed by the prospective relevance marker *the real indictment* and the retrospective *the most telling comment*. Relevance markers overtly show the significance of stretches and provide information about the progression of discourse. Thus, they can be thought of as conveying the point in non-narrative texts.

This detailed analysis of evaluation in non-narrative texts points out that it is much more pervasive than is suggested by the Problem–Solution pattern. It occurs in all clauses or cumulatively across large sections of the text. We can note here that this renewed, more sophisticated view of non-narrative evaluation parallels the developments of research on narrative evaluation. The earlier conception of the notion as a discrete text unit has been replaced by a recognition of its pervasive character in both modes. The metaphor of the wave is particularly illuminating in showing this cumulative effect of evaluation. In fact, Halliday (1985a) has observed that the interpersonal function of language has prosodic or wave-like qualities.

READER ACTIVITY

Analyse text 5.16 in terms of non-narrative evaluation at both sentence and text level. How does evaluation relate to the overall structure of the text? Can you compare your findings with the role of evaluation in the following text?

Text 5.16
Why do I play without the score?
Alas, I started too late having the score in front of me at a concert, though I had long foreseen that this was what I should be doing. It is paradoxical to think that in times past when the repertoire was more limited and less complex, one did as a rule play with a score, a wise custom that was ended by Liszt. Today, rather than being filled with music, one's head is burdened by a useless wealth of information and risks tiring itself dangerously.

How childish and vain, what a source of useless work is this type of competition and feat of memory, when it should merely be a question of making good music that touches the listener! It is a poor routine where false glory takes precedence, as my dear professor, Heinrich Neuhaus, would say. The constant reminder of the score would allow less license for 'freedom', less scope for the performer's 'individuality'.

Without a doubt it is not so easy to be completely free when you have the score in front of you; it requires a lot of time, hard work and habit, hence the advantage of devoting oneself to this practice as early as possible. Here is some advice I would give freely to young pianists: adopt my healthy and natural method, and it will save us, the public, from being bored by the same programmes all through a pianist's life, and will allow pianists to create a richer and more varied musical life for themselves.

(*Source*: Sviatoslav Richter, programme notes, 2 June 1992)

Both the text-structuring role of evaluation and its specific realisations differ across non-narrative genres. This is related to the purposes of communication in each case. Evaluation, in general, varies according to the specific concerns of the text in question. In scientific language, there is a claim for objectivity and precision, which must be combined with the demands for persuasion. The use of implicit and explicit modality is one of the means employed to achieve this. Modality is in fact a means for encoding a text's *evidence* (or evidentiality). Evidence refers to attitudes and claims towards knowledge, to modes and sources of knowledge. It comprises devices which suggest the authority and validity of what is expressed. It constitutes one more category in our already long list of linguistic emotive categories (e.g. see involvement, intensity). Different languages employ different grammatical means in different degrees for the expression of evidence, according to their needs. In addition, as with all expressive devices, different genres may employ different evidential devices. Chafe and Nichols' (1986) study of evidence suggested that academic writing in English, as compared to casual conversation, is more concerned with reliability and deduction (i.e. certainty, objectively verified evidence) and less with belief (unverified evidence), sensory and hearsay evidence (what the speaker saw, heard or was told). Sensory and hearsay evidence have been found to be very important evidential resources in (oral) narratives. Characters' speech presentation is a major means of highlighting the source and authenticity of the teller's knowledge, thus strengthening its reliability, or of mitigating the teller's responsibility for and certainty about what is said (see papers in Hill and Irvine 1993).

In sum, the studies of non-narrative evaluation and evidence suggest that the linguistic choices involved are mainly associated with the categories of distancing, explicitness and involvement through verifiability and objective proof. At the risk of oversimplifying, we could argue that they belong to the opposite end of the continuum compared to the favourable choices in narrative: those, as we saw, were associated with proximity, implicitness and involvement through dramatisation. These differences are well suited to the defining characteristics and communication purposes of each mode. The establishment of generic truth, the objectivity of information presented and the concern with verifiability are essential in most non-narrative texts, in particular argumentative and academic texts. However, we also have to bear in mind that individual non-narrative (and narrative) texts use different patterns and devices to achieve evaluation, according to their specific purposes and other contextual parameters.

5.7 FUNCTIONS AND GENERIC STRUCTURE

So far, we have examined how specific devices serve the expressive or interpersonal functions in narrative and non-narrative. We have also noted the correspondence between these devices and various structural patterns: narrative evaluation for instance is part of a structural pattern (i.e. Labov's narrative structure) which is very different from that of non-narrative evaluation (i.e. Problem–Solution). Here, we will discuss instances of a closer fit between functions and structures. We will look at cases in which a text's purpose of communication and functions dictate certain organisational patterns. This close fit characterises the overall articulation of a text's part into a whole. In such cases, a text's success, efficiency and functionality seem to be judged by the degree of conformity to a specific generic pattern.

The most explicit illustration of this is the case of *iconic texts*, namely texts whose organisation and development closely correspond to or even reflect their content structure (what is described, presented etc.). We have already mentioned apartment layout descriptions and travel brochures. Other examples are biographical parts of obituaries, task-oriented dialogues (e.g. map-reading activities), simple descriptions of an instrument's parts, or biographies like text 5.17.

Text 5.17

Born in Brieg, Silesia, in 1927, Mr Masur studied piano, composition and conducting at the Music College of Leipzig. Upon graduation, he served as an orchestra coach at the Halle County Theater, and later as kapellmeister of the Erfurt and Leipzig Opera Theaters. He accepted his first major orchestral appointment in 1955, as conductor of the Dresden Philharmonic, and in 1958 he returned to opera as general director of music at the Mecklenburg State Theater of Schwerin. From 1960 to 1964, he was appointed the Dresden philharmonic's chief conductor, a post he held until 1972. A professor at the Leipzig Academy of music since 1975, Mr Masur holds honorary degrees from Yale University, the Manhattan School of Music, Leipzig University, the University of Michigan, the Cleveland Institute of Music, Westminster Choir College and Hamilton College.

(*Source*: programme notes, 15 June 1995)

The text above illustrates the close fit between the articulation of content (here, the succession of appointments in Kurt Masur's career) and expression that is characteristic of iconic texts. The text's structure is based on the interaction of an identity chain (*Mr Masur ... he ...*) with a time chain (*in 1927 ... upon graduation ... in 1955 ...*). The pattern of thematic progression also reflects this fit (notice the sentence positions for the members of the participant and time reference chains).

All iconic texts are characterised by this correspondence between what is described (or the articulation of the knowledge base) and the way in which this is done. As a result, every iconic text has a unique pattern to match its content and, by implication, its function. As we saw above, cohesive and other organisational properties follow from this unique pattern.

READER ACTIVITY

How do the cohesive and other organisational patterns in the following text serve its purpose? Are there any cultural or other context constraints that contribute to the text's overall structure?

Text 5.18
Heat up a litre of broth made traditionally or with 1¼ chicken stock cubes. In another saucepan, melt some unsalted butter. Chop a small onion or some shallots finely and fry it lightly in the butter. (You can leave out the onion if you prefer.) Add the rice – about 10 fistfuls for 4 people, stir, add some white wine and stir. When this has all been absorbed start to add the broth a little at a time.

Instructions and other procedural texts also fall into the category of iconic texts, since their basic method of development matches a specific order in the structure of things described. In their case, however, this order is not inherent in the described entities but prescribed by the author or the text-producer. The structure of recipes like text 5.18, for example, is not dictated by the ingredients. Instead, it relates an order of events, as these are prescribed by the writer. Of course, these are ultimately dependent on cultural conventions, for example of what is known to a community of people and what should be explicitly described (cf. Prince 1981). Further-more, the presentation of a recipe depends on certain conventional assump-tions: the ingredients section precedes the instructions section, a temporal succession is followed, certain cohesive patterns are observed etc. What is tellable thus depends on what is usually told.

For the majority of non-narrative texts, the fit between organisational patterns and functions depends less on the articulation of content and more on conventions of presentation. These conventions, which form a part of a speaker's everyday repertoire, constitute the basic characteristics of each genre. Hasan talks of the 'Generic Structure Potential', which is part of a speaker's knowledge of some language (Halliday and Hasan 1985). This is a different configuration of optional and obligatory elements of structure for each genre. Everyday service encounters are a particularly good example of a conventional generic pattern. For instance, text 5.19 can be analysed in terms of corresponding speech acts or 'moves':

Text 5.19

Seller:	Good morning, Mrs Reid.	
Customer:	Good morning, Bob.	Greeting
	Can I have a couple of apples?	Sale Request
Seller:	Is that all today?	
Customer:	Yes, thank you.	Sale Compliance

Seller:	Sixty cents.	Sale
Customer:	Here y'are.	Purchase
Seller:	Thank you.	Purchase Closure
	Goo'day.	Finis: End
Customer:	'Bye.	

(*Source*: Halliday and Hasan 1985: 65)

The full repertoire of moves also includes Sale Initiation (e.g. *who's next? I think I am*).

READER ACTIVITY

Which are the optional and which the obligatory moves in the structure of service encounters? Is there a minimal structure, and how does this correspond to the functions of communication?

As expected, the minimal structure of a service encounter revolves around Sale and Purchase, which is the point of the exchange. However, as we saw in Chapter 2, there are numerous contextual variations from such structures. In Chapter 2, we also saw another example of everyday transaction with a fairly definite match of functions with patterns, namely telephone conversations. Schegloff (1968) has distinguished the following stages in telephone exchanges: a summons–answer sequence, an identification sequence, a greeting sequence, a how-are-you sequence, a purpose of call sequence. Again, the minimal structure here, which corresponds to the basic functions of telephone conversation, can be extended into variants, depending on the context of communication. The conventionality of generic patterns accounts for their being the site of cultural differences. It also accounts for their exploitation for humorous purposes (think of all the TV gags based on the telephone) as well as for the fact that they are less susceptible to change than other aspects of language.

Generic patterns are not restricted to everyday communication. Specialised discourse is also rigorously patterned by conventional generic configurations. It is particularly significant that discourse function is also closely related to structure in these texts. Thus, Swales (1990) observes that categories of structure in academic article introductions are firmly embedded within the localised field of the researcher's previous work. His model posits a number of categories involved in creating a research space for the writer (from which the acronym of the model CARS). These categories can be seen in Table 5.2:

> Move 1:   Establishing a territory
>   Step 1: Claiming centrality and/or
>   Step 2: Making topic generalisation(s) and/or

	Step 3: Reviewing items of previous research
Move 2:	Establishing a niche
	Step 1A: Counter-claiming or
	Step 1B: Indicating a gap or
	Step 1C: Question-raising or
	Step 1D: Continuing a tradition
Move 3:	Occupying the niche
	Step 1A: Outlining purposes or
	Step 1B: Announcing present research
	Step 2: Announcing principal findings
	Step 3: Indicating RA structure

Table 5.2: Structure of research article introductions

According to Swales, the progression from one move and step to the next is characterised by increasing explicitness and a weakening of knowledge claims on the part of the author. This conventional pattern is the product of various formal schemata. Again, the different academic traditions account for the range of structural differences found in academic texts (Clyne 1981, 1987; Hinds 1987).

FURTHER READING

The best descriptions of tropes are, as expected, to be found in studies of literary texts. A useful introduction to the linguistic aspects of these and other literary devices is Leech and Short (1981).

For the use of intensity markers in spoken vs written discourse, see Biber (1986) and Chafe (1985), according to whom not all intensity markers are more typical of written discourse. Gratuitous markers such as *just, really* etc, are more frequent in oral texts.

There are several extant taxonomies of reported speech (e.g. Genette 1988; Short 1989). The most recent comprehensive study is Fludernik (1994), combining work on literary texts with discourse analysis-oriented views. Coulmas (1986) is the standard point of reference for work on reported speech. Research has been concerned with the syntactic forms of reported speech (e.g. Tannen 1989; Yule and Mathis 1992; Mathis and Yule 1994) as well as with its interaction with contextual parameters (e.g. Goodwin 1990; Johnstone 1990) in narratives. Less attention has been directed to the use of reported speech in non-narrative discourse. Tannen's work on constructed dialogue in conversational contexts (1986, 1989) is the exception, which brought forward a change of balance. Studies of speech representation in different contexts include Caldas-Coulthard (1994) for news discourse, Slembrouck (1992) for the Parliament versions of proceedings, Ely et al. (1995) for everyday dinnertime conversations and Baynham (1996) for class-room discourse.

For evaluative categories in children's narratives, additional studies include Kernan (1977), Umiker-Sebeok (1979), Hicks (1990, 1991), Bamberg and Damrad-Frye (1991) and Hudson and Shapiro (1991).

Apart from the classic and detailed Swales (1990), the most up-to-date reference on the analysis of generic patterns is Dudley-Evans (1994). A detailed analysis of the structure of service encounters is Ventola (1987). Many specific applications of this type of analysis can be found in the ELR *Journal*.

Evidence for the cross-linguistic use of patterns in non-narrative discourse comes from an interdisciplinary framework involving language typology, contrastive rhetoric, interlinguistic communicative analysis and composition studies. General descriptions of the complex area of contrastive studies are Houghton and Hoey (1983) and Leki (1991). Two of the most influential paradigms include Kaplan's hypothesis (1983) on the difference of rhetorical contexts and Hartmann's (1980) model of Contrastive Textology.

The best description of the Problem–Solution and other rhetorical patterns is given in Hoey (1983), where further references can be found. Particularly good for the analysis of a wide range of texts is Jordan (1984).

For non-narrative evaluation, there are only a number of specialised articles by genre such as Myers (1989), Thompson and Ye (1991) and Hunston (1993).

Narrative and Non-narrative in Interaction

6.1 CONTEXTS OF INTERACTION

In Chapter 2, we suggested that discourse types lack clear-cut boundaries. They are, instead, dynamic, shifting and mutually influencing. As early as 1929, Bakhtin, a Russian semiotician and literary theorist, drew attention to the ability of discourse to juxtapose language drawn from and invoking linguistic environments of different kinds. This dynamic juxtaposition creates a dialogue of genres, a polyphony of voices (e.g. styles, registers, dialects). The dialogic quality of language, 'heteroglossia' in Bakhtin's terms, is evident at different levels in everyday discourse, including the constant interaction between narrative and non-narrative modes.

In a variety of contexts, the narrative mode precedes, succeeds or is intertwined with the non-narrative mode. Switches from narrative to non-narrative and vice versa constitute an indispensable component of interaction. The two modes constantly intermingle in speech events ranging from TV talk shows, radio phone-ins and conversations to films, news articles and advertisements. In addition, as already seen, any piece of narrative discourse presents embedded non-narrative statements such as descriptions, general orientation, evaluation of events, commentary etc. These parts, as a rule, do not encode events or move the plot forwards. As such, they cannot be considered 'narrative', in the Labovian definition of the term. Their function is to add to the backbone or skeleton of a story's narrative clauses in various ways. In particular, they may complement or highlight the narrative parts, pointing to their relative importance, or they may encode the narrator's subjective stance towards them. The amount of non-narrative utterances embedded in a narrative is not fixed or predetermined. It relates to the overall design of the narrative as planned by individual storytellers. This design may involve the play between suspense and plot forwarding, the amount of interference and background information, the degree of explicitness in the story etc. There is usually a trade-off between 'telling' or explicating narrative action in non-narrative ways and creating a performed and dramatised 'showing' of the events through uninterrupted narrative action.

Contextual factors play a vital role in such choices. Certain environments and cultures favour minimal interruptions of the narrative action, while others present a more systematic intermingling of the two. In numerous cases, storytelling gradually leads to a generalising non-narrative discourse which explicitly puts forward moral conclusions, statements and comparisons.

The opposite is also a common strategy, namely the embedding of narratives in non-narratives. Notice, for instance, the following extract from a recent sociolinguistic book on intercultural communication.

Text 6.1

'Key' is a term borrowed from music to refer to the tone or the mood of a communication. A businesswoman the authors knew once took her young daughter with her to a business meeting. She had told her daughter that they were going to attend a meeting and that she would have to be quiet and behave herself. As it had turned out the meeting had developed a very relaxed key and there was much free conversation and laughing. Afterwards the child said to her mother: 'That wasn't a meeting; it was a party'. When she was asked why she said that, her answer was that meetings were to be serious and parties were for laughing. This young child had understood a significant aspect of two typical speech situations in our culture: that a business meeting and a party normally differ in key.

One very interesting aspect of professional communication, especially when it occurs in an international environment, is that there is so much variability across cultural groups in their expectations about key and about how and when different keys should be expressed. ...

(*Source*: Scollon and Scollon 1995: 26)

An academic book is expected to be an instance of non-narrative discourse. However, as we can see from text 6.1, the non-narrative mode of scientific exposition may be interspersed with narratives with a view to strengthening the effect of the exposition. The story above serves to support the view that our expectations about the key of a situation are culturally determined. In a way similar to the use of stories in conversations, the story owes its effect to the sense of immediacy, involvement and personal perspective. The participation framework invoked also plays a crucial function: the scientific information is nicely couched in a child's voice. (The child is the author, in Goffman's terms.) This is a potentially powerful bid for the readers' immediate support for the view held. The child's voice is more difficult to resist in emotional terms than a rationally-formed statement. In addition, it is more effective in presenting the view as self-evidently true: even a child exhibits a metalinguistic awareness of 'key' in communication. As we will see in the following discussion, narratives are powerful forms of asserting views, shielded from proof, justification, testing and debate.

READER ACTIVITY

How does text 6.1 compare with the following short narrative that opens Stephen Hawking's best-seller *A Brief History of Time*? What is in your view the effect of the interaction between narrative and non-narrative at the opening of this popular scientific book?

Text 6.2

A well-known scientist (some say it was Bertrand Russell) once gave a public lecture on astronomy. He described how the earth orbits around the centre of a vast collection of stars called our galaxy. At the end of the lecture, a little old lady at the back of the room got up and said: 'What you have told us is rubbish. The world is really a flat plate supported on the back of a giant tortoise.' The scientist gave a superior smile before replying, 'What is the tortoise standing on?' 'You're very clever, young man, very clever', said the old lady. 'But it's turtles all the way down!'

Most people would find the picture of our universe as an infinite tower of tortoises rather ridiculous, but why do we think we know better? What do we know about the universe, and how do we know it? Where did the universe come from, and where is it going? Did the universe have a beginning, and if so, what happened *before* then? What is the nature of time? Will it ever come to an end? Recent breakthroughs in physics, made possible in part by fantastic new technologies, suggest answers to some of these longstanding questions. Someday these answers may seem as obvious to us as the earth orbiting the sun – or perhaps as ridiculous as a tower of tortoises. Only time (whatever that may be) will tell.

(*Source*: Stephen Hawking, *A Brief History of Time*
(London: Bantam Books, 1988, pp.1–2)

It can generally be suggested that the intermingling of narrative and non-narrative is not unmotivated but serves strategic purposes. Apart from individual cases such as texts 6.1 and 6.2, we can verify this by looking in a more systematic way into two of the basic contexts of interaction, conversation and news discourse. Conversation has been primarily analysed as non-narrative discourse, mainly consisting of two- (or three-)part exchanges geared towards the exchange of information rather than the retelling of past events. However, conversations are interspersed with longer one-part contributions, the most frequent of which involve storytelling (almost all the oral stories used for exemplification and activities in this book are in fact conversational stories). Narratives in conversations can be thought of as long turns that provide tellers with strong floor-holding rights. As devices fitted into the turn-taking system, they interact with previous and following turns. The realm of conversation does not only shape a story's discourse but also motivates the roles and purposes of telling the story. As a result, narrative and non-narrative in conversation cannot be viewed as two separate and compartmentalised parts.

One of the main uses of conversational narratives is in supporting an argument. As we saw in Chapter 2, the participation frameworks and perspective-taking which stories invoke make them particularly powerful as devices for putting forth views and reinforcing arguments. Through dramatisation and vividness, narratives are capable of compelling belief in various views with minimal risk of argumentative challenges and truth-claims based on testing and debate. Persuasiveness and credibility derive from the overall experiential immediacy which targets the audience's emotions and deters their critical responses (see Witten 1993: 100). An example of a story in support of an argument is provided by text 5.4, a story jointly told by a Jewish couple and collected by Schiffrin (1990). The story essentially puts forward the position that differences between ethnic groups are a cause of trouble for cross-cultural relationships. The end of the story is a disclaimer by the main character: *But he's different! I'm not used t' Gentile boys,* which is highlighted by the storyteller: *That cured her! She'd never go out with one again!* Schiffrin (1990) suggested that in the specific conversational setting the story contextualises and provides the framework for a position that the couple further develop and support in the subsequent conversation. In Schiffrin's words, Jan (the main storyteller) 'tells her story in a way which not only presents Beth's [the character's] experience as a confirmation of her own view, but also allows Beth to actually present Jan's very own views – but in her own individual words' (251). The truth-claims of the story are subtle and embedded in the experienced events; thus, it is more difficult to be objected to.

As we have seen, the roles and functions of stories in conversation are manifold and are not restricted to lending additional authority to an argument. Other functions of conversational narratives include the enhancement of the tellers' conversational profile or their self-exposure, the strengthening of the bonds with the other interlocutors, the exercising of power, the reaffirmation or questioning of culturally-sanctioned values and attitudes, the therapeutic or entertaining sharing, analysing and comprehending of personal experiences etc. In all these functions, stories are *locally occasioned* in their conversational environments, that is, well suited to the needs and parameters of their context, including the sequential organisation of conversation. In other words, every conversational story owes its point to elements of the conversational context.

The ways in which stories are embedded in conversations have been extensively analysed (e.g. see Jefferson 1978). The degree of explicitness in the stories' prefacing and conclusion, the two points of entry into and exit from conversation, is situationally and culturally variable. The expression of the intention to tell a story also exhibits various degrees of explicitness. It can be formulated as a question or an abstract, or appear as a rapid passage into the story at a transition relevance place. Remember that our familiar story about Dan's cooking disaster (text 3.3) started off without an explicit abstract, at a transition relevance place, in which the teller linked her story with the conversational topic, 'spices':

> Nadia: How long do you keep your spices for?
> Alexandra: I don't know. Six months?
> Nadia: Ah, that's fine. After that. 'Cos your mum ((turning to Alex)) had kept some spices ...

All these cases of entry into a story are conditionally relevant on prior turns. Once a teller announces an intention to embark on a story, audience responses are also variable. In certain cases, storytelling can be cancelled just before it starts, due to an explicit audience reaction (e.g. *you've already told me, I've heard that one before*) or an implicit reluctance to grant the storyteller the floor for a long turn. More frequently, the audience goes along with the storytelling act, offering a variable amount of contributions. These may range from verbal and non-verbal back-channelling signals to more lengthy contributions, interruptions and even explicit challenges to the storytelling, depending on culture conventions. Different cultures place different emphasis on joint storytelling; in certain cultures, storytelling appears to be a norm-governed and ritual activity during which interruptions are normally absent. In other cases, audience participation can lead to joint storytelling or co-narration.

The ending of a narrative may be followed by verbal or paralinguistic signals of acceptance, or may trigger another narrative or a series of narratives. These second or third narratives are methodically introduced into the turn-taking system as follow-ups of the type 'that reminds me of what happened ...'. Their functions can be to re-emphasise and elaborate on the point already made or to challenge and disagree with it.

On the whole, conversations are a case of dynamic and shifting interaction of dialogic and/or monologic narratives with monologic and/or dialogic non-narrative texts. Non-narrative is normally realised in the form of snappy conversational turns. However, longer floor-holding turns are also found in argumentation, serving the elaboration of a point (as we have just seen, some of them are examples of narrative discourse). Both narrative and non-narrative turns are complementary means for establishing common information or presenting and supporting a position. In principle, due to the floor-holding rights, it is more difficult for the audience to raise a challenge to a story on-line, as is the case in the turn-by-turn construction of arguments. Nonetheless, both narrative and non-narrative ultimately depend on the audience's participation for putting forth their point.

News discourse is another instance of the interaction between the narrative and the non-narrative mode. Cross-linguistic research has suggested that the degree to which news discourse makes use of narrative is variable.

In principle, the narrative function should be dominant, since news is about something that happened in the past. However, news communication is also concerned with providing background information – especially in newspapers, now that the TV holds sway in breaking the news first. This tension between narrative and non-narrative elements was present even in the earliest forms of news discourse. For instance, street ballads of the eighteenth century, which were used as sources of news, contained a mixture of authentic events and fictionalised supernatural disasters. Pamphlets of the same age also showed a similar tension between real events and fiction.

READER ACTIVITY

Can the following text be identified as a narrative? Are there any non-narrative characteristics? Is there evidence to suggest one or more shifts between the two modes?

Text 6.3
End of the world is apparently not nigh
James Meek in Kiev

There was a great voice, as of a trumpet. And it was a trumpet. Just not the last trumpet. It came from a loudspeaker innocently broadcasting Ukrainian radio in the park on St Vladimir's Hill.

A little further, on Three Prelates Street – close now to the focal point of the end of the world – were four beasts. As foretold in the Book of Revelation, they were full of eyes before but not behind. They looked like stray dogs.

Coming out onto Bohdan Khmelnitskiy Square, dominated by the bell tower of St Sophia's Cathedral, fact seemed to be cleaving to the prophecy.

There was a great multitude of all nations and kindreds, and people and tongues. A great multitude of journalists. A number had cameras trained on the cathedral.

But there was silence in heaven for half an hour (Revelation viii, 1). Then another half an hour. And another.

And not just one, but everyone, was asking: 'What are these which are arrayed in white robes? And whence came they?' (Revelation vii, 13).

The question in Kiev yesterday was not so much whence came the Great White Brotherhood but whither they went. The sun rose and set on the day of prophesied apocalypse, a day with a noticeable absence of earthquakes, seas of blood, last judgements, messianic violence or mass suicide.

With 800 suspected adherents detained by police, their godhead, Maria Devi Christos, in prison after a scuffle in the cathedral on Wednesday and their chief ideologist, Yuri Krivonogov, facing a long jail sentence, the Brotherhood was clearly a spent force by the time the end of the world was due.

It was not clear whether any genuine members risked showing their faces yesterday. Three people were arrested, including a woman who gathered a throng of cameras and tape recorders when she began to explain that she had been expelled from the Brotherhood.

She was snatched by police before she could explain why the world had not ended.

Apart from journalists, the crowd of several hundred was made up of thrill-seekers and Sunday strollers.

Vadim Castelli, a film director now putting the finishing touches to his second feature, The Hunt for the Hetman's God, said: 'I had to be here to decide whether to bother organising the premiere or not'.

Wandering to and fro were relatives of sect members. Sergei Donin, aged 33, came to Kiev from the Rostov region of Russia hoping to find his sister. She joined the Brotherhood a year ago. The family has not heard from her since April.

'If I could see her maybe I could persuade her to come back. but nobody knows where she is', he said.

(*Source*: *The Guardian*, 15 November 1993)

The same blurring of fact and fiction can be found today, especially in popular newspapers or some TV news bulletins, where it is sometimes difficult to distinguish between representations of real and imaginary events. This extensive interaction of the narrative and non-narrative modes is allowed by the generic pattern of news discourse. In van Dijk's research, the typical structural categories of a news article are a mixing of narrative and non-narrative parts, as can be seen in Table 6.1.

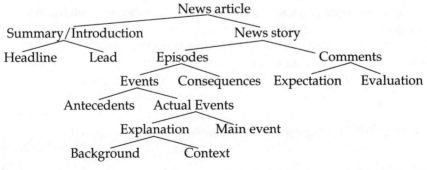

Table 6.1: Generic structure of news article (adapted from van Dijk 1987c: 39)

A typical news article is divided into an introductory section, containing the headline and the lead (*by our correspondent* etc.), and the main news story. The latter consists of a description of events and a commentary on them which predicts what is going to happen next and/or evaluates what happened. The main event section combines a description of what happened with the broader circumstances, namely the antecedents and consequences of events and a possible explanation involving a general background and a more immediate context. The main event part is the core narrative section and the parts of explanation and comment are the usual places of non-narrative exposition. One of the main formal characteristics of the news article is the absence of explicit connectives that allows for the constituent parts to be easily deleted or rearranged. As a result, topics are cyclical or non-progressive; they are made to recur with growing specificity of detail (van Dijk 1987c).

READER ACTIVITY

Can you now analyse text 6.3 in terms of the generic structural pattern described above? What is the order and interaction of narrative and non-narrative constituent parts?

Although the generic pattern of news discourse may stay constant across languages and cultures, the degree of interaction between narrative and non-narrative in it is culturally variable. News reports can be dominated by storytelling tendencies and show affinity with everyday stories. This seems to be the case with Polish and German news reports, according to Duszak (1995), by contrast to American news reports, which draw more on non-narrative discourse.

Considering its overall contexts of occurrence, it seems natural that news discourse should provide an example of interaction between the two modes. Newspapers, for instance, are prominent sites of heteroglossia in that they accommodate a continuum of genres with no clear boundaries. The same is true of the radio or TV context, in which classical stories succeed live reports, and documentaries appear between a stream of advertisements and talk shows. Many of these individual discourse types such as ads are prototypes of heteroglossia, drawing on both narrative and non-narrative resources to make their point (see Cook 1992).

READER ACTIVITY

Consider the interaction of narrative and non-narrative in the following advertisement (public warning) from London Underground. How successful is the use of each mode in increasing the impact of the text?

Text 6.4
A victim's tale
Tuesday

It's difficult to talk about. No one knows what I feel like.
I'd gone into town to pick up a few holiday things.
I really shouldn't have taken the extra cash with me. It was all so fast. I didn't feel anything.
I opened the handbag for a minute. Looked again and the purse was gone.
I'm usually so careful. I can't blame anyone.
Now the holidays won't be the same.

Don't lose out to pickpockets. Keep valuables out of sight. Never carry a wallet or a purse in a back pocket. Keep handbags shut and held in front of you.

The interaction between the two modes extends to the employment of a dynamic mixing of both even in traditional strongholds of one or the other. This mainly applies to narrative discourse in non-narrative domains. Narratives increasingly emerge as ways of challenging the status of knowledge and the epistemological principles of other discourses or, in other words, as alternative ways of analysing and understanding the world. As such, they are recognised as valid voices of disenfranchised groups with restricted access to dominant discourses. For instance, feminist and critical discourse theorists advocate the introduction of personal storytelling into non-narrative domains involving the abstract, analytic form of legal arguments. Their claim is that the use of stories, for example by victimised women in cases of rape, helps to illuminate issues that would otherwise be obscured in a narrow legal context (see papers in Mumby 1993).

The vital role of narrative in combination with non-narrative discourse is also recognised in institutional settings. In medical environments, patients' stories have been found to play a critical role among standard diagnostic criteria. More generally, the narrative construction of illness is a principal way of knowing in medicine (Hunter 1991). Storytelling has also become the focus of research on power relations in professional settings. The recounting of narratives is seen as a powerful form of talk for the imaging of hierarchi-

cal relations at work, the culture of obedience and the parameters and oblig-
ations of employees' roles (Witten 1993).

Finally, it has been argued that the construction of scientific discourse
depends on the exploitation of narrative along with non-narrative resources
in a variety of ways. Not only science popularisations but also all kinds of
research articles rely on narratives for illustration of exposition (see text 6.1).
The range of narrative techniques employed and the related textual patterns
ultimately construct varying views of science (Myers 1994).

6.2 BETWEEN NARRATIVE AND NON-NARRATIVE: NON-PATTERNED DISCOURSE

In the above discussion, we have shown how narrative and non-narrative
fuse or interact with each other in discourse practices. There is, however, a
number of texts that share characteristics of both modes but do not exhibit
structural elements of either. These are, lists (menus, shopping lists etc.), or
list-like texts such as statutes, enumerations of people, things and events in
conversations etc. This large number of texts, which constitute an important
part of our everyday activities, presents a simple, rudimentary concatena-
tion of discourse entities, thus lacking in patterning. Interestingly enough,
list-like discourse is at least as old as narrative discourse: think of the long
descriptions in Homer's *The Iliad* and other ancient epic texts or the lists of
genealogies in the Old Testament. From a developmental point of view, it
also seems to be one of the first stages in a child's acquisition of discourse.

READER ACTIVITY

Can you characterise the following text as narrative or non-narrative?
If not, what would be the necessary changes that you would have to
make in order to turn it into a text belonging to one or the other mode?

Text 6.5
Celebration Menu
Penne alla Arabbiata
OR
Avocado and Prawns
OR
Melon
OR
Minestrone
–
Filetto Farfalla
OR
Grilled Trout

OR
Veal alla Crema
OR
Chicken Romana
–
Sweets from Trolley
–
Coffee

As we have seen, both narrative and non-narrative texts have developed (iconic or not, more or less conventionalised) patterns related to their basic functions and concerns (expression of affect, solution of a problem etc.). Lists and list-like texts, instead, show a flat, non-patterned structure with no elaborate organisation or extensive text relations. At the same time, as Schiffrin (1994b) observes, list-like texts in conversation exhibit similarities with both narrative and non-narrative texts. On the one hand, they occupy an extended turn at talking and are seen primarily as the responsibility of a single speaker. They are also composed of relatively long sequences of structurally simple clauses, reminiscent of narrative clauses. On the other hand, list-like texts also exhibit similarities to non-narrative discourse: they are not organised around a temporal succession of events and they do not foreground evaluation. However, there is a defining difference between lists and the two fundamental modes of discourse. It is the difference between telling about an experience, describing a fact or stating an argument and telling about the organisation of a category such as a menu, items for shopping etc.

This function of lists accounts for the fact that they are built around entities and, linguistically speaking, nominal phrases. Non-patterned discourse thus constitutes an extension of simple repetitive structures characterised by parallelism. The basic text relations are matching contrast or matching compatibility, as we can see in text 6.6, an extract from an interview (A is the interviewer and B the interviewee):

Text 6.6
A: Racing's big around here, isn't it?
B: Yeh.
A: Yeh.
B: Well, you got uh, Jersey.
You got ... Monmouth
and you got Garden State.
Y' got Atlantic City.
A: Mhm.
B: And then uh here you got Liberty Bell.
And they're building a new one up in Neshaminy.

A: That's right. I've never seen that, though.

B: And uh … you got Delaware.
     And of course, if you want to re– be– really go at it you can go up
     to New York.=

A: Mhm.

B: =You got Aquaduct
     and you got Saratoga
     and you have that Belmont y' know
     I mean like uh …

(*Source*: Schiffrin 1994b: 397)

In text 6.6, the category of racetracks is equally organised through repetition (*you got … you got …*) and innovation (*they're building … you can go up to …*). The syntax and discourse order are also significant. As Schiffrin (1994b) notes, the order of items is iconic: the names of the race tracks (Monmouth, Garden State, Atlantic City …) are introduced after the names of the four places in which they are found (New Jersey, here, Delaware and New York). Repetition, innovation and order are the devices characteristically manipulated in list-like texts.

Hoey (1986b) studied a much larger set of similar text-types (including encyclopaedias, dictionaries, cookery books etc.), which he called colonies. According to his basic definition, colonies are discourses 'whose component parts do not derive their meaning from the sequence in which they are placed' (1986b: 4). Colonies share a number of characteristics, as seen in Table 6.2:

1. Meaning is not derived from sequence
2. Adjacent units do not form a continuous prose
3. There is a framing context
4. There is no single author and/or the author is anonymous
5. One component may be used without referring to the others
6. Components may be reprinted or reused in subsequent works
7. Components may be added, removed or altered
8. Many of the components serve the same function
9. They show alphabetic, numeric or temporal sequencing

Table 6.2: Characteristics of non-patterned texts (adapted from Hoey 1986b: 4)

READER ACTIVITY

Characterise the following types of discourse according to the characteristics in Table 6.2 by ticking the appropriate column as shown. Which of these are non-patterned?

	1	2	3	4	5	6	7	8	9
dictionary	+	+	+	+	+				
telephone directory	+	+	+	+					
address book	+	+	+	?					
shopping list	+	+	−						
academic journal									
academic monograph									
classified adverts									
examination paper									
Radio Times									
cookery book									
letters page									

List-like texts can also interact with the narrative and non-narrative modes. For instance, we can interweave stories within a list structure but we can also list events within a story structure. Postmodern literary narration has significantly employed this device by organising a typical story as a list (e.g. a dictionary or an encyclopaedia). This intermingling of modes is a means of undermining narratorial authority and the coherent point of view found in traditional narratives. Comparably, argumentative texts may draw on non-patterned discourse to emphasise a point and increase persuasion. Texts with instrumentative purposes are also close to list-like texts. An important part in the structure of recipes, for example, is occupied by the listing of ingredients.

In Schiffrin's (1994b) view, lists have been developed as means of helping people to discursively create (and store) stable knowledge. This is revealing of the status of knowledge in narrative and non-narrative. Both modes are concerned with the negotiation of knowledge. As already suggested, the point of narrative texts can be negotiated and reshaped according to the requirements of the context. Non-narrative discourse is less negotiable in this respect but allows for a dialogical exchange of information. Non-patterned discourse in particular presents knowledge as stable and not negotiable at all. Furthermore, verifiability is not an issue in this discourse – in contrast to the non-narrative mode, where it can be evidenced by the prominence of relations such as Evidence or Support in argumentative and other non-narrative texts. Non-patterned discourse thus appears to be a third option in the construction of knowledge, although its importance for communication is evidently much more restricted than that of narrative or non-narrative discourse.

6.3 THE INTERACTION OF ANALYSES
We have so far indicated how narrative and non-narrative have become the analytic focus of comparable concerns in the area of discourse analysis. The

analysis of the two modes can be contrasted with regard to three basic issues: text organisation and part–whole relationships; the variety of functions and relations in text; and processes of knowledge in discourse.

Units and Structure

There is a common ground between the basic linguistic entities of narrative and non-narrative discourse. This is true of units, organisational patterns and generic structures. Each of the two modes employs the same repertoire of organisational patterns but both exhibit a preference for a specific set of devices or text strategies. For instance, temporal text strategies are far more important in narrative than non-narrative discourse. This difference is immediately related to the definitional characteristics of each mode. The telling of a story with a beginning, middle and end inevitably leads to an emphasis on sequentiality and temporal as well as spatial relations. In addition, the importance of actors (characters) in the storyworld leads to an emphasis on the linguistic devices that follow their lines of activity. Thus, narrative discourse is built on the interaction between participant, time and place chains; these are major indicators of both individual units and the overall structure. In non-narrative discourse, the goals of imparting information, developing argumentation or description etc. rely on the interaction between given and new knowledge. As a result, non-narrative texts are mainly developed on the basis of lexical patterning which involves the provision of new lexical information in conjunction with the finite repertory of grammatical items, the multiple lexical relations between adjacent and remote items (e.g. cohesion and anaphoric nouns) and the use of prediction pairs or other dialogic structures.

The above preferences for different organisational patterns are also reflected in the use of devices from the pool of linguistic resources. For instance, the employment of discourse markers to indicate discourse structure is a common device shared by both modes. Metalinguistic expressions, however, are favoured by non-narrative discourse and, in particular, written non-narrative texts. In narratives, as expected, temporal adverbials, and participant and tense shifts, are particularly important signals. This has significant implications for text segmentation: narrative units are mainly identified by time, place and character markers. By contrast, the identification of non-narrative units relies on more explicit conventional devices such as paragraphing, metalinguistic expressions and encapsulating cohesion.

The issue of units in the narrative and non-narrative modes needs to be clarified here. So far, we have come across two types of unit. The first type involves units which are defined by formal linguistic (syntactic, intonational, typographic etc.) criteria such as idea unit, stanza and paragraph. These are similarly instantiated in the two modes. Their differences are a question of medium rather than mode: spoken texts (either narrative or non-narrative) have a different range of units from written ones (again, either narrative or non-narrative). In (spontaneous) spoken monological texts, the deployment of units is intertwined with the highly limited capacity of consciousness, its limited duration with respect to any particular piece of information, and its jerky rather than continuous movement (Chafe 1980: 48). In terms of linguistic realisation, spoken paragraphs are defined by a combination of syntactic, thematic and intonational criteria (e.g. intonation key and pauses). The intonational criterion is interrelated to an easily observable property of spoken language, namely that it is punctuated every so often by a sentence-final intonation contour. In Chafe's terms (1980, 1987), this contour signals the completion of the scanning of a centre of interest (see Chapter 3). In spoken dialogic exchanges, the identification of units is further characterised by turn change. By contrast to the above, in written texts the criterion of intonation is non-applicable; identification is based on typographic devices, syntactic and thematic criteria. The ability for planning and the alleviation of time constraints allow information to be segmented in bigger chunks than in spoken texts.

The second type of units can be identified on the basis of the generic structure that characterises the large variety of texts in the two modes. For instance, in narrative discourse we can talk of the units of orientation, abstract, climax and so on, whereas in non-narrative texts we have the units of problem, solution etc. Although the identification of units of this type is supported by the presence of formal linguistic signals, the basic criteria are considerations of the overall structure and the role which individual parts play in it.

The area of overall discourse structure is a locus of divergence for the two modes, since discourse structure derives from different generic patterns. The concerns of plot predominate in narrative discourse, in opposition to non-narrative discourse, which exhibits different patterns according to its different functions (iconic, transactional, problem–solution, claim–denial etc.). However, this divergence does not exclude common patterns across the two modes. First, it can be argued that the problem–solution pattern cross-cuts the narrative versus non-narrative distinction. As Grimes noted, 'both the plots of fairy tales and the writings of scientists are built on a response pattern' (1975: 211). We have seen that, in narrative, the plot develops through an initial disruption of equilibrium that must be restored. This is a variant of a more general problem–solution pattern, which is also found, as we saw, in advertisements, scientific papers, editorials etc. Hoey (1983), who studied the problem–solution pattern in detail, applied it to the analysis of both narrative and non-narrative texts. Second, other common structures may be established in both narrative and non-narrative discourse. For instance, a tripartite structure has been found to be common in conversation (Longacre 1976; Francis and Hunston 1992), lessons (Sinclair and Coulthard 1975), exchange transactions (Ventola 1987), editorials (Bolivar 1994) and other written texts (Sinclair 1988). This is the Initiation–Response–Follow up structure, in the Birmingham School terminology, or Initiating–Continuing–Resolving utterance, in Longacre's terms. Third, there are common content structures in both modes, which affect patterns in the expression planes. Hoey (1992), for instance, has used the matrix organisation of subject matter to analyse both narrative and non-narrative texts. In general, it is difficult to establish patterns exclusive to one mode, as well as purely mode-dependent similarities or differences. Further research is needed in the direction of establishing universal and culture-specific patterns (Berman and Slobin's 1994 and Slobin's 1990 work on developmental universals in narrative discourse are promising studies in this direction). Furthermore, this research should be accompanied by theory-building which would be oriented towards integrated descriptions of discourse.

READER ACTIVITY

Analyse part–whole relations in text 5.7 (from the previous chapter) by using the Problem–Solution pattern. Do the same for the non-narrative text 5.17 by referring to Labov's categories. What does the analysis reveal?

Functions and Relations

All three types of relation between units (i.e. sequential, ideational, interpersonal) are found in the two modes, although there might again be preferences for certain relations over others. For instance, we have noted that stories mainly opt for temporal and causal (*allow, enable, motivate*) relations, while non-narrative texts vary according to the particular purposes of the text (e.g. argumentative texts prefer Justification etc.). Relations and patterns thus constitute a common source of devices for both modes, allowing for different selections according to the needs of each text. Relations function at the level of content, and patterns operate at the level of expression.

A first point of divergence between the two modes arises in the area of interpersonal relations. The differences in prototypical functions of communication between the two modes underlie their differences in the main expressive devices. Performance devices, for instance, are very important for the encoding of narrative subjectivity. Involvement strategies have been looked at in both modes, yielding mode-preferential differences: non-narrative texts are more likely to activate detachment strategies while narrative texts opt for a specific set of devices (such as speech presentation, expressive sounds etc.) which achieve involvement through dramatisation. Evaluation has been associated in both modes with basic parts of their structural patterning; orientation–climax–evaluation in narrative, problem–solution–evaluation in non-narrative. Subsequent research, however, has employed evaluation both as a term that refers to a specific identifiable part of a structure and as a term that covers numerous expressive devices.

READER ACTIVITY

Could you analyse evaluation in texts 5.14 and 5.16 by using the notions developed for the analysis of narrative discourse? Could you do the same for text 5.5, using Hunston's model for non-narrative discourse? What do you conclude?

As happens with other textual mechanisms, the main devices by which evaluation is realised are, as a rule, different in the two modes. As we have seen, in narratives, it is mainly encoded by repetition patterns, tense shifts, speech presentation and (other) dramatisation devices, whereas in non-narrative it relies heavily on explicit lexical signalling.

By contrast, the two modes converge as regards the notion's context-sensitivity and its ultimate dependence on shared norms and values. While being recognised as a vital part of evaluation by both narrative and non-narrative text analyses, the issue has not received as much attention in non-narrative. By contrast, it has yielded a considerable amount of research in the narratives of different languages and cultures. Cortazzi (1993) deplores the compartmentalisation of evaluation studies in the two modes, suggesting that lexical signalling is a crucial area for studying narrative, along with non-narrative, evaluation.

To an extent, the same compartmentalisation characterises the analyses of all subjectivity concepts in the two modes. For instance, while performance devices and their interrelation with contexts of use have been systematically researched in narrative discourse, they have not received enough attention in non-narrative discourse. The same goes for involvement strategies: devices such as speech presentation have attracted a volume of research only in relation to narrative texts, while there is growing evidence that their systematic study in non-narrative texts can be an equally fruitful enterprise (e.g. see Baynham 1996, who focuses on direct speech in non-narrative texts, concerning, in particular, reasoning and argumentation in the classroom).

All the above differences in scope and emphasis are to a certain extent unavoidable in the study of the two modes. The various points of divergence noted are, first, a function of the defining characteristics of the two modes. Second, they are a matter of the different text strategies and organisational patterns associated with the two modes. Finally, as we will see in the next section, they are the outcome of differences in the interdisciplinary affiliations that narrative and non-narrative analysis have formed.

Our discussion so far has not only revealed the relations between the two modes but has also tried to clarify the role and position of individual discourse entities in the construction of text. We can summarise this view by identifying how the different discourse aspects mentioned fit into Hjelmslev's matrix of planes, discussed in Chapter 1. The two planes of content are organised into various patterns of the information base (matrix, tree-diagram etc.) and into discourse relations, as described above. As can be seen clearly in the case of ideational and interpersonal relations, the concern of this plane is with the underlying connections between entities and events. On the expression planes, discourse is organised into generic patterns and units, on the one hand, and organisational patterns, on the other. The former deal with the substance of what is communicated and the latter with the form of communication.

	content	expression
substance	information base	generic patterns and units
form	relations	organisational patterns

Table 6.3: Organisation of discourse planes

It is significant to note here that this matrix has already been used in the analysis of both narrative and non-narrative discourse (by Chatman 1978 and Goutsos forthcoming, respectively). This is further evidence for the common analytical basis shared by the two modes. Further clarification and detailed description of this common basis is one of the most urgent concerns in discourse analysis.

Knowledge in discourse
The third major issue of concern in the interaction of narrative and non-narrative discourse analysis deals with the cognitive processes that shape the linguistic construction of discourse in both its encoding and decoding. Although the emphasis of this book has been on the linguistic mechanisms at work in the two modes and not on the cognitive processes underlying their choice, we have nevertheless frequently invoked notions of knowledge in discourse, mainly in our references to the notions of schemata, scripts and frames. These notions have dominated research in the last twenty years and have been extremely influential in the area of discourse processing. Their main contribution has been in providing a solid theoretical framework for exploring issues of generic structures or superstructures (e.g. van Dijk 1980). Superstructures were argued to be basic organising principles in the production and comprehension of discourse and an integral part of our general knowledge. As we have suggested, this knowledge is to be complemented by contextual information and material provided by the text itself.

The concept of schemata has also provided an influential point of convergence in the study of narrative and non-narrative discourse. With regard to narrative, schematic knowledge has been related to the identification of story-grammar categories. A plethora of subsequent studies has further researched the schematic representation of events, actions, goals and consequences; the recall of stories or story parts; the establishment of causal explanations for events; the reading of texts with complex goal structures; and the culture-specificity of schemata. Current research has tested the initial idea that schemata organise the relations of elements in text by studying the on-line comprehension and reactions of readers. There has also been an increasing recognition of the role of bottom-up processes in text representation. Despite the current consensus that earlier research overestimated the importance of schemata in comprehension (see e.g. Whitney et al. 1995), concepts of schemata still play an influential role in cognitive approaches to discourse.

6.4 INTERDISCIPLINARY AFFILIATIONS AND EMERGING PARADIGMS

Discourse analysis exhibits a multiplicity of approaches and interactions with numerous and diverse academic areas. As Schiffrin claimed (1994a), included in these areas 'are not just disciplines in which models for understanding, and methods for analyzing, discourse first developed (i.e. linguistics, anthropology, sociology, philosophy; see van Dijk 1985), but also disciplines that have applied (and thus often extended) such models and methods to their own particular academic domains, e.g. communication (Craig and Tracy 1983), social psychology (Potter and Wetherell 1987), and artificial intelligence (Reichman 1985)' (1994a: 5). For narrative discourse, interaction has mainly been with sociological, ethnographic and anthropological approaches. Theoretical and methodological influences from these disciplines underlie narrative analysis.

Conversation analysis, in the vein of Sacks, Schegloff etc., is also traceable to sociological theories. Button and Lee sum up this orientation in their assessment that 'the value of conversation analysis to discourse analysis is to be found in revealing the significance of the fact that language-in-use is pervasively a matter of social organisation' (1987: 51). Research in conversation analysis has demonstrated that face-to-face interaction, by being accomplished as a joint effort of interlocutors, can constitute a model of social action and organisation. The organisation of talk as an everyday phenomenon thus offers a unique area of research into social order and organisation.

Narrative discourse analysis has been significantly influenced by the sociological orientation of conversation analysis. First, narratives have been studied in accordance with the main concerns of conversation analysts, that is, as socially-organised orderly affairs within conversations, which have provided a source of information about organisation, structure and rules in conversation and about the social reality in which they are embedded. They have thus been explored as sites for contextualisation of the interlocutors' social identities and relationships. Second, there has been a common concern in both narrative and conversation analysis with the sequential placement of utterances in unfolding talk. This has been considered as the key to the understanding of the actions performed, since conversationalists (and text-producers, in general) are themselves oriented to the sequential placement of utterances in order to interpret discourse. On the whole, important perspectives on discourse have emerged from sociologists interested in systematic analyses of how members of a society build the events they participate in, and how they constitute social order and organisation through discourse. Sociological models have also informed the analysis of narratives in terms of the teller's self-presentation and management of self as a socialised entity. The notion of footing that Goffman developed to capture the different entities which can be invoked by a speaker within a strip of talk has provided a powerful analytical perspective for face-to-face interaction. As we saw in Chapter 2, this analytical focus can also yield a major point of differentiation between narrative and non-narrative discourse.

At the same time, the search for meaning and understanding that sociologically-oriented approaches have identified in the moment-by-moment construction of talk is central to the concept of culture in anthropological and ethnographic approaches. As a result, this topic brings together concerns with social organisation, culture and language use in context. All three components can be analysed as integrated aspects of a single system of action.

This orientation accounts for the focus on everyday oral narrative that has monopolised narrative discourse analyses. Despite their numerous differences, all analyses exhibit a common concern with the interaction between narratives and their social, psychological and cultural contexts. Narratives are explored as 'ways of speaking' (Hymes 1981) which, on one hand, are shaped by their context and, on the other hand, create, shape and mediate contexts. The construction of narrative discourse is seen in interaction with the roles and relations of tellers and audiences and other situational parameters. On the whole, anthropological models underlie the concern with the creation of narrative performances and their relationships with their contexts. A very influential name here is that of Dell Hymes, whose work is a classic instance of the 'ethnography of communication' line of tradition. This approach views narratives as ways of speaking or as socio-cultural activities in different interactional contexts. The ways in which we narrativise our experiences and, on the whole, organise our interactions are argued to be shaped by our cultural knowledge, which is in turn an integral part of our communicative competence as members of specific communities. The notions developed here have included powerful concepts such as participation framework, self and face. These notions have been expanded and made more sensitive to culture-specific norms and expectations. The ethnography of communication has assumed a diversity of structures, functions and styles in different languages, cultures and situations. According to one of the area's main principles, this diversity needs to be empirically attested before any generalisations are made about the patterns of language use.

In view of the above, most studies of oral narrative discourse have started with the assumption that the meaning, structure and use of texts under analysis are socially and culturally variable. This assumption has yielded significant differences in narrative styles between different contexts of occurrence. First, structural patterns have been noted to be context-sensitive: the amount of descriptive or evaluative commentary, the play between implicitness and explicitness of events, and the preferences for specific text-building devices are only some dimensions of contextual variation. The same variability applies to the functions of narrative forms. Different cultures rely on performed and animated narrative styles to a varying extent and by means of different devices. Furthermore, the expectations about the communication purposes of storytelling are also culturally variable. Some communities value the authenticity of the story's events more than the excitement which a competent narrative presentation yields. In other communities, it is the audience entertainment and the teller's display of skill that are at the heart of the storytelling activity, at the expense of the authenticity and verisimilitude (*vraisemblance*) of the events (see Heath 1983). As we have seen, what is considered as exciting narrative material or appropriate, tellable means of narration in one community may be dull, ordinary or inappropriate in another. What constitutes valuable audience participation in the storytelling of a culture may be regarded as rude interruption in another.

We have repeatedly stressed that though culture provides a broad framework of enquiry into our discourse practices, it is only one side of the coin, the other being the local instantiation of discourse in specific contexts. This involves studying how individual actors with specific agendas, goals and purposes in specific situations draw on their background understandings and knowledge about how to mean and what is meant; how they negotiate and locally adapt this knowledge to micro-level concerns, their management of self and the creation of alignments with the audience; finally, how each of their utterances is sequentially relevant to what came before and what comes after. The sociological and anthropological affiliations of discourse analysis call for further work on the relationship between language structure, use and socio-cultural ideologies in diverse contexts. The aim is to establish interpretative links between the forms and functions of discourse and as many settings as possible. This micro-level research is a prerequisite of any informed typology which links linguistic devices, social actions and cultural ethos.

Whereas the interaction with sociological, ethnographic and anthropological approaches has informed narrative discourse analysis, having a definitive impact on research in the area, the affiliations of non-narrative discourse analysis have shown a different orientation. The leading affiliations in this domain have been with cognitive modelling and composition studies. It is not accidental that all contributions in a fairly recent collection of papers on expository discourse (Lindeberg et al. 1992) show an attachment to one or the other direction. Thus, on the one hand, non-narrative discourse analysis has followed the development of notions about knowledge in discourse that has been described above. An abundance of models of discourse comprehension and text generation in artificial intelligence have been developed concerning non-narrative texts. The current shift of emphasis towards bottom-up approaches is expected to bring the aims of modelling closer to the usual concerns of discourse analysis with formal devices, units and functions (see e.g. Knott 1993).

This affiliation has also been related to the approaches which have followed the impact of speech act theory. Spoken and written non-narrative discourse has been particularly amenable to analyses of 'underlying' acts and moves, in contrast to narrative texts, for which there are only isolated attempts at such endeavours (e.g. Pratt 1977). There is a current shift from the pragmatic aspects of speech acts to their contribution to discourse as one of the levels of relations. As a result, the most urgent current issue is to establish the mappings between sequential, ideational, interpersonal and rhetorical relations (Rambow 1993). Further clarification and application of analyses like RST and development of analyses for other types of relations are necessary for attacking this issue. In the field of language generation, the development of theories for representation of text relations and corresponding algorithms are required (Hovy 1990).

On the other hand, the tradition of educational and rhetorical approaches to discourse has culminated in the development of composition studies primarily concerned with non-narrative discourse. The key concerns here have been with the development of literacy and the act of writing, and spoken non-narrative texts have been largely overlooked. Writing is seen as a composite of interacting processes of text-planning, generating and editing within a variety of constraints, which normally take three forms: structural (i.e. conventions for writing text units), content (i.e. ideas which have to be expressed) and purpose (writers' goals, assumptions about readers; see Forrester 1996: 171). This line of affiliation has been influenced by cognitive and developmental psychology. It has emphasised notions of generic patterns and structural conventions as recipe guides to good writing. Lately, the preference for studying the production of written discourse has been replaced by intertask approaches which focus on both writing and reading as interdependent processes (e.g. see Flower et al. 1990). Schema ideas are very important in these approaches: though favoured primarily in reading research, they are also increasingly drawn upon by writing research (as in schema-based knowledge of writing strategies). Another recent shift of interests in composition studies has been towards examining the role of broader contextual and socio-cultural factors in the construction of non-narrative discourse (e.g. Barton and Ivanic 1991).

There is no doubt that one of the most influential emerging paradigms in linguistics is corpus linguistics, which analyses large-scale corpora consisting of vast quantities of text (e.g. 100 million words) by electronic means such as computer concordancing. The emphasis of this paradigm on actual and authentic instances of language use, whole texts and cross-generic considerations (Stubbs 1993) has always occupied a central position in discourse analysis. At the moment, however, this common orientation has not been exploited to any significant extent. This is partly due to the nature of electronic corpus research, which does not respect text boundaries and internal structure. Nevertheless, there are many avenues of research that can be opened. Text annotation is becoming increasingly sophisticated and can provide useful information which will serve as a test bed for discourse theory. In addition, greater care is being taken to provide contextual information (e.g. setting, time, participant details) about individual texts in the corpora. The corpus approach has some significant advantages for discourse analysts: it enables them to test out their hypotheses in an explicit way, putting their analyses onto a firmer empirical footing. It also allows them to quantify the presence of linguistic forms and patterns of forms across different text-types. Furthermore, machine-readable corpus approaches force the analyst to label every single part of a text in a systematic and consistent way, as examples inconvenient to the model cannot be simply disregarded (see Short et al. 1996: 112). On the whole, cross-fertilisation of notions between the two disciplines of corpus linguistics and discourse analysis is bound to yield noteworthy results in the future.

6.5 TOWARDS AN INTEGRATION OF DISCOURSE APPROACHES

In this book, we have isolated the main strands of research in the exploration of structures and functions in the narrative and non-narrative modes. We have identified different methods and concepts in the analysis of the two modes, as well as varying interaction with other paradigms. We have knowingly had to disregard or underemphasise certain theories and tools: it is virtually impossible for any textbook to cover all the different theoretical and analytic perspectives currently in operation in discourse analysis. It is widely held that discourse analysis is not a strictly unified discipline with one or few dominant theories and methods of research. According to some, this proliferation of approaches is a sign of the area's richness, the impressive result of multi-faceted research which has developed a wide range of analytic procedures and tools and provided clear insights into discourse construction. The nature of the subject of discourse is such that 'the goal of a homogeneous discipline with a unified theory, an agreed-upon method and comparable types of data, is not only hopeless but pointless' (see van Dijk 1990b). At the same time, interdisciplinary study is indispensable. Quite simply, it is almost impossible to separate discourse from its uses in the world and in social interactions; as a result, linguistic tools alone are not sufficient for its comprehensive study.

The recognition of the need for pluralism is not incompatible with the need for a more constructive dialogue between different approaches. This need is now becoming apparent in view of an increasing compartmentalisation of the field which makes planning for further development difficult.

The foreseeable danger is that discourse analysis will come to mean loosely any work from diverse analytic perspectives with no common metalanguage, method or technical apparatus. In a similar vein, the various analyses of texts will remain fragmentary and unsystematic, taking too much for granted in terms of theory and method. It is hence widely felt that there is a clear need for a more inclusive strategy, a theoretical and methodological compactness which will tie the loose ends together and lead to integrated accounts of discourse. As de Beaugrande noted (1990, quoted in Duszak 1995: 466), a balance must be struck between what is anecdotal and what is significant in order for discourse analysis to attain the ideal stage of an empirical science.

The plea for comprehensive theories of discourse has been put formally on the agenda for further development of the field by various sources. In a Special Issue of *Text* (1990) on the programmatics of discourse analysis for the 1990s, it was emphasised that what is needed now is a synopsis of the aspects of analysis: 'one of the urgent tasks is to clear up the existing confusion and to propose an integrated theory of discourse which will make explicit the links between different levels, or dimensions of analysis' (van Dijk 1990b: 146). One of the prerequisites for integrated accounts is to explore the common concepts that provide the basis of interaction between different approaches. This has been one of the aims of this book. Discourse analysis gets a high mileage out of a small selection of concepts, namely structure, function and context. All approaches to discourse share these general concerns and make assumptions about the relationship between structure and function, and text and context. Yet these fundamental concepts need to be explained more clearly and the different methodological and theoretical proposals need to be brought together.

Focus on the identification of units and relationships between them can be combined with focus on actions and purposes and the interpretation of social and cultural meanings. According to Schiffrin (1994: 361), though a difficult and delicate task, combining both types of analyses and developing an inclusive attendant methodology may help to balance the weaknesses of one mode of analysis with the strengths of the other. Structurally-based approaches are up against various criterial problems in the identification of units, while functionally-based approaches are clouded by uncertainty and subjectivity regarding the identification of functions. The increase of dialogue between the two will help overcome these weaknesses (ibid.).

The relationship between text and context is another central concern of discourse approaches which can benefit from a more inclusive strategy. Different approaches emphasise different aspects of context in their analyses. They also diverge in relation to how much of the context needs to be taken into account for text analysis. There is much scope for formulating a clearer understanding of the notion of context and a more inclusive view of its relationship with text. This will require a systematic cooperation between all the different empirical analyses of different aspects of texts and contexts.

All the foregoing indicates the need for developing multiple analyses of discourse which would explore how the different levels and entities correspond with each other. This is still a desideratum, though one of the earliest concerns of discourse analysis: the theory of tagmemics is an early example of multi-plane discourse analysis (see Pike 1981), but it was too idiosyncratic to have any large-scale impact in the field. Since then, various steps have been taken in this direction. A prominent instance of analysis at different yet interdependent levels concerns the notion of form–function anisomorphism. This is intertwined with approaches to discourse as a set of systems of structure, function and action, which, although interlocked, can be analytically teased apart for identifying constraints at different levels (see Schiffrin's work, e.g. 1987, 1994).

Text organisation can also be shown to rely on the orchestration of diverse, interacting strategies. Connectivity was conventionally seen as consisting of two separate activities: the linear ordering of connections along a horizontal axis and the projection of this horizontal axis on an implicitly vertical axis (e.g. Karmiloff-Smith 1985; Berman and Slobin 1994). The former orientation works at the local level of adjacent clauses and their boundaries to the right and to the left. The latter is concerned with signalling higher-level relations of saliency, that is, how units are grounded in each other and how they are to be understood with respect to the overarching global theme of discourse. The current tendency is to combine the two foci in more comprehensive accounts of various discourse forms (e.g. Bamberg and Marchman 1991). The combination of the linear and non-linear succession of parts of the text accounts for a text's coherence as a whole. The relative importance of parts is also defined in relation to this global coherence.

A similar combination of approaches underlies current cognitive views of discourse. As has been mentioned, theories of discourse comprehension have placed emphasis either on the idea that pre-existing schema-based knowledge guides comprehension from the top down, or on the idea that comprehension is guided in a bottom-up fashion by the text itself and its explicit information. Currently, there is a broad consensus that both top-down and bottom-up processes are involved in comprehension (cf. Whitney et al. 1995). Similarly, while many research programmes used to focus on only one half of the communication process, either the production or the comprehension of discourse, currently the tendency is to focus on both.

Whether this advance of multi-level discourse analyses is going to be the moving force for the interaction needed between competing and uncontrolled methodologies remains to be seen. At this point, it is almost certain that there is still a long way to go before all the different aspects of text are related to a common system of interacting elements and before an integrated approach is developed with standardised and consistent method, tools and metalanguage.

At the same time as raising radical questions about its state of the art and planning its way ahead, discourse analysis, as an area with a strong input into theories of communication, will also need to meet new challenges. Electronic discourse is one of them, and will indisputably become a major form of communication in the future. Hence, discourse analysis will need to invest more time and resources in studying it. Some of the issues which need to be considered are the differences in structures and functions between electronic texts and spoken or written texts, the place of electronic texts in the continuum of orality and literacy practices, the processes of writing, comprehending and recalling hypertexts etc. (see Foertsch 1995: 301–28). Another by-product of the rapid technological advances in 'western' societies is that of corpus analysis. As already suggested, discourse analysis will need to open up to this expanding paradigm and gain from its insights and tools.

In a recent paper on the state of the art and theoretical development of critical discourse analysis, Kress (1996) drew attention to a fundamental challenge to the area, which is readily applicable to discourse analysis as a whole. He argued that the increasing dominance of the visual medium of expression requires that analyses should start taking fully into account the fact that texts are multi-modal (i.e constituted through a number of semiotic modes). As Kress claimed, 'it is no longer possible to give adequate accounts of texts, even of texts which appear in the print media (let alone those which appear on television, or in cinemas) without transcending, decisively, the hitherto relatively rigorously observed boundaries of the verbal medium' (1996: 20). This issue is interconnected with the increasing importance of texts produced by the media (newspapers, radio, television, film industry etc.) as a major data source for discourse analysts.

The above are only a selective sample of the new challenges and directions for discourse analysis in the 1990s and beyond. They all seem to call for a broad-based approach that applies to language any and all roads to understanding, including introspection, experimentation, theorising, and above all careful observation of the myriad discourse practices within social and cultural practices (Chafe 1990: 21). Discourse analysis needs to be able to combine the rigorous, disciplined and systematic investigation with the attention and sensitivity to the personal and the particular. According to Tannen (1989: 196), there is no reason why the latter should be excluded from a scientific study of language. The theory of language which can derive from discourse analysis is one which will include 'the close analysis of particular instances of discourse as they naturally occur in human and linguistic context' (ibid.). This is the general principle which brings together all different approaches to discourse: the view that discourse is language use interconnected with social and cultural practices. The aim and hope of discourse analysts is that the systematic study of this interconnection will increase awareness of communication and help to create a better world, with fewer barriers, more understanding and more tolerance.

FURTHER READING

One of the best introductions to Bakhtin from a linguistic perspective is Wales (1988), where further references can be found.

On conversation, Sacks 1967 and Sacks, Schegloff and Jefferson (1974) are among the earliest systematic studies. Collections of work include Atkinson and Heritage (1984), Button and Lee (1987). See also references in previous chapters.

For the input of sociological and anthropologial models into discourse analysis, see Cortazzi (1993) and Schiffrin (1994a).

The most detailed description of news discourse from a discourse analysis perspective can be found in van Dijk (1987c, 1987d).

Introductions to advertising from a linguistic point of view include Cook (1992) and Vestergaard and Schroder (1985).

In cognitive approaches, research that combines top-down with bottom-up considerations includes Graesser and Clark (1985) on the role of elaborative influences in text comprehension. Evidence against the monopoly of top-down processes can be found in Abbott, Black and Smith (1985) and Kintsch (1988). The studies by Anderson and Pickert (1978), Dosher and Corbett (1982) and Kintsch and Mross (1985) have also undermined the view that schemata and top-down processes guide a text's encoding. Haviland and Clark (1974) and McKoon and Ratcliff (1992) are among those who support a bottom-up approach in text comprehension and the reader's interpretation.

Research on narrative universals was initiated by story grammars with the controversial results which we saw in Chapter 3. Although the universal impact of certain story categories on comprehension has been quite well documented, story schemas should be thought of as mental processes that contain culture-specific categories: see Harris et al. (1988) and Kintsch and Greene (1978). The other strand of research on narrative universals is related to developmental studies of language communication. Berman and Slobin (1994) is a fundamental work of reference in cross-linguistic routes of development that has established a common transition in the production of stories by children aged 3, 5 and 9 in different speaking communities. These findings are congruent with individual studies on the developmental route of various linguistic forms in different languages, such as Bamberg (1987), Clancy (1992), Hickmann (1980, 1991) and Karmiloff-Smith (1980).

For the ethnography of communication in the tradition of discourse analysis, see Saville-Troike (1982).

A basic introduction to corpus analysis in computational linguistics is Sinclair (1991). Aijmer and Altenberg (1991), Svartvik (1992) and Baker et al. (1993) are some of the best collections of papers on corpus linguistics, with a wide range of issues covered.

Bibliography

Abbott, V., J. B. Black and E. E. Smith (1985), 'The representation of scripts in memory', *Journal of Memory and Language* 24, 179–99.

Abelen, E., G. Redeker and S. A. Thompson (1993), 'The rhetorical structure of US-American and Dutch fund-raising letters', *Text* 13(3), 323–50.

Abrams, K. (1991), 'Hearing the call of stories', *California Law Review* 79, 971–1,052.

Aijmer, K. and B. Altenberg (eds) (1991), *English Corpus Linguistics: Studies in Honour of Jan Svartvik*, London: Longman.

Anderson, R. C. and J. W. Pichert (1978), 'Recall of previously unrecallable information following a shift in perspective', *Journal of Verbal Learning and Verbal Behavior* 17, 1–12.

Ariel, M. (1991), 'The function of accessibility in a theory of grammar', *Journal of Pragmatics* 16, 443–63.

Aston, G. (1995), 'Say "thank you": some pragmatic constraints in conversational closings', *Applied Linguistics* 16, 57–86.

Atkinson, M. and J. Heritage (eds) (1984), *Structures of Social Action: Studies in Conversation Analysis*, Cambridge: Cambridge University Press.

Austin, J. L. (1962), *How to Do Things with Words*, Oxford: Clarendon Press.

Bäcklund, I. (1988), 'To begin with, this is the problem, for example. On some reader-oriented structural markers in English expository text', *Studia Linguistica* 42(1), 60–8.

Bäcklund, I. (1992), 'Theme in English telephone conversation', *Language Studies* 14(4), 545–64.

Baker, M., G. Francis and E. Tognini-Bonelli (eds) (1993), *Text and Technology: In Honour of John Sinclair*, Philadelphia/Amsterdam: John Benjamins.

Bakhtin, M. (1981), *The Dialogic Imagination: Four Essays* (ed. M. Holquist, trans. by M. Holquist and C. Emerson), Austin: University of Texas Press.

Ball, A. F. (1992), 'Cultural preference and the expository writing of African-American adolescents', *Written Communication* 9(4), 501–32.

Bamberg, M. (1987), *The Acquisition of Narratives: Learning to Use Language*, New York: Mouton de Gruyter.

Bamberg, M.(1990), 'The German *perfekt*: form and function of tense alternations', *Studies in Language* 14, 253–90.

Bamberg, M. and D. Damrad-Frye (1991), 'On the ability to provide evaluative comments: Further explorations of children's narrative competencies', *Journal of Child Language* 18, 689–710.

Bamberg, M. and V. Marchman (1991), 'Binding and unfolding: towards the linguistic construction of discourse', *Discourse Processes* 14, 277–305.

Bartlett, F. C. (1932), *Remembering*, Cambridge: Cambridge University Press.

Barton, D. (1994), *Literacy: An Introduction to the Ecology of Written Language*, Oxford: Blackwell.

Barton, D. and R. Ivanic (eds) (1991), *Writing in the Community*, Newbury Park: Sage.

Bauman, R. (1986), *Story, Performance and Event. Contextual Studies of Oral Narrative*, Cambridge: Cambridge University Press.

Bauman, R. (1993), 'Disclaimers of performance', in J. H. Hill and J. T. Irvine (eds), *Responsibility and Evidence in Oral Discourse*, Cambridge: Cambridge University Press, pp. 182–96.

Baynham, M. (1996), 'Direct speech: what's it doing in non-narrative discourse?', *Journal of Pragmatics* 25, 61–81.

Bazzanella, C. (1990), 'Phatic connectives as interactional cues in spoken Italian', *Journal of Pragmatics* 14, 629–47.

Beaman, K. (1984), 'Coordination and subordination revisited: syntactic complexity in spoken and written narrative discourse', in D. Tannen (ed.), *Coherence in Spoken and Written Language*, Norwood, NJ: Ablex, pp. 45–80.

Beaugrande, R. de (1982), 'Story of grammars and grammar of stories', *Journal of Pragmatics* 6, 383–422.

Beaugrande, R. de and W. Dressler (1981), *Introduction to Text Linguistics*, London: Longman.

Becker, A. L. (1988), 'Language in particular: a lecture', in D. Tannen (ed.), *Linguistics in Context: Connecting Observation and Understanding*, Norwood, NJ: Ablex, pp. 17–35.

Berman, R. (1988), 'On the ability to relate events in narrative', *Discourse Processes* 11, 469–97.

Berman, R. and D. Slobin (1994), *Relating Events in Narrative: A Crosslinguistic Developmental Study*, Hillsdale, NJ: Erlbaum.

Besnier, N. (1994), 'Involvement in linguistic practice: an ethnographic appraisal', *Journal of Pragmatics* 22, 279–99.

Bestgen, Y. and J. Costermans (1994), 'Time, space, and action: exploring the narrative structure and its linguistic marking', *Discourse Processes* 17, 421–46.

Bestgen, Y. and W. Vonk (1995), 'The role of temporal segmentation markers in discourse processing', *Discourse Processes* 19, 385–406.

Biber, D. (1986), 'Spoken and written textual dimensions in English: resolving the contradictory findings', *Language* 62, 384–414.

Biber, D. (1988), *Variation across Speech and Writing*, Cambridge: Cambridge University Press.

Biber, D. (1991), 'Oral and literate characteristics of selected primary school reading materials', *Text* 11, 73–96.

Biber, D. (1992), 'On the complexity of discourse complexity: a multi-dimensional analysis', *Discourse Processes* 15, 133–63.

Biber, D. and E. Finnegan (1988), 'Adverbial stance types in English', *Discourse Processes* 11, 1–34.

Biber, D. and E. Finegan (eds) (1994), *Sociolinguistic Perspectives on Register*, Oxford and New York: Oxford University Press.

Black, J. B. and G. H. Bower (1980), 'Story understanding as problem-solving', *Poetics* 9, 223–50.

Blakemore, D. (1988), 'The organization of discourse', in F. J. Newmeyer (ed.), *Language: The Socio-cultural Context*, Cambridge: Cambridge University Press [= Linguistics: The Cambridge Survey, 4], pp. 229–50.

Bloom, R. L., L. K. Obler, S. De Santi, S. and J. S. Ehrlich (1994), *Discourse Analysis and Applications. Studies in Adult Clinical Populations*, Hillsdale, NJ: Erlbaum.

Blum-Kulka, S., J. House and G. Kasper (1989), *Cross-cultural Pragmatics: Requests and Apologies*, Norwood, NJ: Ablex.

Bolivar, A. C. (1994), 'The structure of newspaper editorials', in M. Coulthard (ed.), *Advances in Written Text Analysis*, London: Routledge, pp. 276–94.

Bond, S. J. and J. R. Hayes (1984), 'Cues people use to paragraph text', *Research in the Teaching of English* 18, 147–67.

Bower, G. H. (1978), 'Experiments on story comprehension and recall', *Discourse Processes* 1, 212–31.

Brady, M. and R. C. Berwick (eds) (1983), *Computational Models of Discourse*, Cambridge, MA: The MIT Press.

Brewer, W. F. and E. H. Lichtenstein (1981), 'Event schemas, story schemas, and story grammars', in J. Long and A. Baddeley (eds), *Attention and Performance, IX.* Hillsdale, NJ: Erlbaum, pp. 363–79.

Brewer, W. F. and E. H. Lichtenstein (1982), 'Stories are to entertain: a structural-affect theory of stories', *Journal of Pragmatics* 6, 473–86.

Britton, B. K. and J. B. Black (eds) (1985), *Understanding Expository Text: A Theoretical and Practical Handbook for Analyzing Explanatory Text*, Hillsdale, NJ: Erlbaum.

Britton, J. L., T. Burgess, N. Martin, A. McLeod and H. Rosen, H. (1975), *The Development of Writing Abilities (11–18)*, London: Macmillan Education.

Brown, G. and G. Yule (1983), *Discourse Analysis*, Cambridge: Cambridge University Press.

Brown, P. and S. Levinson (1987), *Politeness*, Cambridge: Cambridge University Press.

Bruner, J. (1986), *Actual Minds, Possible Worlds*, Cambridge, MA: Harvard University Press.

Bruner, J. (1990), *Acts of Meaning*, Cambridge, MA: Harvard University Press.

Bruner, J. (1991), 'The narrative construction of reality', *Critical Inquiry* 18, 1–21.

Bruner, J. and S. Weisser (1991), 'The invention of self: autobiography and its forms', in D. R. Olson and N. Torrance (eds), *Literacy and Orality*, Cambridge: Cambridge University Press, pp. 129–48.

Button, G. and N. Casey (1984), 'Generating topic: the use of topic initial elicitors', in M. Atkinson and J. Heritage (eds), *Structures of Social Action: Studies in Conversation Analysis*, Cambridge: Cambridge University Press, pp. 167–90.

Button, G. and J. Lee (eds) (1987), *Talk and Social Organisation*, Clevedon: Multilingual Matters.

Caffi, C. and R. V. O. Janney (1994), 'Toward a pragmatics of emotive communication', *Journal of Pragmatics* 22, 325–73.

Caldas-Coulthard, C. R. (1994), 'On reporting reporting: the representation of speech in factual and fictional narratives', in M. Coulthard (ed.), *Advances in Written Text Analysis*, London: Routledge, pp. 295–308.

Carter, R. (1987), *Vocabulary. Applied Linguistic Perspectives*, London: Routledge.

Carter, R. and P. Simpson (1982), 'The sociolinguistic analysis of narrative', *Belfast Working Papers in Linguistics* 6, 123–52.

Cazden, C. (1988), *Classroom Discourse*, Portsmouth, NH: Heinemann.

Centineo, G. (1991), 'Tense switching in Italian: The alternation between *passato prossimo* and *passato remoto* in oral narratives', in S. Fleischman and L. R. Waugh (eds), *Discourse-Pragmatics and the Verb: The Evidence from Romance*, London: Routledge, pp. 55–85.

Chafe, W. L. (ed.) (1980), *The Pear Stories: Cognitive, Cultural and Linguistic Aspects of Narrative Production*, Norwood, NJ: Ablex.

Chafe, W. L. (1982), 'Integration and involvement in speaking, writing, and oral literature', in D. Tannen (ed.), *Spoken and Written Language: Exploring Orality and Literacy*, Norwood, NJ: Ablex, pp. 35–53.

Chafe, W. L. (1984), 'How people use adverbial clauses', *Berkeley Linguistics Society* 10, 437–49.

Chafe, W. L. (1985), 'Linguistic differences produced by differences between speaking and writing', in D. R. Olson, N. Torrance and A. Hildyard (eds), *Literacy, Language and Learning: The Nature and Consequences of Reading and Writing*, Cambridge: Cambridge University Press, pp. 105–23.

Chafe, W. L. (1986), 'Evidentiality in English conversation and academic writing', in W. L. Chafe and J. Nichols (eds), *Evidentiality: The Linguistic Encoding of Epistemology*, Norwood, NJ: Ablex, pp. 261–72.

Chafe, W. L. (1987), 'Cognitive constraints on information flow', in R. Tomlin (ed.), *Coherence and Grounding in Discourse*, Amsterdam/Philadelphia: Benjamins, pp. 21–51.

Chafe, W. L. (1990), 'Looking ahead', Text 10, 19–22.

Chaika, E. and P. Alexander (1986), 'The ice cream stories: A study in normal and psychotic narrations', *Discourse Processes* 9, 305–28.

Chatman, S. (1978), *Story and Discourse: Narrative Structure in Fiction and Film*, Ithaca: Cornell University Press.

Chiaro, D. (1992), *The Language of Jokes: Analysing Verbal Play*, London: Routledge.

Churchill, L. (1978), *Questioning Strategies in Sociolinguistics*, Rowley, MA: Newbury House.

Chvany, C. V. (1984), 'Backgrounded perfectives and plotline imperfectives: toward a theory of grounding in text', in M. S. Flier and A. Timberlake (eds), *The Scope of Slavic Aspect. UCLA Slavic Studies 12*, Columbia, Ohio: Slavica Publishers, pp. 247–73.

Clancy, R. M. (1980), 'Referential choice in English and Japanese narrative discourse', in W. L. Chafe (ed.), *The Pear Stories: Cognitive, Cultural and Linguistic Aspects of Narrative Production*, Norwood, NJ: Ablex, pp. 127–202.

Clancy R. M. (1992), 'Referential strategies in the narratives of Japanese children', *Discourse Processes* 15, 441–67.

Clark, H. and S. Haviland (1977), 'Comprehension and the given-new contract', in R. Freedle (ed.), *Discourse Production and Comprehension*, Hillsdale, NJ: Erlbaum, pp. 1–40.

Clark, H. and D. Wilkes-Gibbs (1986), 'Referring as a collaborative process', *Cognition* 22, 1–39.

Clifford, J. (1988), *The Predicament of Culture: Twentieth-Century Ethnography, Literature and Art*, Cambridge, MA: Harvard University Press.

Clyne, M. (1981), 'Culture and discourse structure', *Journal of Pragmatics* 5, 61–6.

Clyne, M. (1987), 'Cultural differences in the organisation of academic texts: English and German', *Journal of Pragmatics* 11, 211–47.

Cohler, B. J. (1982), 'Personal life and narrative course', in P. B. Baltes and O. G. Brim (eds), *Life-span Development and Behavior*, New York: Academic Press, pp. 205–41.

Comrie, B. (1976), *Aspect*, Cambridge: Cambridge University Press.

Connor, U. and R. B. Kaplan (eds) (1987), *Writing Across Languages: Analysis of L2 Text*, Reading, MA: Addison-Wesley.

Connor, U. and McCagg (1987), 'A contrastive study of English expository prose and paraphrases', in U. Connor and R. B. Kaplan (eds), *Writing Across Languages: Analysis of L2 Text*, Reading, MA: Addison-Wesley, pp. 73–86.

Cook, G. (1989), *Discourse*, Oxford: Oxford University Press.

Cook, G. (1992), *The Discourse of Advertising*, London: Routledge.

Cooper, C. (1983), 'Procedures for describing written texts', in P. Mosenthal, L. Tamor and S. Walmsley (eds), *Research on Writing: Principles and Methods*, New York: Longman, pp. 287–313.

Cortazzi, M. (1993), *Narrative Analysis*. London: The Falmer Press.

Coulmas, F. (ed.) (1986), *Direct and Indirect Speech*, Berlin: Mouton de Gruyter.

Coulthard, M. (1985), *An Introduction to Discourse Analysis*, London: Longman.

Coulthard, M. (1992a), 'The significance of intonation in discourse', in M. Coulthard (ed.), *Advances in Spoken Discourse Analysis*, London: Routledge, pp. 35–49.

Coulthard, M. (1992b), 'Forensic discourse analysis', in M. Coulthard (ed.), *Advances in Spoken Discourse Analysis*, London: Routledge, pp. 242–58.

Coulthard, M. and M. Montgomery (eds) (1981), *Studies in Discourse Analysis*, London: Routledge and Kegan Paul.

Craig, R. and K. Tracy (eds) (1983), *Conversational Coherence*, Beverly Hills: Sage.

Crismore, A., R. Markkanen and M. Steffenson (1993), 'Metadiscourse in persuasive writing. A study of texts written by American and Finnish university students', *Written Communication* 10(1), 39–71.

Crystal, D. and D. Davy (1969), *Investigating English Style*, London: Longman.

Daneš, F. (1974), 'Functional sentence perspective and the organization of the text', in F. Danes (ed.), *Papers in Functional Sentence Perspective*, The Hague: Mouton, pp. 106–28.

Davies, F. and T. Greene (1984), *Reading for Learning in the Sciences*, Edinburgh: Oliver & Boyd.

Delgado, R. (1989), 'Storytelling for oppositionists and others: aplea for narrative', *Michigan Law Review* 87, 2,411–41.

Dijk, T. A. van (1977), *Text and Context*, London: Longman.

Dijk, T. A. van (1980), *Macrostructures*, Hillsdale, NJ: Erlbaum.

Dijk, T. A. van (ed.) (1985), *Handbook of Discourse Analysis* (3 vols), New York: Academic Press.

Dijk, T. A. van (1987a), 'Episodic models in discourse processing', in R. Horowitz and S. J. Samuels (eds) *Comprehending Oral and Written Language*, New York: Academic Press, pp. 161–96.

Dijk, T. A. van (1987b), *Communicating Racism*, Newbury Park: Sage.

Dijk, T. A. van (1987c), *News as Discourse*, Hillsdale, NJ: Erlbaum.

Dijk, T. A. van (1987d), *News Analysis*, Hillsdale, NJ: Erlbaum.

Dijk, T. A. van (1990a), '*Discourse & Society*: A new journal for a new research focus', *Discourse & Society* 1(1), 5–16.

Dijk, T. A. van (1990b), 'The future of the filed: discourse analysis in the 1990s', in T. van Dijk (ed.), *Looking Ahead: Discourse Analysis in the 1990s*. Special Issue of *Text* 10, 133–56.

Dijk, T. A. van (1993), 'Stories and racism', in D. K. Mumby (ed.), *Narrative and Social Control: Critical Perspectives*, Newbury Park: Sage, pp. 121–42.

Dijk, T. A. van and W. Kintsch (1983), *Strategies of Discourse Comprehension*, New York: Academic Press.

Dijk, T. A. van and J. Petöfi (1981), 'Editorial Introduction', *Text* 1(1), 1–3.

Dosher, B. A. and A. T. Corbett (1982), 'Instrument inferences and verb schemata', *Memory & Cognition* 10, 531–9.

Drew, P. and J. Heritage (1992), *Talk at Work*, New York: Cambridge University Press.

Dry, H. A. (1983), 'The movement of narrative time', *Journal of Literary Semantics* 12, 19–53.

Dubois, B. L. (1987), 'A reformulation of thematic progression typology', *Text* 7(2), 89–116.

Dubois, B. L. (1989), 'Pseudoquotation in current English communication: *hey, she didn't really say it*', *Language in Society* 18, 343–59.

Du Bois, J. W. (1993), 'Meaning without intention: lessons from divination', in J. H. Hill and J. T. Irvine (eds), *Responsibility and Evidence in Oral Discourse*, Cambridge: Cambridge University Press, pp. 48–71.

Dudley-Evans, T. (1994), 'Genre analysis: an approach to text analysis for ESP', in M. Coulthard (ed.), *Advances in Written Text Analysis*, London: Routledge, pp. 219–28.

Duranti, A. and D. Brenneis (eds) (1986), *The Audience as Co-Author*. Special Issue of *Text* 6.

Duranti, A. and C. Goodwin (eds) (1992), *Rethinking Context*, Cambridge: Cambridge University Press.

Duszak, A. (1995), 'On variation in news-text prototypes: some evidence from English, Polish, and German', *Discourse Processes* 19, 465–83.

Eagleton, T. (1983), *Literary Theory. An Introduction*, Oxford: Blackwell.

Eemeren, F. H. van and R. Grootendorst (1982), 'The speech acts of arguing and convincing in externalized discussions', *Journal of Pragmatics* 6, 1–24.

Eemeren, F. H. van and T. Kruiger (1987), *Handbook of Argumentation Theory*, Dordrecht: Foris.

Eisenberg, A. R. (1985), 'Learning to describe past experiences in conversations', *Discourse Processes* 8, 177–204.

Ely, R., J. B. Gleason, B. Narashiman and A. McCabe (1995), 'Family talk about talk: mothers lead the way', *Discourse Processes* 19, 201–18.

Erickson, F. (1984), 'Rhetoric, anecdote, and rhapsody: coherence strategies in a conversation among Black American adolescents', in D. Tannen (ed.), *Coherence in Spoken and Written Discourse*, Norwood, NJ: Ablex, pp. 81–151.

Fahnestock, J. (1983), 'Semantic and lexical coherence', *College Composition and Communication* 34, 400–16.

Fairclough, N. (1989), *Language and Power*, London: Longman.

Fish, S. (1980), *Is There a Text in this Class? The Authority of Interpretive Community*, Cambridge, MA: Harvard University Press.

Fivush, R. and F. Fromhoff (1988), 'Style and structure in mother-child conversations about the past', *Discourse Processes* 11, 337–55.

Flaschner, V. (1987), 'The grammatical marking of theme in oral Polish narrative', in R. Tomlin (ed.), *Coherence and Grounding in Discourse*, Amsterdam/Philadelphia: Benjamins, pp. 131–55.

Fleischman, S. (1989), 'A linguistic perspective on the *laisses similaires*: orality and the pragmatics of narrative discourse', *Romance Philology* 43, 70–89.

Fleischman, S. (1990), *Tense and Narrativity: From Medieval Performance to Modern Fiction*, Austin: University of Texas Press.

Fleischman, S. (1991), 'Discourse as space/discourse as time: reflections on the meta-language of spoken and written discourse', *Journal of Pragmatics* 16, 291–306.

Flower, L., V. Stein, J. Ackerman, P. Kantz, K. McCormick and J. Paradis (eds). (1990), *Reading to Write. Exploring a Cognitive and Social Process*, New York: Oxford University Press.

Fludernik, M. (1991), 'The historical present tense yet again: tense switching and narrative dynamics in oral and quasi oral storytelling', *Text* 11, 365–97.

Fludernik, M. (1994), *The Fictions of Language and the Languages of Fiction*, London: Routledge.

Foertsch, J. (1995), 'The impact of electronic networks on scholarly communication: avenues to research', *Discourse Processes* 19, 301–28.

Ford, C. (1986), 'Overlapping relations in text structure', in S. DeLancey and R. Tomlin (eds), *Proceedings of the Second Annual Meeting of the Pacific Linguistics Conference*, Oregon: University of Oregon, pp. 107–23.

Forrester, M. A. (1996), *Psychology of Language: A Critical Introduction*, London: Sage.

Fowler, R. (1981), *Literature as Social Discourse. The Practice of Literary Criticism*, London: Batsford.

Fox, B. (1987), *Discourse Structure and Anaphora. Written and Conversational English*, Cambridge: Cambridge University Press.

Francis, G. (1986), *Anaphoric Nouns*, Birmingham: University of Birmingham.

Francis, G. (1989a), 'Aspects of nominal-group lexical cohesion', *Interface. Journal of Applied Linguistics* 4(1), 27–53.

Francis, G. (1989b), 'Nominal group heads and clause structure', *Word* 42(2), 145–56.

Francis, G. and S. Hunston (1992), 'Analysing everyday conversation', in M. Coulthard (ed.), *Advances in Spoken Discourse Analysis*, London: Routledge, pp. 123–61.

Fraser, B. (1990), 'An approach to discourse markers', *Journal of Pragmatics* 14, 383–95.

Fries, P. H. (1983), 'On the status of theme in English: arguments from discourse', in J. Petöfi and E. Sözer (eds), *Micro and Macro Connexity of Texts*, Hamburg: Buske, pp. 116–52.

Fries, P. H. (1992), 'The structuring of information in written English text', *Language Sciences* 14(4), 461–88.

Gee, J. P. (1989), 'Two styles of narrative construction and their linguistic and educational implications', *Discourse Processes* 12, 287–307.

Gee, J. P. (1990), *Social Linguistics and Literacies. Ideology in Discourses*, Basingstoke: Falmer Press.

Geertz, C. (1983), *Local Knowledge*, New York: Basic Books.

Genette, G. (1988), *Narrative Discourse Revisited*, Ithaca: Cornell University Press.

Georgakopoulou, A. (1993), *Binding, Unfolding and Evaluating Modern Greek Personal Storytelling: A Discourse-Analytic Study*, unpublished Ph.D. thesis, University of Edinburgh.

Georgakopoulou, A. (1994), 'Modern Greek oral narratives in context: cultural constraints and evaluative ways of telling', *Text* 14, 371–99.

Georgakopoulou, A. (1995a), 'Women, men and conversational narrative performances: aspects of gender in Greek storytelling', *Anthropological Linguistics* 37, 460–86.

Georgakopoulou, A. (1995b), 'Narrative organisation and contextual constraints: the case of Modern Greek storytelling', *Journal of Narrative and Life History* 5, 161–89.

Georgakopoulou, A. (1995c), 'Everyday spoken discourse in Modern Greek culture: indexing through performance', *Kampos. Cambridge Papers in Modern Greek* 3, 15–44.

Givón, T. (1983), *Topic Continuity in Discourse: Quantified Cross-Language Studies*, Amsterdam/Philadelphia: Benjamins.

Givón, T. (1987), 'Beyond foreground and background', in R. Tomlin (ed.), *Coherence and Grounding in Discourse*, Amsterdam/Philadelphia: Benjamins, pp. 175–88.

Goffman, E. (1979), *Forms of Talk*, Oxford: Blackwell.

Gold, R. (1991), 'Answering machine talk', *Discourse Processes* 14, 243–60.

Goodwin, C. (1993), 'Recording human interaction in natural settings', *Pragmatics* 3(2), 181–209.

Goodwin, M. H. (1990), *He Said–She Said: Talk as Social Organisation among Black Children*, Bloomington: Indiana University Press.

Goutsos, D. (1994), *Sequential Relations and Strategies in Expository Discourse: A Topic Structure Model for English and Greek*, unpublished Ph.D. thesis, University of Birmingham.

Goutsos, D. (forthcoming), *Modelling Discourse Topic: Sequential Relations and Strategies in Expository Text*, Norwood, NJ: Ablex.

Grabe, W. (1987), 'Contrastive rhetoric and text-type research', in U. Connor and R. B. Kaplan (eds) *Writing Across Languages: Analysis of L2 Text*, Reading, MA: Addison-Wesley, pp. 115–37.

Graesser, G. and L. F. Clark (1985), *The Structures and Processes of Implicit Knowledge*, Norwood, NJ: Ablex.

Gregory, M. and S. Carroll (1978), *Language and Situation*, London: Routledge & Kegan Paul.

Grice, H. P. (1975), 'Logic and conversation', in P. Cole and J. Morgan (eds), *Syntax and Semantics 3: Speech Acts*, New York: Academic Press, pp. 41–58.

Grimes, J. (1975), *The Thread of Discourse*, The Hague: Mouton.

Grimes, J. (1983), 'Outlines and overlays', *Language* 48, 513–77.

Grosz, B. and C. L. Sidner (1986), 'Attention, intention and the structure of discourse', *Computational Linguistics* 12(3), 175–204.

Gumperz, J. (1982), *Discourse Strategies*, Cambridge: Cambridge University Press.

Gutwinski, W. (1976), *Cohesion in Literary Texts*, The Hague: Mouton.

Halliday, M. A. K. (1978), *Language as Social Semiotic: The Social Interpretation of Language and Meaning*, London: Edward Arnold.

Halliday, M. A. K. (1979), 'Differences between spoken and written language: some implications for literary teaching', in G. Page, J. Elkins and B. O'Connor (eds), *Communication Through Reading*, Adelaide: Australian Reading Association, pp. 37–52.

Halliday, M. A. K. (1985a), *An Introduction to Functional Grammar*, Oxford: Edward Arnold.

Halliday, M. A. K. (1985b), *Spoken and Written Language*, Oxford: Oxford University Press.

Halliday, M. A. K. (1987), 'Spoken and written modes of meaning', in R. Horowitz and S. J. Samuels (eds), *Comprehending Oral and Written Language*, New York: Academic Press, pp. 55–82.

Halliday, M. A. K. and R. Hasan (1976), *Cohesion in English*, London: Longman.

Halliday, M. A. K. and R. Hasan (1985), *Language, Context and Text: Aspects of Language in a Social-semiotic Perspective*, Oxford: Oxford University Press.

Harris, J. (1980), *Suprasentential Organisation in Written Discourse with reference to Writing by Children in the Lower Secondary Age Range*, unpublished Masters dissertation, University of Birmingham.

Harris, R. J., D. Lee, D. Hernsley and L. Schoen (1988), 'The effect of cultural script knowledge on memory for stories over time', *Discourse Processes* 11, 413–31.

Harris, Z. (1952), 'Discourse analysis', *Language* 28, 1–30.

Hartmann, R. R. K. (1980), *Contrastive Textology. Comparative Discourse Analysis in Applied Linguistics*, Heidelberg: Groos.

Hasan, R. (1984), 'Coherence and cohesive harmony', in J. Flood (ed.), *Understanding Reading Comprehension*, Delaware: International Reading Association, pp. 181–219.

Hatch, E. (1992), *Discourse and Language Education*, Cambridge: Cambridge University Press.

Hatim, B. and I. Mason (1990), *Discourse and the Translator*, London: Longman.

Hausendoff, H. and U. Quasthoff (1992), 'Children's storytelling in adult–child interaction: three dimensions in narrative development', *Journal of Narrative and Life History* 2, 293–306.

Havelock, E. (1982), *The Literate Revolution in Greece and its Cultural Consequences*, Princeton, NJ: Princeton University Press.

Haviland, S. and H. H. Clark (1974), 'What's new? Acquiring new information as a process in comprehension', *Journal of Verbal Learning and Verbal Behavior* 13, 512–21.

Heath, S. (1983), *Ways with Words: Language, Life and Work in Communities and Classrooms*, Cambridge: Cambridge University Press.

Heritage, J. and M. L. Sorgonen (1994), 'Constituting and maintaining activities across sequences: *And*-prefacing as a feature of question design', *Language in Society* 23, 1–29.

Herrnstein-Smith, B. (1981), 'Narrative versions, narrative theories', in W. Mitchell, (ed.), *On Narrative*, Chicago: The University of Chicago Press, pp. 209–32.

Hickmann, M. (1980), 'Creating referents in discourse: a developmental analysis of linguistic cohesion', in J. Kreiman and A. Ojeda (eds), *Papers from the Parasession on Pronouns and Anaphora*, Chicago: Chicago Linguistic Society, pp. 192–203.

Hickmann, M. (1991), 'The development of discourse cohesion: functional and cross-linguistic issues', in G. Pieraut and M. Dolitsky (eds), *Language Bases … Discourse Bases: Aspects of Contemporary French Language Psycholinguistics Research*, Amsterdam: Benjamins, pp. 158–85.

Hicks, D. (1990), 'Narrative skills and genre knowledge: ways of telling in the primary school grades', *Applied Psycholinguistics* 11, 83–104.

Hicks, D. (1991), 'Kinds of narrative: genre skills among first graders from two communities', in A. McCabe and C. Peterson (eds), *Developing Narrative Structure*, Hillsdale, NJ: Erlbaum, pp. 55–87.

Hill, J. H. and J. T. Irvine (eds). (1993), *Responsibility and Evidence in Oral Discourse*, Cambridge: Cambridge University Press.

Hinds, J. (1977), 'Paragraph structure and pronominalization', *Papers in Linguistics* 10, 77–99.

Hinds, J. (1979), 'Organizational patterns in discourse', in T. Givón (ed.), *Syntax and Semantics 12: Discourse and Syntax*, New York: Academic Press, pp. 135–57.

Hinds, J. (1983), 'Topic continuity in Japanese', in T. Givón (ed.), *Topic Continuity in Discourse*, Amsterdam: Benjamins, pp. 43–93.

Hinds, J. (1987), 'Reader versus writer responsibility: a new typology', in U. Connor and R. B. Kaplan (eds), *Writing Across Languages: Analysis of L2 Text*, Reading, MA: Addison-Wesley, pp. 141–52.

Hirsch, R. (1989), *Argumentation, Information and Interaction. Studies in Face-to-face Interactive Argumentation under Different Turn-taking Conditions*, Gothenburg: University of Gothenburg.

Hjelmslev, L. (1954), 'La stratification du langage', *Word* 10(2–3), 163–88.

Hobbs, J. (1979), 'Coherence and coreference', *Cognitive Science* 3, 67–90.

Hodge, R. and G. Kress (1988), *Social Semiotics*, Cambridge: Polity Press.

Hoey, M. (1979), *Signalling in Discourse*, Birmingham: University of Birmingham.

Hoey, M. (1983), *On the Surface of Discourse*, London: George Allen and Unwin.

Hoey, M. (1986a), 'Overlapping patterns of discourse organization and their implications for clause relational analysis in Problem–Solution texts', in C. Cooper and S. Greenbaum (eds), *Studying Writing: Linguistic Approaches*, London: Sage, pp. 187–225.

Hoey, M. (1986b), 'The discourse colony: a preliminary study of a neglected discourse type', in M. Coulthard (ed.), *Talking About Text*, Birmingham: University of Birmingham, pp. 1–26.

Hoey, M. (1991), *Patterns of Lexis in Text*, Oxford: Oxford University Press.

Hoey, M. (1992), 'The matrix organization of narrative and non-narrative text in English', in *Proceedings of the 5th International Symposium on the Description and/or Comparison of English and Greek*, Thessaloniki: School of English, University of Thessaloniki, pp. 215–53.

Hoey, M. and E. Winter (1986), 'Clause relations and the writer's communicative task', in B. Couture (ed.), *Functional Approaches to Writing. Research Perspectives*, London: Pinter, pp. 120–41.

Hofmann, T. R. (1989), 'Paragraphs and anaphora', *Journal of Pragmatics* 13, 239–50.

Holmes, J. (1995), *Women, Men and Politeness*, London: Longman.

Hopper, P. J. (1979), 'Aspect and foregrounding in discourse', in T. Givón (ed.), *Syntax and Semantics 12: Discourse and Syntax*, New York: Academic Press, pp. 213–41.

Hopper, P. J. (1988), 'Emergent grammar and the a priori grammar postulate', in D. Tannen (ed.), *Linguistics in Context: Connecting Observation and Understanding*, Norwood, NJ: Ablex, pp. 117–34.

Hopper, P. J. and S. A. Thompson (1980), 'Transitivity in grammar and discourse', *Language* 56, 251–99.

Horn, L. R. (1988), 'Pragmatic theory', in F. J. Newmeyer (ed.), *Language: The Sociocultural Context*, Cambridge: Cambridge University Press [= Linguistics: The Cambridge Survey, 4], pp. 113–45.

Houghton, D. and M. Hoey (1983), 'Linguistics and written discourse: contrastive rhetorics', *ARAL* 3, 2–22.

Hovy, E. H. (1990), 'Unresolved issues in paragraph planning', in R. Dale, C. Mellish and M. Zock (eds), *Current Research in Natural Language Generation*, London: Academic Press, pp. 17–45.

Hudson, J. A. and R. Shapiro (1991), 'From knowing to telling: the development of children's scripts, stories, and personal narratives', in A. McCabe and C. Peterson (eds), *Developing Narrative Structure*, Hillsdale, NJ: Erlbaum, pp. 89–136.

Hughes, J. and K. McCoy (1993), 'Observations and directions in text structure', in O. Rambow (ed.), *Intentionality and Structure in Discourse Relations*, Columbus: Association for Computational Linguistics, pp. 40–3.

Hunston, S. (1993), 'Professional conflict: disagreement in academic discourse', in M. Baker, G. Francis and E. Tognini-Bonelli (eds), *Text and Technology: In Honour of John Sinclair*, Philadelphia/Amsterdam: John Benjamins, pp. 115–34.

Hunston, S. (1994), 'Evaluation and organization in a sample of written academic discourse', in M. Coulthard (ed.), *Advances in Written Text Analysis*, London: Routledge, pp. 191–218.

Hunter, K. M. (1991), *Doctor's Stories: The Narrative Structure of Medical Knowledge*, Princeton, NJ: Princeton University Press.

Hymes, D. (1964), 'Introduction: Towards ethnographies of communication', in J. J. Gumperz and D. Hymes (eds), *The Ethnography of Communication. American Anthropologist* 66(2). Special publ., Washington, DC, pp. 1–34.

Hymes, D. (1972), 'Models of the interaction of language and social life', in J. J.

Gumperz and D. Hymes (eds), *Directions in Sociolinguistics: The Ethnography of Communication*, New York: Holt, Rinehart and Winston, pp. 35–71.

Hymes, D. (1974), 'Ways of speaking', in R. Bauman and J. Sherzer (eds), *Explorations in the Ethnography of Speaking*, Cambridge: Cambridge University Pres, pp. 433–52.

Hymes, D. (1977), 'Discovering oral performance and measured verse in American Indian narrative', *New Literary History* 8, 431–57.

Illich, I. (1993), *In the Vineyard of the Text: A Commentary to Hugh's Didascalicon*. Chicago: The University of Chicago Press.

Jakobson, R. (1960), 'Concluding statement: linguistics and poetics', in T. A. Sebeok (ed.), *Style in Language*, Cambridge, MA: The MIT Press, pp. 350–77.

Jefferson, G. (1978), 'Sequential aspects of storytelling in conversation', in J. Schenkein (ed.), *Studies in the Organisation of Conversational Interaction*, New York: Free Press, pp. 219–48.

Johns, T. (1994), 'The text and its message', in M. Coulthard (ed.), *Advances in Written Text Analysis*, London: Routledge, pp. 102–16.

Johnson-Laird, P. (1983), *Mental Models: Towards a Cognitive Science of Language, Inference and Consciousness*, Cambridge, MA: Harvard University Press.

Johnstone, B. (1990), *Stories, Community and Place: Narratives from Middle America*, Bloomington: Indiana University Press.

Johnstone, B. (ed.) (1994a), *Repetition in Discourse: Interdisciplinary Perspectives*, vol. 1, Norwood, NJ: Ablex.

Johnstone, B. (ed.) (1994b), *Repetition in Discourse: Interdisciplinary Perspectives*, vol. 2, Norwood, NJ: Ablex.

Jordan, M. (1984), *The Rhetoric of Everyday English Texts*, London: George Allen & Unwin.

Josselson, R. and A. Lieblicht (eds) (1993), *The Narrative Study of Lives*, Newbury Park: Sage.

Kaplan, R. B. (1983), 'Contrastive rhetorics: some implications for the writing process', in A. Freedman, I. Pringle and J. Yalden (eds), *Learning to Write: First Language/Second Language*, London: Longman, pp. 139–61.

Karmiloff-Smith, A. (1980), 'Psychological processes underlying pronominalization in children's connected discourse', in J. Kreiman and A. Ojeda (eds), *Papers from the Parasession on Pronouns and Anaphora*, Chicago: Chicago Linguistic Society, pp. 231–50.

Karmiloff-Smith, A. (1985), 'Language and cognitive processes from a developmental perspective', *Language and Cognitive Processes* 1, 61–85.

Kernan, K. (1977), 'Semantic and expressive elaboration in children's narratives', in S. Ervin-Tripp and C. Mitchell-Kernan (eds), *Child Discourse*, New York: Academic Press, pp. 91–103.

Kies, D. (1988), 'Marked themes with and without pronominal reinforcement: their meaning and distribution in discourse', in E. H. Steiner and R. Veltman (eds), *Pragmatics, Discourse and Text. Some Systemically-inspired Approaches*, London: Pinter Publishers, pp. 47–75.

Kinneavy, J. L. (1971), *A Theory of Discourse*, Englewood Cliffs, NJ: Prentice-Hall.

Kintsch, W. (1988), 'The role of knowledge in discourse comprehension: a construction-integration model', *Psychological Review* 95, 163–82.

Kintsch, W. and E. Greene (1978), 'The role of culture-specific schemata in the comprehension and recall of stories', *Discourse Processes* 1, 1–13.

Kintsch, W. and E. F. Mross (1985), 'Context effect in word identification', *Journal of Memory and Language* 24, 336–49.

Knott, A. (1993), 'Using cue phrases to determine a set of rhetorical relations', in O. Rambow (ed.), *Intentionality and Structure in Discourse Relations*, Columbus: Association for Computational Linguistics, pp. 48–51.

Koch, J. B. (1983), 'Presentation as proof: the language of Arabic rhetoric', *Anthropological Linguistics* 25, 47–60.

Koen, F., A. Becker and R. Young (1969), 'The psychological reality of the paragraph', *Journal of Verbal Learning and Verbal Behavior* 8, 49–53.

Kress, G. (1996), 'Representational resources and the production of subjectivity. Questions for the theoretical development of Critical Discourse Analysis in a multicultural society', in C. R. Caldas-Coulthard and M. Coulthard (eds), *Texts and Practices: Readings in Critical Discourse Analysis*, London: Routledge, pp. 15–31.

Kress, G. and B. Hodge (1990), *Language as Ideology*, London: Routledge.

Kroll, B. M. (1977), 'Ways communicators encode propositions in spoken and written English: a look at subordination and co-ordination', in E. Keenan and T. Bennett (eds), *Discourse Across Time and Space. Southern California Occasional Papers in Linguistics* 5, Los Angeles: University of California Press, pp. 69–108.

Kurzon, D. (1985), 'Signposts for the reader: a corpus-based study of text deixis', *Text* 5(3), 187–200.

Labov, W. (1972), *Language in the Inner City*, Oxford: Blackwell.

Labov, W. and D. Fanshel, D. (1977), *Therapeutic Discourse*, New York: Academic Press.

Labov, W. and J. Waletzky (1967), 'Narrative analysis: oral versions of personal experience', in J. Helm (ed.), *Essays on the Verbal and Visual Arts*, Seattle: University of Washington Press, pp. 12–44.

Lakoff, R. (1982), 'Persuasive discourse and ordinary conversation, with examples from advertising', in D. Tannen (ed.), *Analyzing Discourse: Text and Talk*, Georgetown: Georgetown University Press, pp. 25–42.

Lautamatti, L. (1987), 'Observations on the development of the topic of simplified discourse', in U. Connor and R. B. Kaplan, R. B. (eds), *Writing Across Languages: Analysis of L2 Text*, Reading, MA: Addison-Wesley, pp. 87–114.

Lavandera, B. (1988), 'The study of language in its socio-cultural context', in F. J. Newmeyer (ed.), *Language: The Socio-cultural Context*, Cambridge: Cambridge University Press [= Linguistics: The Cambridge Survey, 4], pp. 1–13.

Leech, G. (1983), *The Principles of Pragmatics*, London: Longman.

Leech, G. and M. Short (1981), *Style in Fiction*, London: Longman.

Lehiste, I. (1982), 'Some phonetic characteristics of discourse', *Studia Linguistica* 36(2), 117–30.

Leith, D. (1995), 'Tense variation as a performance feature in a Scottish folktale', *Language in Society* 24, 53–77.

Leki, I. (1991), 'Twenty-five years of Contrastive Rhetoric: text analysis and writing pedagogies', *TESOL Quarterly* 25(1), 123–43.

Levinson, S. (1983), *Pragmatics*. Cambridge: Cambridge University Press.

Liddicoat, A. (1994), 'Discourse routines in answering machine communication in Australia', *Discourse Processes* 17, 283–309.

Linde, C. (1979), 'Focus of attention and the choice of pronouns in discourse', in T. Givón (ed.), *Syntax and Semantics 12: Discourse and Syntax*, New York: Academic Press, pp. 337–54.

Linde, C. (1993), *Life Stories. The Creation of Coherence*, New York: Oxford University Press.

Linde, C. and W. Labov (1975), 'Spatial networks as a site for the study of language and thought', *Language* 51, 924–39.

Lindeberg, A.-C., N. E. Enkvist and K. Wikberg (eds) (1992), *Nordic Research on Text and Discourse: Nordtext Symposium (1990)*, Åbo: Åbo University Press.

Lindstrom, A. (1994), 'Identification and recognition in Swedish telephone conversation openings', *Language in Society* 23, 231–52.

Longacre, R. (1976), *An Anatomy of Speech Notions*, Lisse: Peter de Ridder.

Longacre, R. (1979), 'The paragraph as a grammatical unit', in T. Givón (ed.), *Syntax and Semantics 12: Discourse and Syntax*, New York: Academic Press, pp. 115–34.

Longacre, R. (1981), 'A spectrum and profile approach to discourse analysis', *Text* 1, 337–59.

Longacre, R. (1989), 'Two hypotheses regarding text generation and analysis', *Discourse Processes* 12, 413–60.

McCabe, A. and C. Peterson (eds) (1991), *Developing Narrative Structure*, Hillsdale, NJ: Erlbaum.

McCarthy, M. (1992), *Discourse Analysis for Language Teachers*, Cambridge: Cambridge University Press.

McCarthy, M. (1993), 'Spoken discourse markers in written text', in J. Sinclair, M. Hoey and G. Fox (eds), *Techniques of Description: Spoken and Written Discourse. A Festschrift for Malcolm Coulthard*, London: Routledge, pp. 170–82.

McCarthy, M. (1994), '*It, this* and *that*', in M. Coulthard (ed.), *Advances in Written Text Analysis*, London: Routledge, pp. 266–75.

Macdonnel, D. (1986), *Theories of Discourse: An Introduction*, Oxford: Blackwell.

McKeown, K. R. (1985), *Text Generation: Using Discourse Strategies and Focus Constraints to Generate Natural Language*, Cambridge: Cambridge University Press.

McKoon, G. and R. Ratcliff (1992), 'Inference during reading', *Psychological Review* 99, 440–66.

McMenamin, G. R. (1993), *Forensic Stylistics*, Amsterdam: Elsevier.

Maier, E. and E. Hovy, E. (1993), 'Organizing discourse structure relations using metafunctions', in H. Horacek and M. Zock, (eds), *New Concepts in Natural Language Generation. Planning, Realization and Systems*, London: Pinter, pp. 69–86.

Malinowski, B. (1946), 'The problem of meaning in primitive languages', Supplement I, in C. Ogden and I. A. Richards (eds), *The Meaning of Meaning*, London: Routledge & Kegan Paul, pp. 296–336.

Mandler, J. M. (1978), 'A code in the node: the use of a story schema in retrieval', *Discourse Processes* 1, 14–35.

Mandler, J. M. (1987), 'On the psychological reality of story structure', *Discourse Processes* 10, 1–29.

Mandler, J. M. and N. S. Johnson (1977), 'Remembrance of things parsed: story structure and recall', *Cognitive Psychology* 9, 111–51.

Mandler, J. M., S. Scribner, M. Cole and M. De Forest (1980), 'Cross-cultural invariance in story recall', *Child Development* 51, 19–26.

Mann, W. C., C. Matthiessen and S. A. Thompson (1992), 'Rhetorical structure theory and text analysis', in W. C. Mann and S. A. Thompson (eds), *Discourse Description: Diverse Linguistic Analyses of a Fund-Raising Text*. Amsterdam/Philadelphia: John Benjamins, pp. 39–78.

Mann, W. C. and S. A. Thompson (1986), 'Relational propositions in discourse', *Discourse Processes* 9, 57–90.

Mann, W. C. and S. A. Thompson (1988), 'Rhetorical structure theory: toward a functional theory of text organization', *Text* 8(3), 243–81.

Maranhão, T. (1993), 'Recollections of fieldwork conversations, or authorial difficulties in anthropological writing', in J. H. Hill and J. T. Irvine (eds), *Responsibility and Evidence in Oral Discourse*, Cambridge: Cambridge University Press, pp. 260–88.

Marchese, L. (1988), 'Sequential chaining and discourse structure in Godie', in J. Haiman and S. A. Thompson (eds), *Clause Combining in Grammar and Discourse*, Amsterdam/Philadelphia: Benjamins, pp. 247–74.

Martin, J. R. (1992), *English Text: System and Structure*, Philadelphia/Amsterdam: John Benjamins.

Maschler, Y. (1994), 'Metalanguaging and discourse markers in bilingual conversations', *Language in Society* 23, 323–66.

Mathis, T. and G. Yule (1994), 'Zero quotatives', *Discourse Processes* 18, 63–76.

Mayes, P. (1990), 'Quotation in spoken English', *Studies in Language* 14, 325–63.

Michaels, S. (1981), '"Sharing time": children's narrative styles and differential access to literacy', *Language in Society* 10, 423–42.

Miller, J. and R. Weinert (1995), 'The function of *like* in dialogue', *Journal of Pragmatics* 23, 365–93.

Miller, P. J. and L. L. Sperry (1988), 'Early talk about the past: the origin of conversational stories of personal experience', *Journal of Child Language* 15, 293–315.

Minami, M. and A. McCabe (1991), 'Haiku as a discourse regulation device: a stanza analysis of Japanese children's personal narratives', *Language in Society* 20, 577–601.

Minsky, M. (1985), 'A framework for representing knowledge', in R. J. Brachman, and H. J. Levesque (eds), *Readings in Knowledge Representation*, Los Altos, CA: Morgan Kaufmann, pp. 245–62.

Mischler, E. G. (1995), 'Models of narrative analysis: a typology', *Journal of Narrative and Life History* 5, 87–123.

Mitchell, T. F. 1957. 'The language of buying and selling in Cyrenaica', *Hesperis* 44, 31–71.

Moffett, J. (1968), *Teaching the Universe of Discourse*, Boston, MA: Houghton Mifflin.

Montgomery, M. (1986), *An Introduction to Language and Society*, London: Routledge.

Moore, J. D. and C. Paris (1993), 'Planning text for advisory dialogues: capturing intentional and rhetorical information', *Computational Linguistics* 19 (4), 651–94.

Moore, J. D. and M. E. Pollack (1992), 'A problem for RST: the need for multi-level discourse analysis', *Computational Linguistics* 18(4), 537–44.

Mumby, D. K. (ed.) (1993), *Narrative and Social Control: Critical Perspectives*, Newbury Park: Sage.

Myers, G. (1989), 'The pragmatics of politeness in scientific articles', *Applied Linguistics* 10, 1–35.

Myers, G. (1994), 'Narratives of science and nature in popularizing molecular genetics', in M. Coulthard (ed.), *Advances in Written Text Analysis*, London: Routledge, pp. 179–90.

Myers, G. and T. Hartley (1990), 'Modelling lexical cohesion and focus in written texts: popular science articles and the naive reader', in U. Schmitz, R. Schütz and A. Kunz, A. (eds), *Linguistic Approaches to Artificial Intelligence*, Frankfurt: Peter Lang, pp. 201–42.

Nwogu, K. (1990), *Discourse Variation in Medical Texts: Schema, Theme and Cohesion in Professional and Journalistic Accounts*, Nottingham: University of Nottingham.

Nwogu, K. and T. Bloor (1992), 'Thematic progression in professional and popular medical papers', in E. Ventola (ed.), *Functional and Systemic Linguistics: Approaches and Uses*, Berlin: Mouton de Gruyter, 369–84.

Nystrand, M., S. Greene and J. Wiemelt (1993), 'Where did composition studies come from? An intellectual history', *Written Communication* 10(3), 267–333.

Ochs, E. (1979), 'Planned and unplanned discourse', in T. Givón (ed.), *Syntax and Semantics 12: Discourse and Syntax*, New York: Academic Press, pp. 51–80.

Ochs, E., C. Taylor, D. Rudolph and R. Smith (1992), 'Storytelling as a theory-building activity', *Discourse Processes* 15, 37–72.

O'Donnell, R. C. (1974), 'Syntactic differences between speech and writing', *American Speech* 49, 102–11.

Olson, D. R. (1977), 'From utterance to text: the bias of language in speech and writing', *Harvard Educational Review* 47, 257–81.

Olson, D. R. and N. Torrance (eds) (1991), *Literacy and Orality*, Cambridge: Cambridge University Press.

Ong, W. (1982), *Orality and Literacy. The Technologizing of the Word*, London: Methuen.

Paltridge, B. (1995), 'Genre analysis and the identification of textual boundaries', *Applied Linguistics* 16, 288–99.

Parsons, G. (1992), 'Cohesion coherence: scientific texts', in E. Ventola (ed.), *Functional and Systemic Linguistics: Approaches and Uses*, Berlin: Mouton de Gruyter, pp. 415–29.

Payne, D. L. (1992), 'Narrative discontinuity versus continuity in Yagua', *Discourse Processes* 15, 375–91.

Payne, T. E. (1993), *The Twin Stories: Participant Coding in Yagua Narrative*, Los Angeles: University of California Press.

Pennington, M. and R. Hastie (1993), 'The story model for juror decision making', in R. Hastie (ed.), *Inside the Juror: The Psychology of Juror Decision Making*, Cambridge:

Cambridge University Press, pp. 192–221.

Peterson, C. and A. McCabe (1983), *Developmental Psycholinguistics. Three Ways of Looking at a Child's Narrative*, New York: Plenum.

Phillips, M. (1989), *Lexical Structure of Text*, Birmingham: University of Birmingham.

Pike, K. L. (1981), *Tagmemics, Discourse and Verbal Art*, Ann Arbor: University of Michigan.

Polanyi, L. (1979), 'So what's the point?', *Semiotica* 25, 207–41.

Polanyi, L. (1982), 'Literary aspects of oral storytelling', in D. Tannen (ed.), *Written and Spoken Language. Exploring Orality and Literacy*, Norwood, NJ: Ablex, pp. 155–70.

Polanyi, L. (1985), *Telling the American Story: A Structural and Cultural Analysis of Conversational Storytelling*, Norwood, NJ: Ablex.

Polanyi, L. and R. Scha (1983), 'On the recursive structure of discourse', in K. Ehlich and H. van Riemsdijk (eds), *Connectedness in Sentence, Discourse and Text*, Tilburg: Tilburg University, pp. 141–78.

Pratt, M. L. (1977), *Toward a Speech Act Theory of Literary Discourse*, Bloomington: Indiana University Press.

Preece, A. (1987), 'The range of narrative forms conversationally produced by young children', *Journal of Child Language* 14, 353–73.

Prince, E. F. (1981), 'Toward a taxonomy of given-new information', in P. Cole (ed.), *Radical Pragmatics*, New York: Academic Press, pp. 223–55.

Prince, G. (1987), *A Dictionary of Narratology*, Aldershot: Scolar Press.

Pu, M. (1995), 'Anaphoric patterning in English and Mandarin narrative production', *Discourse Processes* 19, 279–300.

Quasthoff, U. (ed.) (1980), *Erzählen in Gesprächen*. [= Storytelling in Conversations]. Tübingen: Narr.

Quirk, R., S. Greenbaum, G. Leech and J. Svartvik (1985), *A Comprehensive Grammar of the English Language*. London: Longman.

Rambow, O. (ed.) (1993), *Intentionality and Structure in Discourse Relations*, Columbus: Association for Computational Linguistics.

Reddick, R. J. (1986), 'Textlinguistics, text theory, and language users', *Word* 37, 31–43.

Reddick, R. J. (1992), 'English expository discourse', in S. J. Hwang and W. R. Merrifield (eds), *Language in Context: Essays for Robert E. Longacre*, Dallas: The Summer Institute for Linguistics, pp. 211–24.

Redeker, G. (1987), 'Introductions of story characters in interactive and non-interactive narration', in J. Verschueren and M. Bertucelli-Pappi (eds), *The Pragmatic Perspective*, Amsterdam/Philadelphia: Benjamins, pp. 339–51.

Redeker, G. (1990), 'Ideational and pragmatic markers of discourse structure', *Journal of Pragmatics* 14, 367–81.

Redeker, G. (1991), 'Linguistic markers of discourse structure. Review article of Schiffrin 1987', *Linguistics* 29, 1139–72.

Redeker, G. (1992), 'Coherence and structure in text and discourse', unpublished manuscript, Tilburg University.

Reichman, R. (1985), *Getting Computers to Talk Like You and Me*, Cambridge, MA: The MIT Press.

Reinhart, T. (1983), *Anaphora and Semantic Interpretation*, London: Croom Helm.

Reinhart, T. (1984), 'Principles of gestalt perception in the temporal organization of narrative texts', *Linguistics* 22, 779–809.

Riley, P. (ed.) (1985), *Discourse and Learning. Papers in Applied Linguistics and Language Learning from the Centre de Recherches et d'Applications Pédagogiques en Langues (C.R.A.P.E.L.)*, London: Longman.

Robinson, J. A. (1981), 'Personal narratives reconsidered', *Journal of American Folklore* 94, 58–85.

Rosaldo, M. (1982), 'The things we do with words: Illongot speech acts and speech act theory in philosophy', *Language in Society* 11, 203–37.

Rumelhart, D. (1975), 'Notes on a schema for stories', in D. Bobrow and A. Collins (eds), *Representation and Understanding: Studies in Cognitive Science*, New York: Academic Press, pp. 211–36.

Sacks, H. (1967), Mimeo lecture notes. Now published in Sacks (1992),

Sacks, H. (1972), 'On the analyzability of stories by children', in J. J. Gumperz and D. Hymes (eds), *Directions in Sociolinguistics: The Ethnography of Communication*, New York: Holt, Rinehart & Winston, pp. 325–45.

Sacks, H. (1974), 'An analysis of the course of a joke's telling in conversation', in R. Bauman and J. Sherzer (eds), *Explorations in the Ethnography of Speaking*, Cambridge: Cambridge University Press, pp. 337–53.

Sacks, H. (1992), *Harvey Sacks: Lectures on Conversation* (ed. G. Jefferson, intro. E. A. Schegloff), Cambridge, MA: Blackwell.

Sacks, H., E. A. Schegloff and G. Jefferson (1974), 'A simplest systematics for the organization of turn-taking in conversation', *Language* 50, 696–735.

Sanders, T., W. Spooren and L. Noordman (1992), 'Toward a taxonomy of coherence relations', *Discourse Processes* 15(1), 1–35.

Saville-Troike, M. (1982), *The Ethnography of Communication*, Oxford: Blackwell.

Sawyer, K. (1993), 'The pragmatics of play: interactional strategies during children's pretend play', *Pragmatics* 3(3), 259–82.

Schank, R. (1982), *Dynamic Memory*, London: Cambridge University Press.

Schank, R. and R. P. Abelson (1977), *Scripts, Plans, Goals and Understanding*, Hillsdale, NJ: Erlbaum.

Schegloff, E. A. (1968), 'Sequencing in conversational openings', *American Anthropologist* 70(6), 1,075–95.

Schegloff, E. A. (1986), 'The routine as achievement', *Human Studies* 9, 111–51.

Schegloff, E. A. and H. Sacks (1973), 'Opening up closings', *Semiotica* 7, 289–327.

Schiffrin, D. (1980), 'Meta-talk: organizational and evaluative brackets in discourse', *Sociological Inquiry* 50(3–4), 199–236.

Schiffrin, D. (1981), 'Tense variation in narrative', *Language* 57, 45–62.

Schiffrin, D. (1987), *Discourse Markers*. Cambridge: Cambridge University Press.

Schiffrin, D. (1990), 'The management of a co-operative self during argument: the role of opinions and stories', in A. Grimshaw (ed.), *Conflict Talk: Sociolinguistic Investigations of Arguments in Conversations*, Cambridge: Cambridge University Press, pp. 241–59.

Schiffrin, D. (1994a), *Approaches to Discourse*, Oxford: Blackwell.

Schiffrin, D. (1994b), 'Making a list', *Discourse Processes* 17, 377–406.

Schleppegrell, M. J. (1990), 'Paratactic "because"', *Journal of Pragmatics* 16, 291–306.

Schöttler, P. (1989), 'Historians and discourse analysis', *History Workshop Journal* 27, 37–65.

Schourup, L. (1985), *Common Discourse Particles in English Conversation: like, well, y'know*, New York: Garland.

Scollon, R. and S. Scollon (1995), *Intercultural Communication*, Oxford: Blackwell.

Scribner, S. and M. Cole (1981), *The Psychology of Literacy*, Cambridge, MA: Harvard University Press.

Searle, J. (1969), *Speech Acts*, Cambridge: Cambridge University Press.

Segal, E. M., J. F. Duchan and P. J. Scott (1991), 'The role of interclausal connectives in narrative structure: evidence from adults' interpretations of simple stories', *Discourse Processes* 14, 27–54.

Shaul, D. L., R. Albert, C. Golston and R. Satony (1987), 'The Hopi Coyote story as narrative: the problem of evaluation', *Journal of Pragmatics* 11, 3–25.

Sherzer, J. and A. C. Woodbury (eds) (1987), *Native American Discourse: Poetics and Rhetoric*, Cambridge: Cambridge University Press.

Shippey, T. A. (1993), 'Principles of conversation in Beowulfian speech', in J. M. Sinclair, M. Hoey and G. Fox (eds), *Techniques of Description: Spoken and Written Discourse. A Festschrift for Malcolm Coulthard*, London: Routledge, pp. 109–26.

Short, M. (1988), 'Speech presentation, the novel and the press', in W. van Peer (ed.), *The Taming of the Text*, London: Routledge, pp. 61–81.

Short, M., E. Semino and S. Culperer (1996), 'Using a corpus for stylistics research: speech and thought presentation', in J. Thomas and M. Short (eds), *Using Corpora for Language Research*, London: Longman, pp. 110–31.

Shuman, A. (1986), *Storytelling Rights. The Uses of Oral and Written Texts by Urban Adolescents*, Cambridge: Cambridge University Press.

Sidner, C. (1983), 'Focusing in the comprehension of definite anaphora', in M. Brady and R. C. Berwick (eds), *Computational Models of Discourse*, Cambridge, MA: The MIT Press, pp. 267–330.

Sifianou, M. (1989), 'On the telephone again! Difference in telephone behaviour: England versus Greece', *Language in Society* 18, 527–44.

Silva-Corvalan, C. (1983), 'Tense and aspect in oral Spanish narrative: context and meaning', *Language* 59, 760–80.

Silverman, D. (1993), *Interpreting Qualitative Data: Methods of Analysing Talk, Text and Interaction*, London: Sage.

Silverstein, M. (1984), 'On the pragmatic "poetry" of prose: parallelism, repetition, and cohesive structure in the time course of dyadic conversation', in D. Schiffrin (ed.), *Meaning, Form and Use in Context: Linguistic Applications*, Washington, DC: Georgetown University Press, pp. 181–99.

Sinclair, J. M. (1985), 'On the integration of linguistic description', in T. A. van Dijk, (ed.), *Handbook of Discourse Analysis*, vol. 2, New York: Academic Press, pp. 13–28.

Sinclair, J. M. (1988), 'Mirror for a text', unpublished manuscript, University of Birmingham.

Sinclair, J. M. (1991), *Corpus, Concordance, Collocation*, Oxford: Oxford University Press.

Sinclair, J. M. (1992), 'Trust the text', in M. Davies and L. Ravelli (eds), *Advances in Systemic Linguistics. Recent Theory and Practice*, London: Pinter, pp. 5–19.

Sinclair, J. M. (1993), 'Written discourse structure', in J. M. Sinclair, M. Hoey and G. Fox, G. (eds), *Techniques of Description: Spoken and Written Discourse. A Festschrift for Malcolm Coulthard*, London: Routledge, pp. 6–31.

Sinclair, J. M. and M. Coulthard (1975), *Towards an Analysis of Discourse*, London: Oxford University Press.

Slembrouck, S. (1992), 'The parliamentary *Hansard* "verbatim" report: the written construction of spoken discourse', *Language & Literature* 1, 101–19.

Slobin, D. (1990), 'The development from child speaker to native speaker', in J. W. Stigler, R. A. Schweder and G. Herdt (eds), *Cultural Psychology*, Cambridge: Cambridge University Press, pp. 233–56.

Smith, R. N. and W. J. Frawley (1983), 'Conjunctive cohesion in four English genres', *Text* 3(4), 347–74.

Stahl, S. (1989), *Literary Folklorists and the Personal Narrative*, Bloomington: Indiana University Press.

Stark, H. (1988), 'What do paragraph markings do?', *Discourse Processes* 11, 275–303.

Stein, N. (1982), 'The definition of a story', *Journal of Pragmatics* 6, 487–507.

Stein, N. and C. Glenn (1979), 'An analysis of story comprehension in elementary school children', in R. O. Freedle (ed.), *New Directions in Discourse Processing*, Norwood, NJ: Ablex, pp. 53–119.

Stein, N. and M. Policastro (1984), 'The concept of a story: a comparison between children's and teachers' viewpoints', in H. Mandl, N. Stein and T. Trabasso (eds), *Learning and Comprehension of Text*, Hillsdale, NJ: Erlbaum, 113–35.

Stubbs, M. (1983), *Discourse Analysis. The Sociolinguistic Analysis of Natural Language*, Oxford: Blackwell.

Stubbs, M. (1993), 'British traditions in text analysis. From Firth to Sinclair', in M. Baker, G. Francis and E. Tognini-Bonelli (eds), *Text and Technology: In Honour of John Sinclair*, Philadelphia/Amsterdam: John Benjamins, pp. 1–33.

Svartvik, J. (ed.) (1992), *Directions in Corpus Linguistics*, Berlin: Mouton de Gruyter.

Swales, J. (1990), *Genre Analysis. English in Academic and Research Settings*, Cambridge: Cambridge University Press.

Tadros, A. (1994), 'Predictive categories in expository text', in M. Coulthard (ed.), *Advances in Written Text Analysis*, London: Routledge, pp. 69–82.

Tannen, D. (1982a), 'Oral and literate strategies in spoken and written narratives', *Language* 58(1), 1–21.

Tannen, D. (ed.) (1982b), *Coherence in Spoken and Written Discourse*, Norwood, NJ: Ablex.

Tannen, D. (1984), *Conversational Style: Analyzing Talk among Friends*, Norwood, NJ: Ablex.

Tannen, D. (1986), 'Introducing constructed dialogue in Greek and American conversational and literary narrative', in F. Coulmas (ed.), *Direct and Indirect Speech*, Berlin: Mouton, pp. 311–32.

Tannen, D. (1987), 'Repetition in conversation: toward a poetics of talk', *Language* 63, 574–605.

Tannen, D. (1988), 'Hearing voices in conversation, fiction, and mixed genres', in D. Tannen (ed.), *Linguistics in Context: Connecting Observation and Understanding*, Norwood, NJ: Ablex, pp. 89–113.

Tannen, D. (1989), *Talking Voices. Repetition, Dialogue and Imagery in Conversational Discourse*, Cambridge: Cambridge University Press.

Tedlock, D. (1983), *The Spoken Word and the Work of Interpretation*, Philadelphia: University of Pennsylvania Press.

Thompson, G. and Y. Ye (1991), 'Evaluation in the reporting verbs used in academic papers', *Applied Linguistics* 12, 365–82.

Thompson, S. A. (1984), '"Subordination" in formal and informal discourse', in D. Schiffrin (ed.), *Meaning, Form and Use in Context: Linguistic Applications*, Washington, DC: Georgetown University Press, pp. 85–93.

Thompson, S. A. and R. Longacre (1985), 'Adverbial clauses', in T. Shopen (ed.), *Language Typology and Syntactic Description*, vol. 2, Cambridge: Cambridge University Press, pp. 171–234.

Tomlin, R. (1987), 'Linguistic reflections of cognitive events', in R. Tomlin (ed.), *Coherence and Grounding in Discourse*, Amsterdam/Philadelphia: Benjamins, pp. 455–79.

Toolan, M. (1988), *Narrative: A Critical Linguistic Introduction*, London: Routledge.

Toulmin, S. (1969), *The Uses of Argument*, Cambridge: Cambridge University Press.

Toulmin, S., R. Rieke and A. Janik (1979), *An Introduction to Reasoning*, New York: Macmillan.

Trabasso, T., P. van de Broek and S. Y. Suh (1989), 'Logical necessity and transitivity of causal relations in stories', *Discourse Processes* 12, 1–25.

Trabasso, T. and L. Sperry (1985), 'Causal relatedness and the importance of story events', *Journal of Memory and Language* 24, 595–611.

Trabasso, T. and S. Suh (1993), 'Understanding text: achieving explanatory coherence through on-line inferences and mental operations in working memory', *Discourse Processes* 16, 3–34.

Tyler, S. A. (1978), *The Said and the Unsaid*, New York: Academic Press.

Umiker-Sebeok, D. S. (1979), 'Preschool children's intraconversational narratives', *Journal of Child Language* 6, 91–109.

Ure, J. (1971), 'Lexical density and variety differentiation', in G. Perren and J. Trim (eds), *Applications of Linguistics: Papers from the 2nd AILA Congress*, Cambridge: Cambridge University Press, pp. 443–52.

Vendler, Z. (1967), *Linguistics in Philosophy*, Ithaca: Cornell University Press.

Ventola, E. (1987), *The Structure of Social Interaction: A Systemic Approach to the Semiotics of Service Encounters*, London: Pinter.

Vestergaard, T. and K. Schroder (1985), *The Language of Advertising*. Oxford: Blackwell.

Virtanen, T. (1992), *Discourse Functions of Adverbial Placement in English: Clause-initial*

Adverbials of Time and Place in Narratives and Procedural Place Descriptions, Åbo: Åbo Academy Press.

Volosinov, V. (1973 [1929]), *Marxism and the Philosophy of Language*, New York: Seminar Press.

Vonk, W., L. G. Hustinx and W. Simons (1992), 'The use of referential expressions in structuring discourse', *Language & Cognitive Processes* 7, 301–33.

Wales, K. (1988), 'Back to the future: Bakhtin, stylistics and discourse', in W. van Peer (ed.), *The Taming of the Text*, London: Routledge, pp. 176–92.

Wallace, S. (1982), 'Figure and ground: the interrelationships of linguistic categories', in P. J. Hopper (ed.), *Tense–Aspect: Between Semantics and Pragmatics*, Amsterdam/Philadelphia: Benjamins, pp. 201–23.

Webber, B. (1981), 'Discourse model synthesis: preliminaries to reference', in A. Joshi, B. Webber and I. Sag (eds), *Elements of Discourse Understanding*, Cambridge: Cambridge University Press, pp. 283–99.

Werlich, E. (1976), *A Text Grammar of English*, Heidelberg: Groos.

White, H. (1981), 'The value of narrativity in the representation of reality', in J. Mitchell (ed.), *On Narrative*, Chicago: University of Chicago Press, pp. 5–75.

Whitney, P., D. Budd, R. S. Bramucci and R. S. Crane (1995), 'On babies, bath water, and schemata: a reconsideration of top-down processes in comprehension', *Discourse Processes* 20, 135–66.

Wilensky, R. (1982), 'Story grammars revisited', *Journal of Pragmatics* 6, 423–32.

Williams, M. P. (1988), 'Functional context perspective in the context of systemic functional grammar', in E. H. Steiner and R. Veltman (eds), *Pragmatics, Discourse and Text. Some Systemically-inspired Approaches*, London: Pinter, pp. 76–89.

Williams, R. (1977), *Marxism and Literature*, Oxford: Oxford University Press.

Winter, E. (1982), *Towards a Contextual Grammar of English*, London: George Allen & Unwin.

Witten, M. (1993), 'Narrative and the culture of obedience at the workplace', in D. K. Mumby (ed.), *Narrative and Social Control: Critical Perspectives*, Newbury Park: Sage, pp. 97–118.

Wolfson, N. (1979), 'The conversational historical present alternation', *Language* 55, 168–82.

Wolfson, N. (1981), 'Compliments in cross-cultural perspective', *TESOL Quarterly* 15, 117–24.

Wolfson, N. (1982), *CHP: The Conversational Historical Present in American English Narrative*, Dordrecht: Foris.

Yang, A. W. (1989), 'Cohesive chains and writing quality', *Word* 40 (1–2), 235–54.

Youmans, G. (1990), 'Measuring lexical style and competence: the type–token vocabulary curve', *Style* 24(4), 584–99.

Youmans, G. (1991), 'A new tool for Discourse Analysis: the vocabulary-management profile', *Language* 67(4), 763–89.

Young, K. G. (1984), 'Ontological puzzles about narrative', *Poetics* 13, 239–59.

Young, K. G. (1987), *Taleworlds and Storyrealms. The Phenomenology of Narrative*, Dordrecht: Nijhoff.

Yule, G. and T. Mathis (1992), 'The role of staging and constructed dialogue in establishing speaker's topic', *Linguistics* 30, 199–215.

Index